GROWTH IN COMMUNITY
THROUGH THE POWER OF SPIRIT

COMPILED FROM INTERVIEWS WITH
BRUCE DAVIDSON

EDITED BY
DEVIN LAFFERTY
AND
LLANI DAVIDSON

Copyright © 2018 by Sirius, Inc., Devin Lafferty & Llani Davidson.

All rights reserved. No part of this book may be reproduced in any form on by an electronic or mechanical means, including information storage and retrieval systems, without permission in writing from the publisher, except by a reviewer who may quote brief passages in a review.

Cover photography and much of the photography throughout the book by Joseph McCormack
www.collectionsoflight.com

Cover design and book layout by Devin Lafferty
www.creativ-sense.com

Drawing on page vii by Ben-Christo
www.benchristo.com

CONTENTS

KERNELS OF WISDOM *IX*
A LAST WISH, LLANI DAVIDSON *XI*
INTRODUCTION, DEVIN LAFFERTY *XVII*
PROLOGUE: ROOTS *XIX*

1. EARLY YEARS
   AN IMPOSSIBLE VISION & MIRACLES OF SURVIVAL *3*
2. SPIRITUAL LAND
   LISTENING TO THE SACRED *21*
3. GIFTS AND OBSTACLES
   PARENTING IN COMMUNITY *35*
4. THE LONGHOUSE
   OUR FIRST BUILDING VENTURE *41*
5. THE ECONOMIC SHIFT
   FROM INCOME SHARING TO FINANCIAL INDEPENDENCE *47*
6. GROUP DYNAMICS
   LEADERSHIP & ORGANIZATION *55*
7. PHYSICAL MANIFESTATION
   BUILDING THE COMMUNITY CENTER *75*
8. SUSTAINABILITY
   BUILDING AND INFRASTRUCTURE *91*
9. PERMACULTURE IN ACTION
   GROWING FOOD IN CONNECTION *101*
10. FIRE
    DESTRUCTION AS REBIRTH *115*
11. GARDEN MAGIC
    DEVAS, NATURE SPIRITS & ELEMENTALS *123*
12. INDIA
    LESSONS FROM A SPIRITUAL CULTURE *137*
13. LAWSUITS
    SIRIUS IN JEOPARDY *155*
14. CONFLICT
    LEARNING HOW TO DANCE WITH EACH OTHER *165*
15. THE STONE CIRCLE
    BIRTHING SACRED SPACE *177*
16. THE FALL
    A LIFE-CHANGING ACCIDENT *201*
17. INTO THE FUTURE
    CHANGING FACES IN CHANGING TIMES *229*

EPILOGUE *243*
EULOGY *245*

Blessing

*May this book project fly.
May it land on fertile ground
and stimulate the evolving consciousness
of love, light, and compassion on the planet.
I offer deep gratitude and thanks for
the higher beings and energies
that were present with us through this process,
and for everyone who has helped support it.
Bless it all.*

~ Bruce Davidson ~

*I express deep gratitude
for this experience, for the understanding
and growth that are revealed.
May the wisdom and understanding flow freely out
into the consciousness of humanity,
the planet and the spirit worlds.
May these connections facilitate an abundance
of flourishing, thriving energy
at Sirius and for all.*

~ Devin Lafferty ~

Kernels of Wisdom

This book is not created solely for ourselves. We want to leave lessons for the world and to share experience, understanding and intuition from our work of the last 40 years. This work is the purpose of our lives and the lessons we have learned are valuable.

Without claiming to be perfect, and acknowledging the many different important paths people pursue, we wish to offer the gifts of wisdom and understanding we received from years of practice. Our sharing of this book accelerates and stimulates deeper and more effective growth in ourselves and others.

I hope the information in this book reaches a wide audience and readers taste the kernels of wisdom and spiritual awareness. We want to shine a ray of light on the emerging consciousness already unfolding. In sharing, my dream is to transmit these lessons to help others on their spiritual journey.

May we support you to walk the path without hitting the same pitfalls. May you learn from our mistakes. We hope our lessons support the growth of consciousness on the planet. If it does not stimulate the experience of direct growth in you, I hope it will certainly give rise to questioning and exploration.

My words do not convey brand new concepts and ideas, but rather ageless wisdom evolved through the consciousness of humanity for thousands of years, with great relevance today. We can learn from the elders. The messages in this book touch upon this ageless wisdom. Our gift in this book is that we use this ancient wisdom in our experience of the present time. Without the need to apply the wisdom to today's challenges, reading ageless texts would be enough and we wouldn't need to write this book.

The changing evolution occurring in the world presently calls for a practical application of these teachings. How do these principles and these ideals play out in modern society? How does the modern evolutionary process affect ancient texts? What can we do to develop the wisdom further?

Each new generation accelerates the growth process, taking the lessons deeper and reaching more profound levels than the previous generation. This is part of the evolutionary process and we must understand how these ideals and principles play out in modern society and everyday life.

We recognize we are all in a process of growth. Absoluteness does not exist within any of our lessons. As with any spiritual teaching, these are not ultimate truths, but merely signposts along the way. Ultimately each of us holds responsibility to understand ourselves and find our own truths.

As someone who walked a spiritual path and gained spiritual insight, I hope sharing my learning brings wisdom to others. May people reading about our experience bring forth our lessons. I hope the wisdom will expand through humanity into greater levels of consciousness.

This is my way of giving back for all that I was given.

BRUCE DAVIDSON, NOVEMBER 2015

A Last Wish

BY LLANI DAVIDSON

For decades, my father Bruce Davidson was the public face of Sirius Community and its charismatic leader. He loved greeting guests with boundless enthusiasm to share the mission of community and spirituality. He often cooked the open house lunches, wearing his frilly apron, greeting anyone who came through the door with joy. He tried to hide the sign on the door that read "Cooks only" because he loved talking and sharing with others. When someone complained about losing a part of their life, he always reminded them affectionately, "Well, it's a lesson in detachment." He constantly yet gently tried to offer people a different way of thinking about their lives and the world. Twenty years later people often came back to thank him for his message. While they might not have always been ready to hear it at the time, his words made a lasting impact.

Bruce was a true story teller. Whether sitting over lunch at a picnic table or chatting with a guest group, he delighted in repeating the same tale over and over through the years. He painted pictures of hard work, spiritual tenacity and young idealism. He showed how faith and determination are the foundation for success.

Bruce died about a year before Sirius would celebrate its 40th birthday. He was sick for many years and, despite wishing he could still be here, at some point realized it was time to go. His family and community wanted him to stay, and he always felt he had more work to do in the world, but he ran out of time, and as he was dying, he hoped that others would continue his work.

During Bruce's illness, as he questioned how much time he had left, an idea emerged. He wanted to share the wisdom and lessons he gained during almost 45 years of living in community. The community made many mistakes and learned hard yet valuable lessons. He wanted to share those lessons with others doing similar work in the world to create the new paradigm and make a lasting contribution. He felt that the lessons we learned here might be helpful to others during this challenging time of change on the planet.

My Father

During the early years of Sirius, Bruce focused on community needs and his young construction company, while Linda, his wife, spent time with the children on the land, working in the garden, teaching swimming lessons at the pond and feeding the children endless bowls of "hippie popcorn." Bruce came home smelling of sawdust and gasoline and told endless magical stories of little girls' encounters with flying lions. He chased us around the yard and acted as the human horse. He invented silly rhymes and made beeswax candles in his kitchen with the kids.

Being his daughter brought its own set of rewards and challenges. My mother was still very much in the role of the primary parent. Both my parents were intently focused on birthing the dream of an oftentimes struggling organization. My father was often busy and occupied with other projects and we saw him much less than my mother. He didn't always know how to handle the emotions of children and left much of that up to my mother. Yet I loved the stories he would tell us and he gave us the gifts of play and goofiness, golden aspects of his personality. I loved to roam the land and play in the constructed spaces. They wanted to create a different life for us based on different ideals from the consumer culture that dominates our society.

We didn't watch TV or eat sugar or even know that Halloween was a holiday for many years. We poured carob over our organic homemade fruit ice cream while sitting around raging bonfires in the backyard watching the grownups lead weirdo sacred circle dances.

Other nights after community dinners we played in the meeting room doing gymnastics and gleefully flipping over pillows. We ran in and out of the houses along the street with their unlocked doors and adult buddies as we invented our own games. We found our parents when we wanted something and ran off again to climb a tree. We rode our bikes around the property and played basketball at the neighbor's court before running off to catch frogs and swim in the pond on hot afternoons, or we played in the dust full of nails near the construction site while walls were raised. My father heaped eight kids onto the tractor and drove us around the garden.

As a fourteen year old, I spent my summer up on a roof with a hammer in my hand pounding in nails. My father could build anything and I wanted to be just like him. I hung out with my father's "cool" apprentices, so young and worldly. When they left for other pursuits, I asked to go with them. I wanted to drive across the country or find mountains to climb. I wanted to go see the world.

As a young traveler, I saw the "normal" America for the first time. Tract housing, candy and Republicans... *What was all this? Didn't kids of all ages play together? Who the heck is Ricky Martin?* I worked at a summer camp and another counselor asked me, "So did you, like, grow up with electricity?" I stared at her without a clue where to begin. Of course we had electricity, but what to say? I was just too weird and found myself a foreigner in my own country. Where are all the other community children who understand me?

My parents certainly didn't act like other people's parents. They often sat at the table talking about Christ Consciousness and spirituality, going on and on about karma. Sometimes I thought the eye rolling would never stop. As a college student, when I broke my collar bone, they told me the universe was sending me a message. *No,* I thought, *maybe I just broke my collar bone.*

I did not realize until I was in my twenties how vastly different my childhood was. Didn't everyone's parents teach them to meditate and eat community meals together? I have applied the ideals to my life and now teach many of the values that I grew up with. I often did not realize as a child how much my father's way of being and teaching people mattered to others. To me he was simply my father.

Despite the awkward years, I am grateful for my experience. I explored the mainstream culture and rejected it. I returned to my roots and as I grew older and lost my youthful arrogance, the messages stuck from my alternative childhood as I developed my own inner landscape. I applied my Sirius upbringing to my daily routine. Nature connection, spiritual growth and reincarnation? Why not? I share my parents' ideas and values about the world and embody them in my daily life. Though sometimes I did not like their ideas, I learned to look inward and recognize my own spiritual journey and the lessons of my life. Later in life I also realized how much the lessons mattered to others who spent time at Sirius.

With my father's death I am blessed with the task to bring to others these spiritual lessons he instilled in me and offer them as a recipe for the future of humanity.

The Vision Manifested

So you are holding in your hands the preview of Bruce's last words' desire and dying wish. This book started with recorded interviews put together in 2015, about two years before the end of his life. Devin Lafferty, the co-editor, recorded them in Bruce's home over the course of the winter months while he was already sick. They explored the history of the community, the many challenges, the astounding miracles, the financial struggles, the blossoming beauty. They outlined how to create community socially, financially and spiritually. We are here to finish his work in the world and make sure that all the messages are not forgotten or lost. This book is the work and collaboration of a number of people. We are blessed to be putting forth this publication as Sirius celebrates 40 years.

In this book, Bruce offers a look at both the 40-year history of the community along with the intense, sometimes painful lessons learned along the way. He desires to tell a story, paint a picture and help readers save the time of reinventing the wheel or making the same mistakes in their own lives. He wanted people to understand what has enabled our community to survive over the last forty years when so many other communities failed.

The recorded interviews begin with the decision to purchase land. To provide context, I included a history of Bruce's early life before the founding of Sirius. Once they arrived on the land, Bruce picks up the story in his own voice. He offers insight into the history of the community and highlights the intense, sometimes painful lessons learned along the way, including the financial and interpersonal struggles of making community happen socially and spiritually. He delves into spiritual truth and wisdom referring to ancient spiritual masters and current teachers. He highlights his own path and spiritual journey, including the lessons learned from his long illness and his relationship to pain.

With his death, we continue this vision. His stories offer insights and wisdom for all of us. We have worked to edit and transcribe this information in a format that offers insight and inspiration to inform your own endeavors in the world.

Most of the information comes directly from the recordings of Bruce. We transcribed and edited the interviews into the form of a book, adding details and rearranging stories for ease and flow. Occasionally we changed names to protect people's privacy. While much of the words and organization of content are ours, the message and insights belong to Bruce. Though some information in the following pages may be inaccurate, we used our best ability to record events as they happened. Details vary in the collective memory, and we recognize the information is Bruce's perspective and how he remembered it. Bruce also often quoted other spiritual teachers and forward thinkers, and we did not verify them as direct quotes but see them as interpretations through Bruce's eyes.

This book is the work and collaboration of a number of people. While Devin and I are the editors, others offered insight and wisdom. We confirmed and verified stories with people who lived them, including Bruce's wife Linda and the other co-founders of Sirius, Bruce's brother and sister-in-law, Gordon Davidson and Corinne McLaughlin. We consulted Bruce's mother and her memory. The project was also made possible by a compassionately generous donation from a former member of Sirius from the 1980s, Jamie Babson.

The original ideas of Sirius were ahead of their time. In the early years our work was on the fringes and the margins of society, inciting suspicion and distrust of our alternative way of living. Now more people are seeking out Sirius to use as a model and provide a recipe to reduce their own footprint.

These lessons hold great importance for our time. People want hope and want to feel that their existence matters, in a world that increasingly tells them they are expendable. In an era when people begin to experience the devastating effects of climate change, society recognizes more of the values of Sirius, as people seek alternatives, collectively and individually. They recognize we live on a finite planet with shrinking resources and we must change our ways in order to survive and thrive.

Community is not a new idea. We lived in villages for thousands of years, where the good of the whole depended on all members of the group. The concept of "one family, one household" is fairly new, and the amount of depression, isolation and despair it creates is unprecedented. In modern society, we don't realize what we have lost in sacrificing community. Our world is shifting and changing, and the time for positive, inspiring alternatives is now. In order to keep living on the planet, rugged individualism no longer serves us. We are moving into an era where community is again essential and we cannot continue on the path of endless capitalism that is destroying the planet. We must learn to get along interpersonally and create systems for the well-being of all humans rather than a few at the top.

I hope that this work will inspire you and lead you further on your own spiritual journey so that we may all have a brighter, better future.

Introduction

BY DEVIN LAFFERTY

I feel blessed with the great honor of helping to bring the message of such an inspiring man of wisdom into the world. Almost five years ago, in search of an elder for guidance and a community for me to sink my hands into the earth, I attended what would be the last tour of the community that Bruce's body would allow. Moved by his wisdom, sensitivity and humor, in addition to the collaborative community and sacred land, I decided to stay.

I remember my worry about disturbing such an important person, before I knew him well. I desired to hear his stories and learn from him, but didn't want to waste his precious time. In reality Bruce was so welcoming and loved to share. I felt excited when he invited me to join the building, grounds and maintenance crew, and even more grateful when he asked me to help him in his healing garden.

Connecting with Bruce over the ensuing years offered me wonderful delight. Helping him in the healing garden that he started outside his house, I experienced the incredible power of manifestation with which he worked. I marveled at the way we slowly enhanced the energy in the garden as beauty blossomed forth. His excitement for the natural world sparkled as he eagerly peeked to see if his lotus plant would bloom. When we hit an impassable rock beneath a garden bed, he guided me to keep turning and prying it up until we could rest it on the ground to accent the edge of the bed. He always found a way to lightly laugh at the most difficult experiences.

The meditations he led opened a powerful channel of healing, a gift for the whole planet, and I listened attentively when he gave input about opening the channel of light in group meditation.

Feeling called to share the valuable lessons and stories of Sirius, I interviewed Bruce over several months. But once we completed the interviews together, the project lay in hiatus. I was astounded to learn that the main reason Bruce extended his life through the insufferable pain for so many years was to ensure the publication of the book we had started. Eventually Bruce received the guidance that this project was being taken care of, and he was free to go. So he let go of this life. Soon after, a man of great generosity offered the funds to complete the project and bring it into the world.

Bruce recognized he had his own faults. At the 40th anniversary of the community, I spoke with Deborah Wilson, an energetic teacher of mine, and a person who also received great inspiration from Bruce in their connection over the decades. She described seeing a vision of his legs energetically tangled in heavy black cords, until we began working on this book. It appeared as if the initiation of offering the gifts of his experience in service to the world finally released him from past baggage, and the cords began to disappear. He later came to Deborah in another vision and shared his gratitude for the unconditional love from his partner Linda when he was sick, which finally liberated him.

I also talked with his brother Gordon, who tearfully spoke of Bruce, their mother Josephine and Corinne. All three powerful, loving people passed away in the last year. Gordon received the understanding that from another state of consciousness, the three of them are working together to create an energetic bridge, strengthening the positive, loving relationship between humanity and the nature kingdoms.

It is with incredible gratitude that I immerse myself in the words of wisdom, collaborating with Bruce's daughter Llani, to offer these stories of so many benevolent people over the years who contributed to the service of building community and growing in spirit together. As I worked on this project, I noticed how each bit of wisdom I sit with astoundingly applies directly to my life and helps me with the specific challenges that arise in the moment. I imagine you may find similar sources of inspiration to understand from a new perspective whatever arises in your life. With appreciation for all the people and beings who helped bring this forward, I invite you to bask in the enlightening illuminations we have to share. Enjoy!

Prologue: Roots

BY LLANI DAVIDSON

Family

Bruce's grandparents faced devastating poverty in Poland at the turn of the century. They found hope in a minister who immigrated to the New World and established himself on rural land. He wrote back to the old country and spoke of new farm endeavors with the potential to sustain a livelihood and live a better life. Drawn by this promise, Bruce's grandparents on his mother's side abandoned their lives in Poland and settled in Minnesota. They lived on rural farms with large families, speaking Polish and living a rudimentary life. They lacked electricity and indoor plumbing and grew most of their food, raised animals, and attended church.

Bruce's mother Josephine, the youngest of nineteen children, was born in 1920. In her childhood, horses and buggies were the most common form of transportation, phones were scarce and electricity was rare. She was ten when she saw her first car as the times began to change. By the time Josephine was a young woman, the old ways and the Polish language of her childhood faded out. The younger generation did not remember their roots, eager to assimilate into America. Josephine left home at 16 and started working in the domestic service in exchange for board while attending school. She enrolled in the University of Minnesota before joining the Marine Corps. As one of the first women to be enrolled as a private in the United States, she supported the war effort that swept over the country, deeply saddened to see her brother's name appear on the death list, among many other young men she cared about.

At the beginning of her job, Jo was dispatched by the officer in charge, Dave, and he told her to clean the windows. Jo insisted, "If I have to do it, you have to do it too." He helped to clean the windows and they started flirting. For many years to come they shared this story of their first meeting. She married Dave during her time in the military.

Dave, Bruce's father, grew up in relative poverty on the South Side of Chicago. His father was a shopkeeper and Baptist minister, and his mother had a strong, intense, overbearing personality. When Dave was four years old, his father disappeared from the shop, and no one ever saw or heard from him ever again. The police investigated and found the shop unlocked, all the lights on and nothing stolen.

This tragic incident shaped Dave's personality, and the shadow of a missing father hung over his life during his childhood years. When Dave died many years later at the age of 69, Josephine studied his birth certificate in detail and she realized the word "Jewish" had been blacked out. The anti-Semitic sentiment was strong and perhaps his disappearance was connected to a hidden Jewish identity, but whatever happened to Dave's father remains a mystery.

Josephine and Dave had a military wedding and married in full uniform in 1944. Like many soldiers and servicemen coming out of the war at that time, they made by with little money. Their life together started frugally as they established themselves; the five cents for school lunch was sometimes more than they could afford. Sometimes Josephine wore Dave's pants to save on expenses. Dave read meters for the utility company and eventually moved up through the ranks to spend his career working for and installing electric poles and utility lines.

While still in the military, they started a family. Their first child, Gordon, was born in 1944 when Dave was out at sea with his platoon. At six weeks old he almost died from the wrong kind of medication. Despite this, Gordon survived his near fatal start and Bruce, his younger brother, was born four years later. They settled in the coastal town of Plymouth, Massachusetts.

Gordon and Bruce were both children of the '50s. The expectation at the time left the wife at home to do most, if not all, of the child rearing, and Jo's family was no exception. She had dinner ready on the table every night by 5:30, while Dave made all the financial decisions.

Dave, with an authoritarian personality, was a harsh disciplinarian. He ran a tight ship and used his masculine power to control the family. Josephine claimed that he was just another big baby to look after and dealing with him took as much work as the children.

She played the proper part, but managed to find some power through clever tricks. When they renovated the dining room, she asked for five-inch-wide window sills in the initial design, so she could place her African violets in the window. Dave bossily told her he would design it his way. Later in the process, when the work started, she suggested the window sills be seven inches wide. He retorted he would make them five inches wide.

Childhood

Bruce, a sensitive little boy, was shy and easily overwhelmed, but he formed a strong connection to nature. He loved being outside with the plants and collected rocks, which he brought into bed at night. When they fell on the floor he cried until his mom came and put them back under the covers. When he turned eleven, he brought a magnifying glass into the grassy field near his home. Fascinated, he caught the sun through the lens, marvelling at the grass starting to smoke, until it actually caught fire. Stunned, he ran off as the entire hill caught fire. He hid in the woods while the local fire department came to put it out.

As a shy awkward kid, he was a poor student and a day dreamer who focused more attention out the window than in the classroom. Teachers complained he did not apply himself. Convinced he was stupid, he spent his grade school years unable to learn the lessons and flunked out of several classes. Sensitive to the world around him, he was easily overwhelmed by the intensity of people's energy. When his parents had company and friends over, he hid in the closet until the guests left.

Gordon and Bruce fought continuously and argued over everything, even which end of the dog to pet. Their father drew a line down the middle of their shared room and told each of them to stay on his own side. Dave wanted both of his sons to follow in his footsteps and work for the utility company, but they had other ideas; in their adolescent years Gordon rebelled first. During his time in college, he found interest in politics and edited the school newspaper. He discovered spirituality and joined the peace corps, which brought him to India, close to many of the world's spiritual traditions.

In high school, Bruce worked at a tourist seafood restaurant washing dishes, where he discovered women and alcohol. His social awkwardness improved and the alcohol numbed the intense sensitivity he felt. Integrating into the world of parties, he bought a jeep and drove it up and down the beach near the ocean, often with many people hanging off the back during big beach parties and campfires.

Spiritual Emergence

He grew into an adult as the United States geared up for the Vietnam War. His school record was so terrible, he was told he could never go to college. About to be drafted, he decided to enlist before his number came up in order to choose which branch of the military to join. He joined the Marine Corps and spent the beginning of his military life training in California until he was shipped overseas. Halfway to Vietnam, they changed his orders. Later he laughed, "I guess God had other plans for my life." He spent the war years living on a base in Japan working as a mechanic on airplanes. The longer he was in the military, the more he abhorred it as he sabotaged the industrial war machine from the inside. He concluded that a corrupt corporate system killing innocent people didn't deserve his skills. Despite his underhanded behavior, he was promoted to sergeant before his four years finally ended.

After he left the military in the early '70s, Bruce would experience the most traumatic experience of his life. In a night of heavy drinking, he caused a severe car accident, the details too disturbing to disclose. Flooded with guilt, Bruce sank into a deep depression, full of thoughts of suicide.

While recovering from a broken leg, he followed a friend's recommendation to see a spiritual healer. The woman told him she could perform hands-on healing. He scoffed at the idea, but let her do her work anyway. Her treatment greatly improved his condition, which caught his attention. The woman shared about spiritual ideas such as meditation, reincarnation and karma and gave him several books to read. She emphasized the spiritual component to life and shared about the sacredness of all life. She told him if he really wanted to know truth, he would have to look within to find himself.

Inspired by a new hope for meaning, he grew hungry for more, and abandoned his former life attached to drinking, women and sports cars and motorcycles. He dropped out of society as he sought answers to fundamental questions about life and spirituality.

He asked, *"Is there a god? What am I doing here? What is my purpose?"* For two years he aimlessly hitchhiked around the country by himself. He trekked through Yellowstone National Park where a ferocious snowstorm almost took his life. Later while camping on the beach, he left his backpack outside his tent, and someone stole all his possessions. He spent a winter in San Francisco reading books about spiritual teachings of the world and took up meditation, spending most of his time alone. His years of drifting completely transformed his life.

On one particular trip to the Sierra Nevada Mountains, he experienced an epiphany that shifted his perspective and shaped the rest of his life. Sitting shivering under the stars in the black cold of night, he gazed into the points of illumination held in vast emptiness. He realized a deep sense of oneness of all that is, embracing the interconnection of all life. He understood that spirituality weaves itself through all creation. We are souls having human experiences, and our lives are lived in relation to a Divine Presence. He made an agreement between himself and God that he would dedicate the rest of his life to the pursuit of spiritual principles. He would care for the planet and help others realize how we are all connected.

After this epiphany, his meditation practice increased with new depth, and he traveled to Hawaii where he spent six months living in a Zen Buddhist monastery. Here he meditated daily for hours on end, integrating the lessons he learned. He felt a profound shift in his consciousness and decided that in order to continue his journey, he needed to travel to India, a Mecca of spiritual wisdom and teaching. Before he left, he heard about a spiritual community in Scotland called Findhorn and decided to take a detour on his way to India to see what Findhorn was all about. Bruce did not make it to India for another 25 years.

Findhorn

When Bruce arrived at Findhorn, he walked up to the entrance and was struck with a vision of his future of leadership in spiritual community if he took another step forward. Startled, he froze in his tracks and immediately turned around. Totally freaked out by the path he saw, Bruce sat on the beach trying to decide what to do next. He pondered and meditated as the day passed, eventually night came and he went to sleep there on the beach.

By morning he had processed through his fears and fully embraced his mission. Rejuvenated with clarity, he packed his bag and headed to the entrance of Findhorn. When he arrived, he was greeted by the guest coordinator.

"I'd like to stay for a while," Bruce said.

"Oh! I'm sorry, but we're all full," answered the coordinator.

Stunned, Bruce didn't know how to respond. "But I came all the way from the US!"

"Sorry, I don't know what to tell you."

Bruce proceeded to describe the deep calling he had received to be at Findhorn at this time, that the importance extended beyond his personal desires. He recounted his full day of meditation and clear guidance to be a part of the community. Miraculously, the coordinator could hear the conviction and trusted a deeper plan was in order.

"I suppose we could find some space for you," the coordinator accepted.

Bruce ended up staying for four years. During his time at Findhorn, his meditation practice deepened as the insight opened his consciousness and spiritual wisdom poured in. At times the dramatic shifts in his consciousness left him disoriented, but he steadfastly paid close attention and listened to new messages, allowing daily integration of his spiritual awareness with his personality.

Though he was still young, others sought him out for counsel and advice. Peter, the founder of Findhorn asked him to facilitate the Core Group, where he learned group process and spiritual consensus. He ran the guest department at Findhorn and developed his carpentry skills, building caravans for the community and working on the sewer lines. He focalized 50-person guest weekends and worked in personnel, in addition to working construction at Cluny Hill. He focalized events at Drumduan and Cluny Bank, while continuing to meditate four hours a day.

Partnership

During this time, Bruce stayed in touch with his mother Josephine. Some of the letters she and Gordon received seemed strange and out of character as Bruce talked about love and light and the magic of Findhorn. Fearing he joined some weirdo spiritual cult, they decided to visit Findhorn and learn more about the place, in case Bruce was in trouble. Instead of confronting a cult, Gordon experienced his own spiritual transformation and found his life partner.

Bruce lived in the caravan park with a housemate named Corinne who also worked in the guest department where Bruce focalized big groups. When Gordon came to visit, he and Corinne felt immediate attraction for each other and both loved to talk. They started dating shortly after meeting and took a trip together to London, which started their long-lasting relationship. Gordon returned to New York to close up all his affairs and moved to Findhorn to be with Corinne.

While working for the guest department, Bruce encountered an application not filled out properly from a woman named Linda but let her attend anyway. As part of community experience week, participants push their edges as they are led through many games and exercises. One such activity involved gazing into a stranger's eyes for a minute to break down barriers and help people get to know each other on a deep level of vulnerability. Linda refused to participate. Bruce thought she was weird and didn't know how to interact with her. He didn't realize he was looking at his life partner.

Linda grew up in California in a trailer park and married a military officer at age 19. Marriage provided her an opportunity to get out of her parents' house and break out on her own. By the time her daughter was three, she was a divorced single mom, trying to make a living. She went to Ananda, a yoga community in California and worked hard to make a life for herself. She learned gardening skills and lived in the back of a bread truck, as it was the housing provided. Her ex-boyfriend, who was still interested in her, visited Findhorn and enjoyed his experience, so he bought her a ticket to visit as a gift for her birthday, thinking Linda would also enjoy her experience there. Linda traveled to Findhorn with her friend Kay Lynne Sherman looking for a spiritual experience. At this point in her life, she was considering becoming a nun. Despite this, when she met Bruce, she thought he was supermodel gorgeous.

Their friend arranged for the three of them to take a walk on the beach and Bruce and Linda both showed up but their friend did not. One walk on the beach started 41 years of shared life, building a family and creating community together. Kay Lynne later joked that she went to Findhorn to find a man and Linda went for a spiritual experience. She said she had the spiritual experience and Linda got the man. With time, Linda joined Bruce at Findhorn along with her nine-year-old daughter from her first marriage. From the beginning they had a strong understanding their relationship was based on spiritual principles and would involve positive work in the world together. They believed that by helping to change consciousness, they could help change the world.

Even though Bruce, Linda, Gordon and Corinne were deeply enmeshed in Findhorn, they understood that their eventual work was in the United States. Bruce, during his meditation, received guidance that his work at Findhorn was coming to a close as he felt urgings and saw visions to start something similar in the US. When all four of them discussed their future, everyone had similar feelings they were being called elsewhere. Their visa status was becoming complicated and they felt pressure to leave the country. They wanted to promote community, change consciousness and help create a better future for all children and the planet as a whole.

In 1978 Bruce returned to the United States with Gordon and Corinne, Peter Caddy and Linda Siconolfoli to conduct workshops about Findhorn's message. He felt torn leaving his family but persevered knowing he was doing the work God called him to do in the world. His partner Linda stayed behind at Findhorn, pregnant with their first child. When Bruce first found out he was going to be a father, without saying a word, he left the house and didn't return for 12 hours. He was brought face to face with all his unresolved conflicts and feelings about his relationship with his own father. Eventually he accepted the idea and stepped into fatherhood joyfully. He returned from his travels for the birth. Elana was born at Findhorn, where she spent the first year of her life. Before Elana's birth, at the precipice of the search for land, our story begins.

Early Years

AN IMPOSSIBLE VISION & MIRACLES OF SURVIVAL

I

The First Vision

An impossible yet unstoppable vision gripped our hearts and refused to let go. My brother Gordon and I, and our wives Corinne and Linda, foresaw ourselves creating a self-sustaining spiritual community in the United States, which on a rational level made absolutely no sense. We had no money, no land and no jobs.

We traveled around the country leading workshops, earning only enough to get by. Despite our lack of funds, we had this sense that somehow we would create something out of nothing. With no logical basis, our ambition came from a very deep intuitive place within us. We wondered, *How will we possibly get any land when we have no money to put down?* Sometimes impressions or intuitive feelings call you to complete certain work in your life. It was one of those impressions, always there, constantly building internal pressure for us to follow through.

Letting go of the idea should have been easy because it seemed so ridiculous; without the necessary resources, we could have dismissed it as some whimsical dream. But the dream would not leave us alone. It kept strongly impressing on us, and every time we meditated, we sensed that we were meant to accomplish this feat together.

Land for Sale Across the Street

We set out traveling and the very first destination we came to was in the hills of the Pioneer Valley in Western Massachusetts. We planned to teach a workshop at Hampshire College, and we had met a woman at Findhorn, the community in Scotland that inspired our dream, who lived nearby. She offered, "You are welcome to stay at my house while you give your workshop."

Then she added, "By the way, if you want to start a community, *the land across the street is up for sale!*" It was the middle of winter with two feet of snow covering the ground. So we trudged across the field and knocked on the farmhouse door. No one answered. We saw a little sign that read, "Don't break down the door. If you want to look around, the key is under the doormat."

We opened the door and peered in, admiring the wood floor and the tall stone fireplace. While the space looked nice, Gordon and I looked at each other and said, "Who wants to create community in freezing New England? You can't hardly grow food in this rocky soil!" We grew up dreading New England winters and strongly believed we could find a nicer place. So we finished our workshop and went on our way, traveling all over the country.

We traveled out west to California, teaching workshops, looking for the ideal piece of land to start community. For nearly a year we searched, but alas we came up empty handed. Meanwhile, my partner, Linda, was pregnant with our daughter in Scotland and I eventually set my gallivanting aside to go give her my support. Even when I left, a strong sense remained that Gordon and I would create something special together.

I said to Gordon, "When you find land, I will come back to America. We will build our community."

So we agreed, and I traveled back to Findhorn for the birth of my daughter. Gordon and Corinne continued traveling longer looking for land, searching and searching. They could not find anything. Nothing would emerge; not even the vaguest possibility, so they started to give up and decided they would also return to Scotland, back to Findhorn.

They stopped back at the Pioneer Valley to teach one last workshop before resigning themselves, again staying at the same woman's house in Massachusetts who had shown us the land nearby. One morning Gordon sat in meditation when he was overcome by the most intense vision. He received direct guidance to go over and buy the piece of land we had originally visited. He accepted the call, even though rationally he knew it would be a joke to approach the landowner without any money.

He and Corinne went over to the land, now with the first green sprouts of spring color emerging. The owner, who had been gone all winter, had returned to the property.

They approached him and said, "We'd like to buy the land."

The owner said, "Wonderful! I'll hold it for three days and then I'll want a $30,000 deposit."

They agreed right away. But as they walked back across the street, they scratched their heads, wondering how they could come up with the money. They stopped in the bank to ask for a loan, and the bank literally threw them out! Not only did they have no job and no credit, they had no address in America. The bank told them to get lost, unwilling to even talk to them about a loan.

Meanwhile, people excited about spiritual communities were flocking to a conference in New Hampshire related to Findhorn. Gordon and Corinne drove to the conference and asked several people if they would be willing to support a community project in America similar to Findhorn. Amazingly, two people said yes. They received a $10,000 donation and a $20,000 loan on the spot. Within three days they had the money they needed in their pocket.

They came back to the landowner and said, "We can give you $30,000 right now. But we encountered a problem. The bank refused to give us the mortgage."

The owner said, "Well, it's okay, I like your community vision, and I'm disgusted with the idea of chopping up the land into tiny little house lots along the road. I'll tell you what; I'll give you a ten-year mortgage at half the going interest rate." In 1978 the interest rate was 13% and he offered the mortgage at 7%! He continued, "Not only that, but because I really like the idea of what you're doing, I'll sell you the whole lot at half price."

What we thought was 86 acres, later turned out to be 90 acres of land. In 1978 it was valued at $140,000, which included a house and two garages. He sold it to us for $70,000, and that was the beginning of Sirius.

Gordon wrote to me and said, "We got the land! Can you come back now? We're ready to create the community here."

I couldn't come back immediately because I was deeply involved in Scotland. Findhorn was experiencing big changes in leadership, which I played a key role in facilitating, so Gordon and Corinne settled on the land for six months before Linda and I joined them, along with another woman who had also been living at the Findhorn Community.

When Gordon and I had first looked at this land, we said to each other, "Oh this is a nice place," but we didn't have a deep sense of it. We liked it, but our personalities spoke for us, as we concluded, *"Let's find a warmer place!"* We weren't listening deeply on a soul level at that moment. Because it was winter with two feet of snow, we didn't walk the land that much and didn't experience deep resonance.

Interestingly it was the absolute first place we came to when we started our search for land in America, as if a divine hand was guiding the whole plan. Gordon and I tuned into a divine intent, combined with our own desire, knowing we wanted to do something that was of value, and our soul wisdom motivated us to do it here. It wasn't a personality choice; it was intuitively listening to a deeper soul calling.

Miracles of Survival

Once we all arrived on the land, we immediately started growing food in the Shanti Garden, which had already been cleared by the previous residents. None of us had any jobs or income, and Linda was pregnant with our second daughter. But we came to the land with absolute faith that somehow we would succeed. Our leap of faith led to powerful, interesting experiences.

In the first few years, we pooled all of our resources together. We used whatever money any of us had, paying the mortgage or buying food. After a month or two, the mortgage was due of maybe three or four hundred dollars. The owner was a very nice, wonderful guy, great sense of humor and very supportive, but when the payment was due, he would ask us, "Where's my check?"

Three days before the mortgage deadline, we got together and put all the money we had on the table. It was twelve dollars and some change. Far short of the four hundred required, we considered going out to get jobs, but we knew we couldn't make that kind of money in three days.

We felt that we were doing everything in our power to make our vision happen. We were working twelve hours a day, building community so we decided that it was in the hands of the Divine. Whatever was going to happen next was out of our power.

We shared our fears of getting thrown off the land into the street, homeless, but we knew that wasn't the right attitude. We meditated together to release our fears and let go and acknowledged it was in the hands of the Divine. Whatever happens will happen; all we can do is trust. And we went back to work on the land, building our meditation room and creating the gardens.

The very next day we received a telephone call from a woman in Connecticut whom we had met at Findhorn. She said, "I hear you're creating community, can I come out for a visit?"

So we said, "Yeah, sure!" She added, "Oh, by the way, I have a check for five hundred dollars that I'm bringing with me." She arrived the day the mortgage was due and we took her check, drove to the bank, cashed it, drove over to the owner, and paid the mortgage.

This experience was a real affirmation for us, and it gave us great inspiration to receive what we needed at the last moment. We learned a deep spiritual lesson in trust, and it inspired us to know we were doing the right thing. We knew we were on the right track.

We were young, in our late twenties, and had a certain naivete, but our innocent perspective benefited us. Our optimistic faith and inspiration were accompanied by a passionate drive to do everything in our power to succeed.

When the money came through at the last minute, it blessed us with one of our earliest experiences with manifestation. When someone does what is right, not merely for personal gain, but for the collective higher good, the universe supports such an endeavor, and we felt completely uplifted by it.

For the first two years that we lived here on the land, none of us worked any jobs outside of the community, as we invested all our energy here full-time. We relied on donations and the money we were able to scrape together from Gordon and Corinne's workshops and public talks. We often had no idea even where food was going to come from, yet people kept arriving at serendipitous moments. Random people would graciously arrive with money for materials, food and other necessities. Eventually we all separated our income, and every family became responsible for their own finances, each contributing a monthly amount to cover the mortgage costs. But in the meantime, we relied on miracles.

Saved by Nuns

Another experience totally blew our minds. We would all take turns cooking in the communal kitchen at the farmhouse, and my turn to cook came around. I looked in the cupboard where we kept all the food, and I found only enough food to prepare one meal for everybody, but nothing else. I used up the last morsels of food as I prepared the meal, and while we ate I mentioned to everyone, "Well, I just want to let everybody know, there's no more food in the pantry; what you are eating is the last of our rations."

Everybody paused, forks in the air, looking at each other in silence for a moment, and then kept eating. Very little conversation commenced as we quietly acknowledged the situation. We understood not to lose our heads worrying about this dilemma, but to calmly hold the reality in our consciousness.

We all went back to work the next day and honored a moment of silence. People did not act upset or agitated. We thought, *Here is an opportunity to find a way to meet our needs and trust that the Divine will come through.* We fasted that day.

Amazingly, the next day we received a telephone call from two Catholic nuns in their 60s. They wanted to start a healing center and thought they could learn from us. They lived in the monastery for most of their lives, and the Catholic Church gave them permission to visit us. When they called, they told us, "Oh by the way, the church has given us $500 to cover your expenses." They arrived that very day.

The expectation that we might get a check from the Catholic Church to support what we were doing was far beyond anything imagined. We were surprised the Church would support our work, but the three nuns turned out to be some of the most joyful, funny, hardworking people. We had a wonderful, wonderful time with them and they were willing to do anything, always happily working away.

We realized we must not limit possibilities of how to receive answers to our problems. This experience showed us to stay open and be willing to receive whatever guidance or resources we need to receive, from any source. These kinds of experiences kept happening throughout the history of the community, affirming our alignment to the right path of service.

Educational Mission

Throughout the entire history of the community, we've always been graced with guests and visitors. In the early years, We didn't have great accommodations, but people came anyway. People were genuinely inspired by what we were doing, so we ran a number of our own workshops, in addition to inviting presenters in alignment with our mission.

We committed to such workshops and teachings when we incorporated as a 501(c)(3) nonprofit educational organization, and we embraced the requirement of what we truly wanted to do.

From the very beginning, we planned to incorporate as a nonprofit. With this label, we can receive grants and tax deductible donations. It also helps us with the zoning regulations from the town because nonprofits in the state of Massachusetts receive the same zoning exemptions as schools and churches, posing less restrictions. With this early intention, we contacted a neighbor and friend of ours, Terry Mollner, who understood the legal considerations of nonprofits, and he walked us through all the procedures to file the legal paperwork, establishing us as a nonprofit.

It was a very wise decision and though the classification presents some limitations, what we gained far outweighed the negatives. If people want to build a house here, they can't get a bank loan, as all the property is owned by the nonprofit rather than individuals. It may not be the best strategy for every ecovillage or community, but it served us to pursue our goals and vision as a community.

Through workshops we received a bit of income, and we gained tremendous inspiration from the reciprocal nature of teaching. To bring people in with a fresh energy and new ideas both supported our endeavors and energized our inspiration by providing us an opportunity to give meaningful lessons to others. To be able to give to others is the invocation of our soul.

Peter and Eileen came and spoke about their experiences at Findhorn. Dorothy Maclean enlightened our guests about the consciousness of plants and spiritual explorations. David Spangler came and offered his spiritual wisdom. But the vast majority of the educational programs we provided ourselves. Gordon and Corinne ran an ongoing Spiritual Science course about integrating spiritual life and meditation.

I do not want to paint the picture that our whole experience flowed easily, because we endured great pains over long periods of time, which proved tremendously difficult to overcome. The interpersonal challenges would test our resolve, determining whether we would survive as a community or dissolve in ruin.

Challenges: *Commitment to Spiritual Growth*

Significant challenges involving interpersonal relationships arose between all of us, and we plumbed the depths of our own being, searching for compassion, love, and acceptance of each other, going deep into our own inner landscapes. Quite a bit of conflicts emerged among us, but we also celebrated joyful, harmonious moments together. The mixture of challenge and ease swirled back and forth.

The community's only chance to continue depended on our commitment to our own spiritual growth, individually and collectively. Without that commitment, the intensity of interpersonal relationships would split us apart and the community surely would perish. Committed to recognizing our own inward responsibility no matter what crazy conflictual dynamics arose, we faced considerable confrontations.

The Group

Some of the interpersonal dynamics that we struggled through were magnified by the personalities of the people who were here. Gordon and Corinne, Linda and I, and another cofounder, Suzanne, all had powerful, fiery personalities. We were young and bold, with all this passionate intensity within us.

Our fifth co-founder also lived at Findhorn, and when she learned what we were envisioning she asked in excitement if she could be a part our future, so we invited her in. Her name was Suzanne Garden, and she indeed worked in the gardens at Findhorn.

She participated in the formation of Sirius for a number of years and brought a strong sensitivity to nature, which presented some challenges for our personalities. She insisted on frequent attunement, but when we didn't attune as much as she desired, she got upset. We worked through the relationship issues that arose, and by the time she left, she seemed quite harmonious with the community.

During the first years, people heard about our work and asked to join the community. We attracted people who felt strongly about deep spiritual practices, and who were drawn in by the powerful transformation we were practicing. The people who were showing up came to realizations in their own lives and wanted a stronger relationship to Spirit. Individually they desired an environment where a spiritual way of living and practice were held commonly as a community.

Three new members were drawn in because of this focus. Konnie Fox came from Georgia, and even though we had no space to offer her housing, she wanted to participate so badly that she lived in her tent until winter arrived. She currently still lives nearby, maintaining a friendship with the community. Another couple from Oregon also arrived in the first year. John and Cheri, pregnant with their first child, drove across the country to join us. We rented a house across the street, and while Gordon and Corinne lived in the farmhouse on the land, the rest of us moved in before winter.

In the beginning, we focused on spirituality as a community more than being a sustainable ecovillage, although we believed all life is sacred and everything is interconnected, which makes an ecological mindset important. We meditated several times every day and shared our practice of attunement to nature.

We upheld this practice vigilantly throughout the first two years. We were all here in the community 24 hours a day, dedicated to our spiritual practice, regularly discussing our intentions. Considering the challenges we would face, we would need the blessings of every one of those meditations!

Early Transformation

We experienced tremendous transformation in those early years among the initial group. We didn't arrive as fully integrated spiritual beings, harmoniously creating community with love and compassion. Instead we showed up as a collection of personalities bashing against each other with deep seeded ideals and personal misunderstandings flaring up, often yelling at each other through all the tensions.

We battered the personality issues out of each other, and through all its challenges, the process proved beneficial to our evolving souls and personalities. Perhaps we didn't do it very graciously, yet it was who we were; it was authentic. We had to resolve and work through our issues, and our motivation soared sky high. We knew if we didn't move through the conflicts, we weren't going to succeed as a community. The lessons revealed were perfect for us, even though it didn't always feel that way. To guests our behavior seemed outrageous, yet we knew we needed to work through these issues.

It wasn't that easy initially but gradually we smoothed out the process and became more loving and compassionate with each other, and with ourselves. The unfolding process of learning was beautiful to watch. We learned to ease off of yelling at each other and find less intense and damaging ways to communicate.

Moving your personality in new directions is a long process. We can formulate ideals around our perceived growth, but to respond with understanding on a day-to-day basis when people push all your buttons takes work. The idea of "nonviolent communication" did not exist yet but we knew we valued love and compassion in relationship and agreed to commit to those values, determined to find a way to work it out.

We discovered ways through our experience to communicate that honored and affirmed each other with love, rather than reading the concepts in a book. When somebody screams in your face, the opportunity arises, and you must choose how to respond in an instant. Much of the conflict we faced arose from the incredible challenges of power and hierarchy.

Community Structure

When we first started the community, we practiced egalitarian consensus. We all agreed every individual had absolute equal right, equal say and equal money. This was our vision of the ideal society. In practice, we realized our vision wasn't so ideal. The right of any newcomer to claim equal say about the whole direction of the community forced us to be *extremely* picky about who joined us.

People asked to join, and we replied, "No, you're not ready yet."

New people didn't understand everything about our deeper mission and focus, they just felt good on the land and wanted to be with us. They didn't usually want to make big decisions, so we changed our model, giving people incremental power.

We created the Core Group in the second year as more people joined us. We gave the Core Group authority to make decisions about our purpose and direction, in addition to finances.

Only later did we realize how much the Core Group model pushed people's buttons. People felt powerless when the Core Group handed down decisions. People cried out, "The Core Group makes decisions that affect us all, and we don't get an opportunity to say anything about it!"

How terrible!

People rebelled, insisting, "This doesn't work. We don't like it at all!"

We thought about all the reasons we didn't like the process, and we could see that keeping this system was to the detriment of the whole. So we changed it. We discussed and imagined how to maintain integrity with our purpose as we empower our collective, without being completely at the mercy of new arrivals.

In the new agreement anybody in the community receives the power to challenge Core Group decisions, and we allow the discussion to continue until everyone feels heard. Sometimes the people *did* change the mind of the Core Group.

I didn't notice any significant difference in the quality of the decisions, but people's mentality shifted. If the Core Group goes crazy, we now have avenues to address it.

Our systems are not perfect! We made some unconscious decisions, because our evolution demands going completely unconscious at times.

Yet if you look hard and you wade through the debris, perfection exists as a thread of light weaving through the whole. Glimpses of that elusive light kept us going.

Each of us carried leadership qualities, including tenacity and fire, which is necessary to create something of significance because there are so many challenges to overcome. But because of the fire in our interpersonal relationships, we would easily get angry or upset about the actions of the other people around us. So those dynamics were emerging on a very regular basis, particularly between Gordon and me.

Brothers

Gordon and I faced all kinds of issues. Our volatile childhood prevented us from getting along well as brothers, always fighting. We grew up with an abusive father who regularly beat and yelled at us.

We definitely were not buddies. I quietly and meditatively reflected in introspection, while he burned forward, the extrovert, the fire. He actively wanted to push ahead all the time, hating to be stopped. Our worlds constantly collided as we each tried to find a way to escape our father's torment. We routinely lashed out at each other in an attempt to claim our own scrap of power in a home that denied our basic right to be ourselves.

All the trauma and issues those experiences caused resurfaced in our community relationship. Old dynamics emerged which led to constant conflict. We excelled at violent communication rather than nonviolent communication.

Sometimes we erupted into yelling matches, facing off in the kitchen with clenched fists while onlookers watched frightfully. We revealed deep-seeded issues in our personalities that needed to be transformed. People today would be shocked by what went on in those early days. We were stumbling around, trying to make our way through the conflicts.

Our commitment to collective growth helped us through those challenges. We seized each opportunity as it arose, forced to look at it head-on, or we couldn't proceed. We knew long-term investment was essential to create what we truly wanted to create together, and that drove us to persist.

Gordon embodied the most fire of us all. And while I was more contemplative, I had my own fire going too. Conflict would arise when Gordon did whatever he wanted without consulting the group first, a typical quality of a passionate leader. You have so much energy; you just want to go for it. Group consensual process takes patience and humility. It requires thinking about the greater good. You need to move beyond your own desire and ask, "What do we *all* believe?" We must notice what we receive when we all attune and meditate together.

Gordon struggled with this, and often he charged ahead doing what he thought was right. From my perspective, sometimes he was right and sometimes he wasn't. His disregard for conferring with the group brought up conflictual issues among us.

Linda and I especially valued connection to the nature kingdoms, listening with sensitivity to the trees. Gordon showed less sensitivity to nature than others in the group and he pushed forward with an attitude of, "We're just going to get on with it and do what we need to do!"

When Linda and I first arrived, we saw that Gordon had cut down many trees without even attuning to them. We were shocked! Aghast, we demanded, *"What about communicating? What about attuning to them?"*

He replied, *"Well, I needed to get it done!"*

We talked about it and made an agreement in the future to engage in a meditative process whenever we cut trees or significantly impact the land. And he agreed, although the damage had already been done.

Other conflicts arose when I felt Gordon did not think through the repercussions of his actions. Gordon built a gorgeous passive solar house on top of the hill with big picture windows overlooking the garden and a beautiful lawn. He wanted the lawn to thrive, so he poured chemical fertilizer on it.

From an ecological perspective, the damage this causes is unacceptable. The lawn may look nice and green, but the chemicals kill not just the weeds, but also the earthworms and the microorganisms in the soil, interrupting the interconnected spirit of life. It violated our principles and everything we were working to accomplish.

I called him on the phone, my hands shaking, and started screaming at him. We clashed in a loud confrontation as he defended his desire for a nice lawn. From my perspective, we worked hard to develop sensitivity and awareness to the interconnectedness of nature, and harsh chemicals cause severe repercussions in the natural world. In our work, we considered the good of the whole, including the essential microorganisms, and Gordon disregarded all of this!

The event sparked every kind of conflictual, philosophical dilemma between us, but eventually we resolved the issue and he agreed not to use such products again. He recognized if we wanted to demonstrate methods for healing the earth he could not commit such destructive acts.

We battled through our profound power dynamic for a long time. Gordon was the more dominant personality, but something arose in me that blocked dominance to rule over me any longer. In my transformational process, within my being a resolution formed that refused to submit anymore.

We danced with each other, consciously wrestling with the dynamic tension between us. We worked with it the best we could, but the underlying tension remained. Our connection wasn't smooth and loving but a struggle for power and leadership, testing all the challenges of building a common vision together.

Yet we were driven by a deep desire to create beautiful community together. We knew it would help our growth and the planet as a whole. As we recognized this truth beneath several layers, our relationship began to shift and we connected on a deeper level. The superficial, irritating personality dynamic dropped away as new appreciation for each other created a thriving, communicative relationship. We found ourselves happier and more content.

The process of resolution was mysterious and gradual. I learned to let go, and saw this garbage arising in me wasn't for my highest good. Similarly Gordon learned to slow down and develop love and compassion. No one single event triggered the transformation; it emerged from a slow process.

When Gordon eventually married Corinne one summer out in our community garden, he asked me to be the best man. In our current relationship we both had developed absolute respect for each other and chose wholeheartedly to honor our intricate personalities. We recognized that, though very different, we still lived as brothers walking a spiritual path together.

Our appreciation of each other came from a deep place of being, and though we had never gotten along very well, we completely resolved our issues and tensions to become great friends. When unresolved tension finally came to completion, it positively changed the dynamic within the community as greater inspiration and flow emerged, demonstrating one of the first important lessons we learned as a community.

I was asked recently if Gordon left the community burned out and defeated by our disagreements. On the contrary, when Gordon left we were very positively connected with each other. Just as I learned about fire, he learned about water and his fire was transformed by his experiences, as we mutually evolved together.

When Gordon and Corinne finally left the community for good, their new direction felt in alignment without friction. Karmically, spiritually and personally we worked through lifetimes of baggage. Since then we have been harmoniously connected and good friends for many, many years. Reaching such harmony required me to uncover my own wounds from authority.

Past Wounds

During the early years of Sirius, much of our tension arose from power dynamics and past wounds with authority such as parents or teachers. I brought many of my childhood wounds because I always thought I was stupid growing up.

In school I was picked on and I didn't have any friends. The teachers accused me of daydreaming while they smacked me with a ruler when I didn't pay attention. I spent my time staring out the window wishing I could explore outside because I was bored out of my mind. If I sat in the back, my attention drifted further so they moved me right in the front row. My report card said, "He just doesn't care." One teacher, whom I appreciated, made similar comments, but also saw my light, holding faith that I would eventually find my inspiration.

Because my learning process was intuitive rather than rational, I left school defining myself as stupid. The whole system told me I wasn't bright and reinforced my self-doubts. They told me I failed at my assignments because I didn't easily remember facts and figures. I hated algebra and geometry, flunking both subjects.

When I graduated high school, they told me, "You're not university material; you'll never succeed in college." I came of age during the Vietnam War, and I was about to be drafted into the service. I decided to join the Marine Corps, and upon entering they gave me aptitude tests to determine my placement. New recruits went through the training and we took all the tests as a whole group. One test measured our IQ. Afterwards a sergeant had a stack of papers in his hand. He looked at us, and shouted, "Hey you! The smart one over there, take these papers and give them to the drill instructor when you get to Paris Island."

He looked directly at me. Looking around bewildered, I wondered, *Who is he talking to? Why is he looking at me?* He took the papers and threw them at me, demanding, "Take these and go!"

I was stunned; did he just call me what I thought he did?

I found out later that I performed excellently on the test, better than anyone else in the room! I felt little pressure to succeed since it wasn't a college entrance exam. Because my experience from my education anointed my self-image as stupid, that I couldn't get anything right and couldn't learn, this incident inspired a huge revelation in me. Shocked to realize my own level of intelligence, I puzzled for days in complete astonishment. Just because I didn't learn well in the school format didn't mean I was stupid. In fact I was pretty smart!

I brought this new image of myself into my later leadership roles in life and saw how others were wounded by similar experiences.

Wounds Emerge

Other members forming the community also brought childhood issues and wounds from our authoritarian society. In today's competitive society, our egos demand to see, "Who's going to win all the power? Whose idea is right or wrong?" Rather than recognizing that two different points of view hold value, we see only winners and losers. We fear that our rival's ideas will damage the group. This threat provokes our critical minds to lash out rather than honor our diverse perspectives.

Some issues run deep, perhaps deeper than our current lifetimes. It's possible the others we encounter in community worked together in past lives and shared traumatic events. We had to work with it and see it. I believe in reincarnation and karma, and when that energy came up, we confronted past life experiences that surfaced, working on them to resolve the tension.

Our soul battled our personality in a bout of inner conflict. The personality hung onto the creation of conflict, as the soul exclaimed, *"No, that's not where we need to go with this!"* We made this dynamic conscious, as we recognized, "Wow this really isn't working, this isn't the higher ideal, the way we truly want to live together." As we invoked our souls to live in more aligned consciousness, our personalities reared up against it.

Yet because we were all so committed to moving through our personal transformation in order to do our work in the world, we asked,

"Okay, if you say you want to be a more loving and compassionate person, how will you handle *this*?" But our perseverance provoked the challenges with greater intensity. We had little idea of the extreme challenges we would face in subsequent years.

Working through those conflicts proved difficult as we danced with each other and worked with the tension. We would wrestle with the issues that arose, but the extended underlying tension fed our irritation. It wasn't a smooth, loving connection; it was a struggle.

Underneath the superficial imperfections of our personalities lived a deep soul commitment to work through our challenges. We dealt with the tension the best we could, meditating both individually and together with some success. When intense difficulties arose, we overcame them through mindfulness. Even as this unresolved inner tension kept pulling at our being and intense clashes arose, our underlying commitment frequently enabled us to rise above and accept each other. We constantly shifted back and forth between judgmental charges and compassionate understanding.

As intense as our judgments toward each other could be at times, we committed not to fix the problems we perceived in each other, but to transform ourselves. We knew we needed to practice the qualities we aspired to create in community. In order for the relationship to deepen, we absolutely needed to accept our differences. We knew we would never be alike, but each of us exhibited unique qualities to offer to each other and to the process.

We had to recognize and accept each other as our truest selves. When all these projections and judgments would come up, all we could say was, *"Why are you acting this way? What is wrong with you?"* Many challenging years passed before unconditional love poured in and we could see each other clearly.

All those aspects were in the mix, and we watched various kinds of results emerge as we sorted out our personalities, sometimes consciously and other times unconsciously. Some issues took months or years to completely resolve, but eventually our interactions lightened up.

The land where we formed our community holds us as we work out our conflict together. The safe container of the forest provides an environment that allows our subconscious defenses to relax enough to face our challenges. And the spiritual energy embodied in the land pushes us to open up in the fire.

Spiritual Land

LISTENING TO THE SACRED

2

When I returned from Scotland with Linda and our daughter after Gordon and Corinne purchased the land, something about the land was deeply moving me. Everybody who walked into the forest here similarly felt as if we had stepped into a subtle spiritual vortex of energy.

Once I had fully arrived, I spent days wandering the land, communing with the rocks, trees and flowers. I studied the driest spots, observed sun patterns and noticed how the land looked after being bathed in rain. Wandering the land for the first time and seeing those sacred sites, I thought, *There really is something special about this place.*

I found many sacred places still hidden in secret today. Some woodland edges are dotted with peculiar rows of stacked stones, called cairns. Some stones are placed with a rocking stone on top, so that when somebody stands on it and rocks back and forth, the stones speak.

Three "hearthstones" stand near different water elements, stone structures featuring an opening where one might light some sage, its smoke drifting up through a shaft that opens into the heavens. A quartz crystal rests in the base of one, perhaps to channel the energy of specific spirits. Two of the structures connect to old hand-dug stone wells, revealing round walls stacked with mossy rocks. They descend eight feet into the earth, tapping into spirits of the underworld. Two more stone structures stand slightly off the property of Sirius, also near various water elements.

We recognized the land already held a sacred space, which we didn't want to disrupt, instead seeking ways to enhance its spiritual expression. And we wanted to develop parts of the land to construct the Community Center, build more living space and design more gardens, so together we mapped out the land.

We sat together with paper and markers and everyone drew red hearts on locations they thought were special or significant. We agreed to honor and preserve those places as sacred space. We decided to develop other parts of the land that felt less special or desirable and infuse them with our conscious intention. We understood that when nature interacts with conscious human beings the space also becomes sacred.

Affirming our intuition, Veronica Multon, head of the local historical society said, "These stone structures were built by the native people. They probably didn't live here, but I believe they practiced sacred ceremonies here. Would you please respect these structures, and not destroy them?" We would never have harmed them, but we appreciated her insight.

Some think these structures were built by settlers to build fires, but their construction would render them almost useless for such a function and they feature no charred marks on their interior. James and Mary Gage, who study indigenous stone structures, identified specific themes in their construction that reveal their native origins from different time periods. In my wandering I sat and meditated and developed relationships with these places.

Very few native people live in this area in recent times and we did not gain much wisdom from them because they were gone by the time we founded Sirius. Many died of disease as white settlers intentionally gave the native people blankets contaminated with smallpox to kill them. The survivors fled to Canada because they were so mistreated.

After we purchased the land, the nephew of the man who sold us the land came and visited. He told us he was half Native American. He knew of the land through his uncle and was happy to see what we did with it. We showed him around and he stayed for a while to absorb what we were doing. As a boy, he had stayed here on the land and was pleased that we honored the land and developed it in a conscious way. Other visitors would astonish us with their insights of the land.

Energy Insights

David Spangler, one of the spiritual teachers most respected at Findhorn, came to visit. While meditating he tapped into a reservoir of spiritual energy radiating from the land that called out for an avenue to be expressed in physical form. The energy existed, in potential, ready to manifest as sacred gatherings, gardens, community meals or ponds.

An energetic field availed, conducive to our spiritual work in creating community. Many people who came to the land here who were quite sensitive also picked up on the same energy. They would say, "Something's going on here!"

These spiritual vortexes exist all over the world in the form of ley lines, which are the energy meridians crisscrossing the earth. The human body also has energy meridians aligned and tracked by Chinese medicinal acupuncture. They cross at major energy centers in the body called chakras. Similar to the body, meridians on the earth cross at the earth's major energy centers.

One day, right at the beginning of the community, a rough, burly guy walked up the driveway. Unrefined, he uttered, "You don't know me and I don't know you, but I'm doing a research project on ley lines. A bunch of 'em cross around here in Shutesbury. I saw your sign and I wondered if I could come look around. Did you know anything about this? *There are two or three of them that cross right here where you are!*"

He belonged to the American Society of Dowsers in Vermont who use rods to energetically determine where the ley lines meet on the earth. When the rods are used on the land, and the dowser taps through an energy meridian, the rods cross dramatically. Their society plots ley lines all over the planet.

We invited him in, and he shared his research with us. He had a great sense of humor, and we enjoyed his company as he shared and laughed about his work. He didn't take it too seriously, but he did have deep understanding and knowledge about his area of expertise.

His presence was an affirmation of our already existing feelings, and he appeared out of the blue. The guy had never heard of us, and was just traveling around following ley lines. When he left, we asked ourselves, *"Who was that guy?"*

Thirty years went by, and on one visit, my friend Henry McClain, the architect of the Community Center, brought a man whom he knew from the Society of Dowsers. We were taking a sauna and the guy said, "Oh yeah, I came here many, many years ago to plot ley lines."

Surprised, I started to realize who he was, inquiring, *"Are you the guy...?"*

"Yeah that was me!"

I never expected to meet him again, but here he was! A new refinement and maturity about him gave him a deeper sophistication. I strongly felt some presence deepened in his beingness.

We engaged in a long discussion, as he was impressed with what we accomplished, and he grew especially excited about the Stone Circle we built. In alignment with their interest in ley lines, dowsers celebrate an appreciation for stone circles, which intensify the energy meridians through the land. He saw the Stone Circle was a powerful addition to the land, and he could see what forces drew him back to visit us thirty years later. He had no idea what we had become and he loved the energy here.

That was a beautiful affirmation from him. Connections like the dowser randomly showing up in our driveway happen all the time here, begging us to understand the science of synchronicity. Can science somehow explain the seemingly unlikely happenings that mystify conventional wisdom?

Radiating Energy

Countless visitors of the last 39 years have felt the of vortex of energy here. Spiritual places all over the planet provide these centers of light, and most ancient cathedrals were built on these energy meridians. Plot them with a ruler and many line right up, following ley lines. The old builders and designers knew about these concepts. They would pick a spot to build a cathedral energetically compatible to the idea of spiritual upliftment.

We were guided here because of the potential energy that would greatly enhance and support the work that we planned to do.

According to the documentary, *Lost Lightning*, scientists have been recording the resonant human frequency on the earth since the '40s. When massive thunderstorms form, they send high voltage lightning bolts into the stratosphere, which affect the resonant human frequency. Every one of these lightning strikes affects everyone on the earth simultaneously. No matter where you stand on the planet, your energy field is altered by one blast of lightning.

This discovery proves we truly are all connected. When we meditate, we send our energy out as a healing force, creating a vibrational field that reflects that energetic force. We realize that yes, the subjective level *is* having an impact. We *are* doing something important. Visitors come here and say, "I don't really understand what you're doing, but keep it up!"

In my personal life I recognize my internal action has just as much significance, if not more, than what I do externally on the planet. We consciously work with the questions: What are we doing here, and what kind of impact are we having on the whole? Recognizing how small our group is in the context of the planetary whole, we wonder, are we really going to have an effect on the planet? We came to the realization that we *are* having an important impact. Physically it may not always be that easy to see in the world, but our sense is that inwardly and subjectively we have a significant impact.

Part of the evolutionary cycle of the community helps us be spiritual beings connected to our spiritual selves. We explore what pathways open that connection. We dig into our personalities to see what gets in the way of that connection. And we pursue how to anchor that quality of real spiritual depth and connection into the very things we are creating and the very community we are building together.

This is already a sacred land to begin with, and the fact that we use it for sacred work enhances the quality and the frequency of that energy force. Over time we began to gain an understanding of that reality. One moment when we sought to build a new structure, the land carried us on an exhausting adventure as we sought to listen to its guidance.

Listening to the Sacred in Physical Form

We took our relationship to the land seriously, and without imposing our conceptual images of what we wanted, we would meditate, listen and intuit what seemed the best course of action.

Early on in the '80s we felt the need for a little spot out in the woods to meditate in privacy and feed our spiritual growth. We decided to build a meditation retreat house to keep us dry and warm in the winter when we wanted to go in seclusion. Six of us were assigned to find a place to build, so we went out on the land. For many hours we wandered through swampy areas covered in moss to the top of the hill under towering white pines, following faint deer trails together, searching. We came to a location that some liked, but others rejected. Then we would find a spot that the others admired, but the previous admirers wouldn't accept. We simply could not get any agreement! After hours of mulling about in disagreement, bitten by mosquitoes, we grew cranky and tired.

Close to giving up, we wandered to a spot we hadn't encountered yet. We viewed a small rocky ledge sloping away into open forest full of tall beech trees and we all stood still a minute. We looked at each other and said, "Yes! This is the place." That we could get consensus so fast seemed impossible as every prior location attracted several dissenters, but not a soul among us objected to this spot.

In our search we earnestly tuned into the land, listened to our intuition and tried to be open to receive from nature. When we finally found the spot, it felt like a miracle. We looked at each other in disbelief, wondering, *What happened? How did we finally agree on someplace?* In hindsight, the location turned out to be the ideal home for the retreat house.

After this experience, we formed a land use committee that works with this principle. The Community Center, Cob House, gardens, greenhouse, Stone Circle, and all the other structures, we sited with intention. We always wandered the land, meditated on the proposed site, and listened to our guidance.

A general consensus emerged that certain sites on the land held unique power. Many people were having powerful experiences with the swamp at the top of the hill, as if the land was commanding some strong, energetic force. We agreed to observe and respect the sacred spaces that were already delineated by the land itself.

At times we acted out of alignment, however, and the land surprised us by shutting down our misaligned ambitions. One time in particular, when we attempted to bring our egoistic ambition to the most sacred part of the land, the spirit of the land spoke to us loud and clear.

Sacred Swamp

At the swamp, one of my favorite places, I feel a deep connection to the land. Filled with grassy hillocks and tall hemlocks, water unusually collects right near the top of the hill in the center of the property. Roots of the hemlock protrude from carpets of moss to form tiny fairy houses, dense with bushes climbing out of standing water.

I recognized that the swamp would be an asset for our spiritual work, as three locations on its edge, a raised outcropping of rocks, a sheltered flat spot under an exceptionally large hemlock, and a space enclosed by mossy, protruding roots, channel a special vortex of energy. The whole land emanates powerful energy, but the field concentrates in certain spots. Perhaps the ancients performed a transformative ceremony there or maybe the ley lines cross as part of the energy meridian system of the planet.

When we first arrived, we came up with the brilliant idea to open up the swamp. Overgrown with blueberry bushes and shrubs, we wanted it to be more expansive and filled with light. Equipped with our chainsaws, clippers, boots and gloves, we attuned and got to work, but immediately something felt off. As soon as we started to try to clear the space, everything went wrong. The branches and twigs snagged and whipped us as we began to argue with each other. Our chainsaws malfunctioned and our clippers dulled. Our boots got swallowed by the mud, and the more we worked, the more uptight we grew, with every action proving more difficult. Finally everyone stopped, dropped the tools and sat down. We looked at each other and asked, "*What the hell is going on?*"

We gathered in a circle and began a long attunement, listening closely to the Spirit of the land. In my meditation I saw little nature beings, the swamp spirits, all dancing around us in a circle singing, "*They're listening, they're listening, they're listening! The human beings are listening!*"

We each experienced various visions in the attunement, but

everybody opened their eyes and thought, *We can't do this; this is wrong.* To listen to the divine nature of the land together offered us the most beautiful, magical experience. We stopped our work and decided we needed to leave this place alone. So we turned around and walked away, never to touch that part of the land with our tools again.

After many years of maturing our process of attunement, we again attempted to clear a part of the land to manifest our vision. We hoped our dedication to deep listening would guide us in opening up a space for an orchard.

The Tree Speaks

We decided to clear a patch of forest so we could start a permaculture orchard. We meditated together and this time we received clear permission to cut the trees. Because we were cutting *all* the trees in a big open space, we gave them notice and waited two or three weeks. We communicated our intention, expressing the purpose and how we planned to carry through.

After a few weeks, we went in to work. We progressed very slowly, cutting the smaller growth out first, and eventually we started cutting bigger trees, returning once a week to go in and cut some more.

One week we started cutting, but in our attunement we heard, *"No, not yet!"* We were all ready to work, adorned with our boots and gloves, clenching our chainsaws, all oiled and fueled up. But we let our eagerness subside as we submitted and put away the chainsaws. When we came back a week later, we heard, "Yes, now is the time."

We learned the lesson that the energy of the trees and nature needed time adjust after we changed the landscape. The energy must redistribute itself into other trees and other parts of the land. We could see that the energy does not completely withdraw, but realigns somewhere else. The web of life was readjusting to the changes that we were making.

By slowing down, we allowed this process to happen and could feel this dynamic as the energy moved. When we pushed too hard, it felt disruptive and fractionated the web of life. But by doing it in a very respectful, slow way we allowed the shift to happen. By the time all the trees were cut, everyone visited the site and said, "Wow, this is beautiful!"

No one who stepped into the clearing thought it had been

fractionated or jarred; instead it felt completely undisturbed, even though we cut down to the last tree. We left blueberry bushes and other plants and ferns, and everybody who entered saw only beauty.

Over the years I've connected with different places on the land, and different qualities of energy exist in each one. Sometimes I guide people to the places where I feel the special energy. Without overemphasizing what they should feel, I let people experience it for themselves.

The gift of these sites is fundamentally useful, and when people enter the energetic space, a certain levity helps free one's consciousness. The collective layering of thought forms typically limiting our perspective is loosened.

With this levity, to expand our consciousness and speak with new illuminated understanding becomes easier. When I go out in the world I feel stressful, limited thought forms invade my thinking, and when I return to the land my consciousness returns to freedom. I connect to spirit, shedding the layers of all these collective thought forms and limitations. Lightness, openness, and buoyancy happen. We live on special land here, and it supports the work that we do. As with many sacred places around the world, it offers a lightening that lends protection as it helps lift the limiting collective thought forms.

Sacred places of the world

Similar spiritual vortexes of energy exist all over the world that expand and uplift your consciousness simply by being in them. Sirius is one of those places as we hold intention to break free of the collective limitations in consciousness that most of humanity still holds onto. We say, "No, there is a different way of being, of living, and of experiencing life." Being in a place where mental constructs are looser frees our attachments to them, compared to a city, for example, where we are bombarded with countless collective thought forms.

Beautiful mountainscapes in the world hold a similarly powerful energy. Exceptional caves and valleys, lakes and streams, emanate an indistinguishable quality of brilliant lightness. Energy has been anchored and maintained in the sacred space.

When I go to sacred mountains or rivers, I feel a joyful lightness of being that fills me and my environment, as if a weight has lifted. Many different places I visited all over the world bring this joy. The St.

Columba Hermit Cell on the sacred island of Iona off the west coast of Scotland holds incredibly powerful energy. Hills covered in waving grass, blown by the ocean winds, house a small ancient church on the three-mile island. Sheep wander the hillsides freely grazing. Thousands of people pilgrimage to the island each year. Irish saints visited through the centuries to sit and meditate. As soon as one walks into that circle an unbelievably magical presence opens in one's consciousness.

The cell rests way out in the sheep pastures, standing right out in the open, and yet sometimes it can be almost impossible to find. I brought a group there from my conclave. We spent two hours looking for the cell but, despite all our efforts, could not find it. I visited this place twenty times before and now it escaped my sights. Finally the group grew frustrated and left. I turned around and walked right to it! It lay completely veiled, because for some reason I wasn't meant to bring them there. As soon as they left, it magically appeared out of nothing.

Tearing the Etheric Web

Humanity's approach to nature is generally one of domination. With no sense of cooperation, the attitude prevails, "We're just going to remove the mountaintop and get all the coal." People mutilate the living energy and tear apart the web of life. For centuries, humanity operated believing domination is the right path. *"We shall dominate over the earth!"* is an attitude that has created many problems.

I visited clearcut forests in the Northwest where the loggers clearcut everything with absolute disregard, leaving behind total destruction and devastation, including burning everything living on the land. I was in a war zone in a raw, painful experience, and I felt sick being there. The energy was so ragged, raw and rough, I wanted to scream, *"Oh my God, I've got to get out of here!"* because it felt so horrible.

In contrast, being here where we clearcut the trees for the orchard felt in perfect harmony. I wasn't the only one who felt they were bathing in beauty when they came to this clearing. I believe the way we work with it makes a huge difference.

When Linda and I first arrived after Gordon and Corinne bought the land, and I saw the area that Gordon had clearcut full of stumps, I was terribly upset. I felt the harshness and the tear in the etheric web.

Today I can laugh at the whole experience, but at the time my mind went wild, *I can't believe he did that! Did he really do that? Where is his consciousness at?* The incident created tension between us and while it didn't necessarily seem unfixable, I felt shredded.

Every day, life is a spiritual teacher. We deeply contemplate how to attune to a tree, exploring, *How do you cut down a tree consciously? What quality of energy are you bringing to build a structure? What are the repercussions of ignoring that quality of energy? What elements are involved?* We work consciously with all these questions.

We learned that you *can* cut trees because part of their purpose is to serve humanity, but the method must be respectful and honor the energy, rather than disregarding the powerful life force. We can work and not jar or disrupt the interconnectedness of the web as long as we listen and tune in. I have cut a lot of trees myself, and when I work with nature it doesn't feel like the web has been ripped or destroyed, because I attune with nature using patience and care for the landscape. Sometimes we don't always listen closely because we get fired up and we want to forge ahead. But the nature beings understand that we do try to listen and work with them rather than dominating.

Areas that have been clearcut can be healed, but the healing happens more slowly when the method is disrespectful. Because so many ancient tree are gone, cutting any today always disrespects the spirit of the forest. If the forest was all big ancient trees, we could cut some, but unfortunately most of those ancient beings have been destroyed. Respecting the ones that remain is essential because they channel specific energy different than smaller trees. To stand tall and powerful 300 feet up into the air, hosting entire ecosystems in their massive crowns and rooting deep down into the earth, creates a tremendously powerful vibrational quality important to the earth.

When standing small and insignificant in the presence of a great tree I am awed by their remarkable presence as I wonder, *Oh my God, the energy of this being is so tremendous, how could anybody even* think *about cutting it down!* While that awareness is often ignored, more people understand those experiences. The paradigm shifts when people wake up and have firsthand experiences with the presence of nature. When people feel the presence in their own souls, they will honor and protect it. We must help people receive firsthand experience of the spirit of nature, because it facilitates change.

I attended a Quaker Buddhist retreat center, and during attunement one of the founders offered her blessings and gratitude to all beings. In meditative sincerity, she expressed, "I give my deep, deep gratitude to the microorganisms in the composting toilets." The consideration of our impact, even on such a microscopic level delighted me. Are we adding chemical fertilizers to the environment that *are* killing the microorganisms in the soil? How do we honor that aspect of life? As a community, relating to our care on various levels has been an evolutionary process.

The Jains in India devote themselves to *total* nonviolence and some of them refuse to eat roots for fear of harming microorganisms in the soil. They wear masks to prevent swallowing any microorganisms when they breathe. Every time we take a breath we kill millions of microorganisms.

While Linda and I tend to stand on one end of the scale, though not this extreme, others move toward the other end, yet within everyone here resides an acceptable level of conscious sensitivity.

Understanding nature grew in me because I spent long hours meditating, cutting trees and working with the land. My awareness of nature kingdoms evolved with the community. As a community we've grown into a deeper sensitivity. Still some people don't understand completely, and don't honor it to the degree that we'd like, but we feel the care in the work in the gardens and on the land.

When someone acts unconsciously, we discuss the action and work with changing the approach. Some people don't share the same level of sensitivity that Linda and I do, which we have had to come to accept.

The dynamic is definitely changing, and people are remembering to respect the sacred web of life. In the new paradigm we cooperate with nature and create mutually beneficial relationships instead of domination. We won't have any less of what we truly love.

Slow Down and Attune

I push hard for the attunement process, while others complain we could complete our endeavors much faster. This question was a point of tension at times, but paying attention to efficiency versus the patience to listen has balanced our approach. We may have taken it to the extreme a few times and gone over the top, but not often.

Linda and I hold the fire energy to go out and get projects done.

Though I pushed for the necessity of attunement, I also had the ambitious fire burning inside. *I want to get this done too!* Internally for me I find balance, but I believe I err more on getting it done than too much attunement. Sometimes in rare circumstances I slowed down the group process because of an attachment to the way it was done, but even within me as a human being I want to just go do it, rather than hold back and wait to go through the attunement process.

Sometimes I have been ready to go, and people have stopped and asked, "Hey are you going to attune?"

"Oh yeah!" I try to listen to that too.

At times I wish we had attuned more, especially in the garden. With trees, we proceeded with more sensitivity because of their size and because they were here first. When I've been working in the garden, yanking up plants, I jolt to a stop as I recognize, *"I didn't do that with the greatest amount of sensitivity!"* I can feel the response come back, a jarring fragmentation of the living web. These experiences remind us how essential it is to be in nature, in harmony with the beautiful existing energy.

We can heal the energy when we recognize what happened and slow down. Very quickly the web harmonizes again. When I realize my unconscious mistakes, I just stop my work, or I meditate more. Nature offers forgiveness and when the general level of intention is clear, it allows room for mistakes. We learn and reflect: *Maybe I should have taken more time here. This is a good lesson.* The inner Spirit speaks directly to us and we realize, *Ohh, okay...I need to go a little slower with a bit more sensitivity.*

Building a Labyrinth

My mother Josephine and Jean Marie came across some ancient books that describe the mystic power of labyrinths. Architects of labyrinths lay geometric patterning on the earth, and when a participant traverses these patterns, the journey raises one's consciousness, allowing one to connect with the earth and heal oneself. The ancient knowledge of labyrinths has been understood and respected for a long time, as designers of old cathedrals in Europe built labyrinths into their tilework floor structure. Fascinated by this ancient tool of wisdom, Josephine and Jean Marie decided to create a Cretan labyrinth.

When we traveled to Brazil, I saw a labyrinth laid out on the floor of a large pyramid structure. The people treat the labyrinth with great respect, and at lunch time all the businesspeople come and eat their lunch. They walk the labyrinth to heal and reenergize before going back to work.

The shape of the labyrinth here at Sirius was laid out with strings. We dumped a big pile of stones from the land by the entrance, and each time someone walked the labyrinth, we asked that they take a stone and place it somewhere around the edge. Many people over time, with one collective intention, actually placed the stones that outline the labyrinth.

People come to experience the effect of the labyrinth when we do ceremonies. We have gathered in the center of the labyrinth and performed rituals for full moons, equinoxes, solstices and other celebrations. It remains a great addition to the community, bringing in a certain quality of spiritual attunement and alignment. Many different spiritual centers and retreat places I've attended build these labyrinths because of the presence they hold.

When we built the labyrinth I felt skeptical, because I didn't understand these ideas. But once it was built, I walked the pattern, and I truly felt a shift in my consciousness. I felt my consciousness opening, allowing me to connect with the healing power of the earth. Within my being, a deeper alignment organized itself. I felt a positive, healing presence moving through me, and my respect for the medium grew as I began to understand its power.

Gifts and Obstacles

parenting in community

3

When we first arrived on the land, only one house with two bedrooms existed, and we needed more living space. Gordon brought a house trailer to the land without knowing at the time that it was highly illegal. The town has an ordinance against house trailers and the aftermath caused a huge problem in our relationship with the town officials.

Upon our arrival, Linda and I, with the kids and Suzanne all moved into the illegal house trailer while John and Cheri joined Gordon and Corinne in the Farmhouse.

Once we found out it was illegal, we meditated as a group about the trailer and we had the sense that we needed to keep it. We went to a zoning board of appeals to get a zoning variance to keep the trailer, and quickly realized there was absolutely no possible way it would be accepted. Since we felt that it was right, we insisted on our way, sabotaging our relationship with the town, while ultimately forfeiting the trailer.

Obviously that revealed itself as not the best decision, and we confronted our learning discernment early on, realizing not all whole group decisions come from a higher place. As we made decisions, the feedback of how aligned are decisions proved to be would come back to us. We realized, *That really was not the best idea!* Despite this, the feedback gave us information about the town's response to the community and how to deal with similar issues in the future. While a microcosmic mistake, the lesson proved to be an important learning experience.

When the town came knocking and finally demanded that we remove the illegal trailer, a house across the street came up for rent. Linda and I, John and Cheri, and Konnie moved into the larger house across from the garden while Suzanne joined Gordon and Corinne in the farmhouse. We rented the house for several years while the kids were little. On short notice we found out the house was sold right out from under us and we needed to move. We couldn't find any other space available nearby, so we built a little cabin on the land and lived there while we built the Longhouse.

A tiny one-room cabin was not sufficient for a family of five. Rebecca, our eldest daughter in her teenage years, could not stand living in a tent outside the cabin, so as we designed the Longhouse, we decided the top floor would be residential. We finished the kitchen and living area first and moved in as a family before finishing a connected dorm and additional rooms. The progression of building more and more living space for people had begun.

Time for Families

Raising family in community brought challenges, especially in the beginning when we were broke, holding onto a vision and scarce resources. I needed to dedicate time to my family in addition to the community and to find time to balance both proved painstakingly difficult as I struggled immensely. While I probably gave more energy to the community than to family, I also felt blessed by the powerful and beautiful experience of raising a family here.

I came from an unconscious, abusive childhood and family situation with an authoritarian father who smacked us around made it hard to be with people. Being particularly sensitive, communicating was difficult as I picked up everybody's feelings and thoughts. I worried something was terribly wrong with me. Up until age 15, I spent much of my time alone in the woods, but in nature I never felt alone, I felt surrounded by friends and nature beings. To cope with the overwhelming invasion of other people's energies as an adolescent, I started drinking alcohol and it shut down all my sensitivities. Unfortunately as I got older, alcohol became the problem.

When I merged back on the spiritual path, all my sensitivity started to return. By the time I left Findhorn, people helped me to process my sensitivity. They explained to me, "You have sensitivity, but the emotions of others don't have to affect you so negatively." They offered tools and strategies to keep from feeling so overwhelmed. I visualized a field light around me for protection. Gradually I learned that as long as I held myself in a vibration of love and spiritual light, the energy would pass through without affecting me. I was not vibrated by it. It was there, but it flowed around me like water and left me still whole.

Without any methods to understand my sensitivity as a child, I wanted to offer better support for my own children. By surrounding them with like-minded, aware adults and providing ample nature connection, we hoped to nurture them in a better way.

Despite my best efforts, patterns from my own childhood wounds emerged anyway. I claimed, *I'll never do this to my children!* but quickly found myself doing what I sought to prevent. Yet because I was so committed to be a spiritual, compassionate being, I dedicated myself intensely to correct those contradictions. Despite my strong beliefs against the practice, I spanked my daughter once. I felt so traumatized from the experience as it brought up the horrible memories of my father hitting me and I never did it again. I think the spanking affected me more than my daughter. As part of my evolutionary cycle, I evolved both as a parent and in in my relationship to the community.

Both our children as adults expressed to us we should have better prepared them to go out into the "real world." They went from community right into Waldorf education, which is also cloistered, and when they emerged into the rest of the world, they were both shocked and dismayed by how differently the world treated them compared to the perspectives held here at Sirius or in the Waldorf school. It took them a long time to adjust to mainstream culture, and they often expressed that they felt like foreigners in their own country. They may still be adjusting but are mostly integrated now. It was a hard lesson learned, that children in community need preparation to understand what is going on out in the rest of the world.

They also sometimes complained that the community competed for our attention and we were unable to focus on their needs and desires as much as other parents.

Despite the challenges, raising family in community has been rewarding because it takes more than just a couple to raise a child.

There's truth in the famous quote, "It takes a village to raise a child." Our children experienced an expansion being around so many conscious, engaging adults and played often with their community aunties and uncles, in addition to growing up with loads of other kids to play with. In the first generation of the community, eight other children from two other families lived on the land, with several other kids coming and going through the decades. They all experience a free range childhood, often going off to play around the land, ride bikes, swim in the pond or run through the backyard remotely supervised.

Some of our parenting styles across the community varied, as some kids ate more sugar and watched television; some attended the local public school while others went to Waldorf. But we trusted each other and knew our kids were safe in the presence of all the adults in the community. We all agreed on the same behavior for children during community time and we created shared boundaries and discipline. The benefits outweighed our differences, and we shared carpooling, meals, childcare and many parenting responsibilities that made aspects of parenting much easier.

While we ate most of our meals as a large community, we set aside one night of the week to eat dinner at home as a family, and some evenings I would tell my daughters stories or make candles with them. My younger daughter took to learning carpentry as a teenager and loved helping on the crew and hanging out with my young apprentices. While we could have spent more time with them and prepared them better when busy creating community, we tried to do the best we could.

As we were building the Longhouse, I also started a worker-owned cooperative business separate from Sirius called Rainbow Builders, building passive solar houses and greenhouses for people in the local area. I would work all day in the construction business, come home to eat dinner and work here till two in the morning before returning to work. Young and full of energy, I fulfilled double shifts since we desperately needed a place to live in addition to earning some income.

My older daughter didn't like it much. She yelled from the bed "It's two o'clock in the morning! *What are you doing?*"

"Sorry, sorry!" I would call back.

Life is a dance and a constant learning journey; when you stop learning, you die. It's not always easy. You make missteps, with parenting, with other people, with your work, and you fall down, get back up and brush yourself off. Don't forget to keep laughing and loving, moving and dancing. There's not much else to it. Sometimes you fall down and it's hard to get up, but eventually that's what you have to do, just keep going.

I've faced the tremendous challenge of getting up from some devastating falls a few times and it wasn't that easy but I tried to keep dancing. Unless you're reborn as an enlightened master, you're mostly growing and learning, but even the masters are growing and learning.

The Longhouse

OUR FIRST BUILDING VENTURE

4

Sustainable Materials

Stemming from our deep sense of spiritual connection, we care immensely about ecology and the environment, so when we built the Longhouse we practiced care daily. When you believe all life is sacred and interconnected you become a deep ecologist because you recognize we live together on this beautiful, vibrant planet, and everything we do affects our home.

We took our spiritual principles and grounded them into powerful collective creation. The integrated way of living motivated us to consider every choice we made. *What kind of buildings shall we erect? Shall we slap out a bunch of junk buildings that mess up the planet and devour tons of energy? Or shall we harvest real local, sustainable materials to energize our efficient construction with potent, powerful purpose?*

This mentality guided our building process as we conducted research. *Can we find a local source for this? How might we approach this in a way that is more environmentally sound?*

Most of the Longhouse construction materials came from repurposed sources. Our attention to second-hand materials was partly driven by economic factors as we had little money, but our beliefs also informed our construction practice and we tried to buy nontoxic materials and use sustainable practices as much as possible.

As a builder, I hadn't yet tried passive solar building; I only studied and read about it, inspired by boundless possibilities. The two most important sustainability strategies included passive solar heating and better insulation. Later we created sustainable systems with electricity, heat, and hot water sources, but we did not realize their importance at first. As we are committed to honor our sacred interconnectedness, we decided any buildings built on the land must be energy efficient and passive solar.

People cleared space for their gardens and solar devices, letting us pick up the trees for wood, which were milled at the local sawmill.

I wondered how we would find glass, quite an expensive commodity, for the many large, double-paned windows we needed, and another miracle arrived. An employee of Anderson Glass Company visited and told us, "I'm about to throw these thermal windows in the dumpster, do you want 'em? If you pay my gas I'll bring 'em up here!" He felt concerned about wasted materials, so he hauled three truckloads of windows up the hill to our site, and we paid him $28 for gas. The repurposed and donated materials we used in the Longhouse slashed our expenses down to only $20,000!

Once we completed the wood shop, we started using it immediately, which, along with the new residential space, provided additional income for the community. Providing my family a place to live, securing residential space for others, and introducing a woodworking shop brought us a great sense of completion. A great feeling of affirmation radiated as we proved, *Wow, we can do it! We have the power to manifest our vision!*

Our lack of funds added personality to the structure. We made one of the beams in the shop out of an old railroad tie because we were short on wood. When we dug the well, we told the company to drill only as deep as we could pay for, which was only fifty feet. On hot summer days, the well runs out of water for an hour sometimes, so I had to build additional systems for rainwater catchment in my garden. For some reason we constructed the building on top of the well, which never allowed us to drill it deeper at a later date.

Composting Toilets

Slowly, as we developed new projects and pushed the edges of acceptable building methods, some of our practices became seen as less strange and more accepted by the building industry. When we first came to the land we wanted to build composting toilets and opted to add one into the Longhouse. Flush toilets are an ecological disaster. Pooping in clean water that we can drink, then spending vast resources to remove it, is completely unsustainable.

When we first arrived, we had the difficulty of getting any composting toilet model approved. The law allowed composting toilets only if an entire septic system and regular flush toilet also existed in the building.

In the Longhouse, we installed a flush toilet only because it was the law. We also installed a composting toilet. I closed the lid on the flush toilet and built a bookshelf on top of it so it would not open. When my youngest daughter first went to school, she was used to our composting toilet. I was there with her at school the first time she went into the bathroom. She came running out asking, "Daddy, Daddy, which one is for pee and which one is for poo?" Many perspectives abound on how we raise our children!

Within a few decades, the state of Massachusetts passed a law approving and legalizing composting toilets. While not every variety is approved, there are commercial models allowed without requiring a flush toilet in the building as well. We probably were not directly responsible for this change, but our presence and forward thinking did stimulate conversation on the state level.

The compost toilets we use here on the property work effectively, known as moldering compost toilets. They compost in two different holding chambers. The urine goes into several tanks on the basement where it is stored until the tanks fill up. The solid waste drops down a long tube into a concrete box. When the concrete box reaches capacity, we close the toilet from above and the excrement sits in the box for two years to break down. We open up the other chamber and let it fill up while the other breaks down. When both are full, we shovel out the solid waste. Because the waste mixes with sawdust over two years, the smell vanishes and the waste begins to look like soil.

In order to make sure the material contains no pathogens, we place it in black barrels for another two years and it breaks down further. Eventually we layer the fertile resource under the fruit trees in the orchard and cover it with three inches of wood chips. Because it processes for so long, we eliminate any health risk. As an added precaution, we never use it directly on any of the annual crops.

Urine on the other hand is a great fertilizer, which comes out of your body sterile. A great source of nitrogen, we pour off the tanks in the basement and collect it in five gallon jugs. We water it down and use it in the garden in the spring as a foliar feed and soil drench. We also pour it in wood chip piles, add it to the empty garden beds covered in leaves in the fall and mix it in the compost piles. We never put it on crops we are actively eating.

We win both ways because we cut down on the waste stream while also receiving valuable fertilizer. We hope this becomes the model for the future, as human waste presents a huge problem all over the world.

Addition

Quite a few years later, our daughters outgrew their tiny bedroom with bunk beds. I inherited some money and decided to invest it in building an addition for the girls. We added one room and while the girls still shared a room, they were not right on top of each other. The girls grew up there but it was also the front door where all the visitors came knocking, so I often received feedback on the poor design. They did not appreciate lying in bed undressed while some community member came looking for us.

The room sat empty for a long time after they took off to travel and find their own adventures. They would return for a few months off and on for years, appreciating that they always had a place to come back to, so we left it empty for them to crash. We let the guest department use it and hosted our own personal guests in the space, but it was seldom used because of its inconvenience.

About six years ago our daughters marveled, "This is stupid! That room doesn't hardly get used at all. We passed the travelling phase and we're more settled now, so we rarely need that room. Why don't you build a wall here and make an entryway?"

I replied, "If we did that we would be using the room all the time and you wouldn't have a place to live." They pondered the consideration, "Oh, oh yeah," before exclaiming, "You should do it anyway!"

I asked, "You sure?" And they both answered, "Yeah!"

After it was built they became so upset when they didn't have a place to crash anymore.

"*We have to stay in the guest space? What's that all about?*" they complained. But they were the ones who told me to do it! I just laughed as I could see the archetypal adult maturation of letting go. They still wanted connection, but their adult self spoke forth, *"Do it!"*

Building the Longhouse built our confidence, so when the next big idea emerged, we believed we could do it. The Longhouse proved to be an essential lead up to the Community Center. I learned post and beam construction from a book and when you walk through all the different buildings, you can observe my learning curve and how much my skills improved with each decade. The leap in consciousness required to start another project shrank every time, and it all started with our first abode and workshop. The Longhouse has been serving ever since.

The Economic Shift

From Income Sharing to Financial Independence

5

After struggling to make ends meet for two years with an income sharing model, we received guidance in our meditation to shift to individual financial independence. When we decided each family would control its own finances, some of the women with children stayed and worked in the community full time, tending the gardens, caring for the children and cooking. Some were running the guest services, and everyone was very busy, so not everyone had time to earn money outside of the community.

We set up new financial systems, settling on a minimum monthly membership fee that every family paid. We decided that as the members of the community, we were the bottom line, and we must make the community work financially. When we needed more money to pay all the bills, monthly membership fees increased, sometimes even doubling. No matter what the financial needs were, we agreed to contribute for financial success.

The new model opened up the inspiration for a revitalized flow of energy in teh community. In order to meet this new model in which we shifted away from everybody living and working on the land all the time, we started a construction business run as a worker-owned cooperative.

Rainbow Builders: An Innovative Workers' Co-op

We were blessed with an excellent bookkeeper, Evie, who trained as a CPA and lived with her family at Sirius. She kept the books for our business in addition to the community, and she would let us know our financial status on a month-to-month basis. In order to meet all our financial needs each month, she would tell us we needed to contribute X number of dollars that month. Oftentimes our contribution surpassed the minimum; sometimes it jumped much higher, and we would just pay what was needed to make it work.

While the transition brought significant challenges, the shift strengthened the community and increased our interaction in the neighborhood as we formed new relationships. During the two years of the communal economic system we were isolated from the rest of the people in the neighborhood, as we did not connect with hardly anyone else socially or economically.

The construction business required a connection with the local business owners, customers and other local contractors. Those same people and businesses later supported the construction of the Community Center.

To take the spiritual principles that I learned about for years and invest them into a construction business was very empowering for me. These principles were not restricted to living in a spiritual community, but could apply to running a successful business.

Rainbow Builders became a community in itself, and we all supported each other to get our needs met. Many employees said it was the best working experience they ever had. The business supported the needs of the people while we made money and had fun. To see universal spiritual principles work in business was a great affirmation. When you bring love and connection into your work while supporting the wellbeing of people and the planet, abundance flows.

The business we created was an equal share, worker owned business. We stepped outside of the industry's norms as we employed women, attuned together, and worked with a consensus decision making process. While some people in the business lived at Sirius, we also hired local tradespeople.

Because we applied the spiritual principles of interconnection and the sacredness of life, we worked on supporting the needs of the people in the business. We believed we could do something good for ourselves and for the planet by building passive solar houses and greenhouses that are less toxic, more environmentally friendly and use better building materials.

The male-dominated construction industry fuels itself on a fast-paced, speed-driven attitude. We decided to work at a slower, more relaxed pace, with an intention of having fun. Because of the high level of competition in the construction business, we decided we would take lower wages if necessary to work at a more reasonable speed. With this choice, nobody felt extremely tense or pressured while we worked.

We boldly experimented with wages. The normal practice for wages bases its scale on seniority and skill, but we changed the model and decided people would earn a wage determined by need. If somebody had a family to feed with several children, they would receive more money to care for their family.

Despite my status as one of the most skilled people in the business, I decided to be paid the least amount. I wanted to keep my income low enough not to pay taxes I disagree with as a war tax resister. I personally haven't paid any war taxes for almost 40 years. This decision created an interesting dynamic in the business, as we looked at wages and labor from an entirely new perspective.

Together we experimented and decided each individual could decide their own personal salary. Because everybody was an equal share owner, we all knew exactly what everybody else got paid and the production and skill level of each person. If you wanted to change your pay rate, you participated in a peer review by all members of the business. People gave feedback about your work, your timeliness and the harmony of your relationships with others in the business, plus a general review of your performance as a member of the worker owned cooperative.

Once you went through that process, you decided how much you got paid. It was a controversial arrangement, but nobody took advantage of the situation. Everybody acted responsibly, taking the money they deserved in relationship to their performance. The interesting experiment seemed to work. Some people made more money than others, but because we decided together, without top down authority, everyone invested oneself in the model.

As a worker owned cooperative with equal share ownership, if we made money, everybody made money, and if we lost money, everybody lost money. So we took our responsibility seriously. With no boss-employee relationships, we pulled together, worked hard and fully invested ourselves to find success.

The experience proved tremendous for all of us, particularly for women who typically had a hard time entering into the male-dominated, fairly harsh construction business. Many women wanted to get involved and, when given the chance, turned out to be some of the best contractors and finish carpenters. I watched with joy as other people felt empowered, owning and running a business. It was a remarkable experience and we expanded to a community of 15 people working together successfully.

While benefiting Sirius, the construction business wasn't directly related to the community, existing as its own entity with its own bookkeeping and group process. Sirius gained information to source building materials, met contractors, and received leftover materials, while Rainbow Builders benefited from the space to host meetings and events.

Skills we learned through the business also supported the community. I eventually applied the experience I gained from the business in the construction of Sirius buildings, especially the Longhouse and Community Center. One day all the people in the business provided a huge boost to the community when they volunteered to work on the Longhouse.

Separating Finances

When we moved into the Longhouse, everyone was trying to figure out how to get our finances in order as we moved away from a communal economic system. The community was active and busy, especially for me, because I worked a full-time job outside of the community, while still completing the house.

Once we separated our finances, we came back together as a community and reevaluated our identity on a new level. No longer tied together by this economic need, and independently economically stable, we still wanted to grow as a community, but with evolving ideas of what community meant to us. As we formed new connections and relationships with people in the extended neighborhood, we matured to recognize that we are part of the world we live in, even though some of our values may differ.

The spiritual component of the community became paramount, as we wanted to work together and deepen our connections. With improved finances, the additional money gave us more flexibility. We redefined the community in more alignment to our spiritual aspirations, and not based on making money together.

Ownership, Equity and Neighborhood Expansion

The Question of Owning Land

Sometimes individuals who come here have different visions for Sirius that do not align with our overall mission and purpose. One example of clashing ideas appeared with homesteading. Individuals wanted a tract of land to build a house, with ownership and autonomy to make their own decisions regarding developing and selling their property. While we seriously considered the idea, it was impossible under our current governance model. The zoning limited our options because we would need to chop the land up into tiny bits and separate from the nonprofit in order to give individuals complete ownership. Each plot would require 250 feet of road frontage, forcing us to lose pieces of the land that we wanted to keep.

However, people who lived at Sirius instead bought houses in the neighborhood and remained involved in the community, expanding Sirius in other ways we didn't imagine. This wonderful expansion of the community allowed more people to be involved without such intense commitment. The neighborhood supports the energy of Sirius and adds to the social setting.

Certain limitations *do* still exist within Sirius, and in order to maintain essential aspects of the community, we need to work within some of those limitations. We all need to accept some of those limitations, such as not dividing up the land and selling off little parcels. Huge ramifications would result and we could lose our tax exemption status, which would deny our use of the Community Center, our ability to receive tax exempt donations, everything!

When people want to make fundamental changes to our structure, we must consider if the changes truly contribute to the good of the whole, not only in the short-term, but over time as well. The Core Group is not perfect at making those decisions. Sometimes we can be deluded but we do the best we can while considering everyone's needs. Some of our meditative decisions may have surprised all of us at the time, but our experience in retrospect reveals that most of our decisions benefited a higher good, seen or unseen.

Building with Equity

To meet people's desires about owning a house, we agreed that if people build a house here, then whatever they invest in the house, including sweat equity, they would eventually get back from the community. We considered the investment a loan. When they leave, the community pays them back over time from the residential fee of the house they leave behind. Unfortunately we originally conducted this proposal verbally without articulating the details on paper and greatly regretted the blunder when misunderstandings ensued years later.

Two other key families joined us by the early 1980s and chose the option to build houses on the land. Ed and Evie Pless came from Indiana with their five children and lived across the street for many years while they built their house. Ed, another key carpenter, worked with me at Rainbow Builders. Ed also embraced a deep connection to nature and we related on many levels. Using old barn beams, from his own constitution he decided to design the house with ten sides, featuring funky corners, curved walls and homemade bathtubs. Ed was ambitious but not a finish carpenter. His family moved into the house with sheetrock missing from the walls and a rough plywood floor as he periodically continued to work on the building. Eventually the family moved out and the house remained unfinished. Twenty years later the building crew continued to install window sills, seal up the basement, and complete other house necessities. Still to this day, none of the closets have any doors, and squirrels sometimes sneak through hidden cracks in the walls.

Another family, Norman and Georgette, and their three boys, also joined us and lived here for about 13 years. The family lived across the street while building their house. Georgette worked extensively in the gardens with Linda and spent many hours with all the kids. An innovative musician, Norman installed a recording studio in the house where he recorded a Grammy award winning album with his friend and accomplished jazz musician Yusef Lateef!

When Norman and Georgette split up, they left the community and their house behind and wanted their investment returned. A dozen years had passed since they made their agreement with the community, and the details were hazy and unclear. We had the house appraised and its value came in way under what Norman and Georgette thought it was worth. It didn't cover nearly the amount of time, money and labor that they expended to build it. They also wanted their money in one lump sum rather than over the course of a decade, which the community could not provide. Much conflict ensued, and though we came to an agreement eventually, no one left especially happy with the result. Sirius strained to find the funds to pay for the house immediately, and Norman and Georgette felt they did not receive what they deserved.

Sirius took out a personal loan to avoid paying 13% interest and paid them. They unfortunately left angry after more than a decade of sharing community together. Our kids all grew up and played together, we shared meals, sweat and history, and it ended poorly.

Evie and Ed also divorced eventually and Evie continued to live in the house with her kids. When she left, with the help of an appraiser, she settled on a fair price with the Core Group, of which she was a member. We wrote up an official agreement and paid back her investment slowly over time.

We learned hard lessons and because of the conflict and confusion from both these houses, all future agreements about houses were spelled out in great detail. When we arranged to rebuild the Phoenix House, everything was signed, documented and counted, including paying the heirs if the homeowner died.

Community Expansion in the Neighborhood

While building a house exemplified one model to build equity, others who wanted home ownership decided to build or buy houses along the road, which also expanded the community. The population of the community shifted over time as members of the community moved nearby. Many neighbors are still very involved here, and they even offer their service in the garden, building structures and making financial donations.

We didn't foresee that shift, and it has enriched and strengthened us to have that larger sense of community and connection with the people living nearby. It broadens the social aspect of the community while surrounding us with supportive friends.

Different people have different levels of involvement, some intimately engaged and others more peripherally. But we feel the presence of all our friends nearby, and sometimes they all come together for big celebrations and such.

Group Dynamics
LEADERSHIP & ORGANIZATION
6

Individual vs. Group Delusion

As we worked creatively together through a group meditative process, our bad decisions based on delusional perceptions lessened considerably. In any meditative or intuitional process, one individual might act completely off the wall, but it is much less likely for the entire group to lose itself in delusional perception.

We decided that even if we believed the guidance we received in meditation came from a deep place, it remained disputable. We gave ourselves permission to question each other's deepest sense of reality. Our commitment belonged to truth, not to placating our personalities. We sought the root of understanding, and when someone made a proposal, we gave ourselves permission to speculate, "Well, how's your day been, and what state of consciousness are you in today? Do your statements come from a deep place or from some personal charge?" People receiving guidance might exclaim, "I am transmitting the unquestionable word of God!"

And we rebut, "No you're not!"

Stunned, they retort, *"What do you mean?"*

In a group context, when one member expresses one's deepest sense of truth, the task proves tremendously difficult for another to respond with, "Well, maybe that's not entirely right." Trust and love need to combine with effective communication skills in order to address our concerns without attacking each other's deep vulnerable places.

Our current society often dismisses the source of our spiritual guidance as nonsense, rather than honoring its wisdom. Feeling the pain from the dominant culture's denial of our intuition, at Sirius we intend to stay sensitive to judgment. We choose to guard and protect the vulnerability of speaking to our deeply felt truth.

Yet any of us will be deluded at any time. In our imperfections, our deepest innermost reality can be tainted by unresolved personal issues. Guidance in meditation may not necessarily be the word of God, but the possibility to tap into a higher perception and receive pertinent, powerful information lives strongly in our being.

We hear guidance like radio receivers; the static that convolutes the communication through the line lies in our own internal misperceptions! The clearer we are, the clearer reception we hear from these higher levels of consciousness. When I'm having a bad day, my emotional charge distorts the channel, tuning out from those higher levels of conscious awareness.

We must work through our life patterns and clear up the interference in order to receive spiritual understanding clearly. We attune in this way constantly to become pure channels of spiritual light and love, and we can apply it to our group work. Still today we have a commitment to question each other, which requires great trust and vulnerability.

One time, the hungry deer provided a surprising scenario for an outside guest to speak up and confront us with clear wisdom…

Lesson from the Deer

In the early years, considerable unresolved tension still remained, particularly between Gordon and me. We all worked in the garden fulltime and built round beds like saucers, planting them full of peas, lettuce and kale. We harvested some lettuce, but soon the deer came and devoured the whole garden!

We tried every trick in the book to keep them out, erecting fences, urinating on the edges, sleeping in a tent nearby and blaring a radio. We even asked the deer in meditation to stop eating up our whole garden but nothing worked. Then a guest came along and said, "Your group process is like the deer. The deer are coming and eating all the tender lettuce just like you nibble on the tender parts of each other." He clearly looked at us with a strong sincerity in his eyes and said, *"You need to resolve the interpersonal dynamics of the group."* We all paused in silence and nobody said a word.

Then we acknowledged, *"We think you're right!"*

In that moment, the truth hit us clearly, as we realized Spirit provided no choice but to pay attention and look inside ourselves. Expressing criticism like this might be unpopular but it creates clarity and power, and leads to a deeper perception of reality. We need to cultivate enough trust and understanding to give people courage to express their unpopular insights. People need reassurance they will still be loved and accepted by the group.

As we heeded the reflections from our guest and nurtured the tenderness in each other, we witnessed absolute miracles from the deer in the garden! We continued to meditate with the deer, expressing that the plants we grew were essential for our nourishment and survival. The next year, instead of devouring the whole garden, the deer only ate half.

We continued to reflect on respecting and caring for each other's vulnerabilities as we encouraged the deer to find their forage in the wilderness. We invited them to rest in the sanctuary of the land, requesting that they leave our garden alone. That year the deer ate only a quarter of the garden. With more compassionate attention to each other and our four-legged friends, the deer returned to eat only a small fraction of the garden the following year.

After several years of mindful practice, our major interpersonal challenges resolved, and we held each other with more compassionate understanding. The day after hunting season opened, we saw deer beds as they found sanctuary on the land, yet not a single plant in the garden had been disturbed! The deer went on their way, never to return again. I still see deer in the neighborhood, but they haven't bothered us in decades.

The process with the deer was slow, taking many years as we learned our lessons. Learning to communicate with nature or animals is reflected in our own nature. We needed to learn about ourselves and also to communicate with the deer. We recognized our obstructions in creating meaningful relationship among ourselves in addition to the animal and plant kingdoms. The process was deep, and the real clarity emerged when a courageous new voice spoke truth to leadership.

Becoming a Leader

I went to Findhorn in my mid-twenties after spending six months at a Zen Buddhist center in Hawaii. Before I arrived at Findhorn I had studied some spiritual teachings but still considered myself a novice. I had continual intense inner experiences that brought me understanding and wisdom, facilitating my awakening. Each time I sat down to meditate, spiritual concepts flooded my mind.

Once at Findhorn, I excavated so deep, I felt as if I died! I lost sense of who I was, spiraling into an identity crisis. I meditated for four hours a day and the flooding awareness completely disoriented me. My past identity and personality completely shifted. I saw my true nature as a spiritual being, with insight and understanding in a way I never experienced before. Everything changed so rapidly inside of me. I never before studied the concepts, yet they flooded my consciousness, and I became aware of spiritual ideas beyond the grasp of the experienced spiritual teachers around me. I learned simply by tuning in, not from studying the teachings.

People noticed and they came to me for advice, asking about concepts I had just learned, which gave me tremendous power. Four years into my spiritual journey and two years after my arrival at Findhorn, the founder asked if I would focalize the Core Group. Bewildered, I looked at him unable to comprehend why I would have the knowledge and experience for this role. To gain that kind of responsibility frightened me because people expected me to get everything right, sometimes loading me with blame when reality disappointed them.

I was a lost American kid in my 20s, thrust into a position of power in a prominent community. I realized much of my wisdom came from my past lives as I recapitulated old knowledge in my soul. I tuned into my true identity as a spiritual being. All the other phases of my personality that I passed through in this life became exposed as garbage layered over my true self.

The revelations totally disoriented me. Imagine all your ideas about who you are dissolving away and some entirely different reality flooding in.

The rapid change turned me into a complete emotional wreck desperate for some comforting familiarity. I recovered slowly over many months as I had to recognize and accept I was someone completely different from who I thought I was. I started running into trouble communicating with others because I was completely thrown off. I wretchedly cried, *"Oh my God, spare me this horrible terror!"*

Gradually I worked through the disorienting fear and arrived at a sense of empowerment as I saw a spiritual side of life. My reborn perspective stood in stark contrast to everything that I had been told about life while growing up and in the military. The new wisdom gradually elevated me to a position of power and authority which was uncomfortable and new because I didn't know how to sit in power. Eventually I encouraged myself, *Well you can do it, it's okay.*

Soon after, an existential crisis in Findhorn's leadership would utterly test the volition of my realizations and demand me to put my new skills to work.

Intuition and Confronting Leadership

When we become spiritual leaders we are all at risk of distortions. I've met many powerful spiritual teachers who on one level had such great insight and connection, but on another level faced a huge distortion in their personalities. Not all, but some of what they perceived was off. The guidance distorted when it filtered through the personality.

Perhaps souls exist on this planet who have enough purity and consciousness to be free of such distortions, but I have only encountered one or two if any. The extremely rare exceptions are pure beings such as Gandhi, Martin Luther King, Jesus Christ and the Buddha.

Tremendous problems arise with many spiritual teachers around the world. A teacher might have great insight and understanding in one area but when translated, it becomes distorted in various aspects of their life such as sexual relationship. To use your individual discernment and discrimination in any particular situation, especially with spiritual teachers, is essential. While the wise masters *should* be honored, don't ignore your intuition and follow the flock simply because they offer great insight.

When people put spiritual teachers up on the pedestal and exclaim, "This guru is infallible!" whatever fallibilities or distortions they have in their personality get translated through the whole system. To come to a deeper understanding of reality is easier when we work through a group process rather than as one individual. The danger of distortion and illusion also decreases if a group is self-actualized, as members work with their own power to integrate into a sense of connection with the whole. Without this maturity, all the people become followers, and group distortion flourishes.

I experienced this treacherous obstacle at Findhorn with Peter and Eileen, two of the community's founders and spiritual teachers. With brilliant insights, they established themselves as wonderful, powerful spiritual teachers, yet serious personality distortions began to protrude from the surface.

All kinds of thoughts float in and out of your consciousness, and our spiritual growth process helps us learn to discern and understand what's going on within oneself. On a personality level it's easy to be swept away in false beliefs, tagging them as deeply spiritual messages. I saw this distortion with Peter and Eileen.

Appointed head of the Core Group, the community's decision making body, I felt averse to the role because I would be responsible to face the contradiction I saw. Despite the Core Group's authority, everyone followed Peter's lead. I decided Peter was acting off the wall and I stood up and said no. Because I was a young kid I feared I would appear as if I didn't know what I was talking about, and it was difficult to speak up.

Throughout the formation of the community, Eileen channeled guidance she received in meditation and transmitted it for Peter to enact. The guidance obviously illuminated truth, as the partners' efforts produced surprising miracles in the blossoming of the community. One day, however, the guidance Eileen received ended, and she said to Peter, "I'm sorry, I have no more direction to offer you."

Lost and dismayed, Peter sought guidance from a psychic who told him, "You are overlighted by St. Germain! Everything you do and say is in direct relationship to this higher guidance." So Peter began to act from his ego, leading the community in misguided directions. The missteps started causing problems in the community, exposing the obvious distortions in his perception. When I confronted Peter and Eileen saying, "I don't think your perception is entirely correct," immense tension ensued.

I confronted the whole governing structure and they dismissed me, saying, "You just don't understand." I questioned myself, *Do I really understand?* But the guidance I received was, *You need to stand up to this. You need to speak your truth and be here, even though you're being pushed back so strongly."*

I get a kick out of this: For a while, I was accused of blocking the manifestation of the community because I refused delusional misdirection and had to just sit with the accusation while sticking to my opinion. After one meeting, I walked away thinking, *Either I'm a completely whacked out nutcase, or they are!*

At the time, I honestly didn't know whether I was blinded in illusion or they were. I faced extreme difficulty as I questioned myself and my own sanity, even my own ability to ascertain who I was. I willed myself to object to power and authority, when most everyone else insisted on the opposite. I leaned into a powerful stance as I declared, "No, this is not okay! These actions are not right; they are misaligned with Spirit."

These were the founders of the community! Who was I to question them? Yet through the strong soul connection I was experiencing at that time, I received clear insight.

Gradually others saw the truth of the situation and spoke up as well. The dynamic slowly shifted, and eventually everyone acknowledged the system needed to change. The Core Group established its power and Peter stepped back in allowance.

The blind acceptance of a leader's complete infallibility is one of the great dangers in group dynamics, but to deny my feelings would have been in direct conflict with my intuition. What I confronted at Findhorn revealed the truth of my insights, but only after enduring heart-wrenching pains over a dreadfully long period of time.

One might think this experience would guard me from falling into the same trap that caught Peter, but I have had significant distortions in myself as well. When I assumed a role of leadership at Sirius, seated in the reverse position, I faced a similar sight of dissatisfied members dishing me their accusations. Now I stood as the confronted authority figure.

My Own Leadership Confronted

"This isn't right!" insisted the members of the community. The trial had begun.

Secret meetings had been organized in the community to talk about Linda and me, and we weren't invited. We found out about them of course, because no secrets survive in small communities. Pissed off, we reacted extremely defensively before we realized, *No that's not going to work. We just need to listen.* My previous experience of confronting leadership allowed me to stay open to criticism.

As often arises in any group, my power, authority and leadership were questioned. While these qualities are necessary and useful, I had to pay attention to the reflections I received. Without reaction, we said, "Okay, what are the issues, what are the problems?" We sat down and listened to every single person in the community who came to us to explain the problems they saw. We heard many people reiterating some of the same concerns, exposing some validity.

Some concerns clearly reflected our personality distortions, but some we saw as projection. Half projection mixed with half clear reflection, the people aired their grievances, and our willingness to listen and implement changes helped dissipate the intense charge. We appreciated people's courage to raise their concerns directly to us.

Speaking Up

In my life, I had similar experiences where I was called to speak up, and I've made a lot of mistakes. But rather than whimsically ranting, the questioning comes from a deep space within me, from a depth of soul recognition and spiritual understanding. Sometimes these thoughts are bogus and delusional, but when they persist they have a deeper nature and spiritual significance.

Whenever we are motivated to speak up only to discover our objections are based on illusion, powerful learning occurs as we learn discernment, understanding and the deeper nature of spiritual reality.

Because we might be wrong in our insight, it's difficult to speak up in a group of peers, with people we respect, especially when pressured by the group. We want to belong, to be loved and accepted. Even if we feel a deep calling within to say no, the personality comes along insisting, *They're not going to love me if I say this.* Often we let go because we believe we lack spiritual understanding or insight. Rather than trusting our intuition, we defer and assume the teacher is too highly evolved to be questioned.

We all perceive profound principles of what's really true. We experience gut feeling and a deep truth yet resist our intuition. To effectively create a dynamic group process, it is essential to have the power within ourselves to speak what we truly feel. Our opinion may not always be right, but it is important to put it out there and acknowledge our perception. This courage demands a strong level of spiritual development and self-actualization because it often goes beyond the personality's basic needs to be liked.

The whole group will be working on a decision and one voice on the side speculates, "I don't think this is right." Individuals in the group might recognize, "There's something important here that we're not seeing, and maybe it's what *I'm* not seeing." Yet that discrimination can be a blockage too sometimes. The group consciousness process is a dance with irreplaceable value.

None of us have reached the level of spiritual enlightenment of being completely unaffected by our personalities, which is okay. All part of the dance, I don't become a bad person when a distortion in my personality leads me to make the wrong decision. The error doesn't reduce me to anything less than my truest self, it simply illuminates where I am in my growth and what I'm moving through.

Core Group Decisions

A key objection that people raised when they confronted Linda and me rested in the fact that no process existed for the community to give feedback on Core Group decisions, and people recognized that Linda and I expressed strong voices in that body. When the Core Group came to a final agreement, that was the end of the story. We handed down our decision and everybody had to live with it.

No one else was even allowed to attend Core Group meetings, while the Core Group retained ultimate decision making authority over topics that affected everyone in the community. Tremendous reaction ensued as people abhorred the arrangement, exclaiming, "I didn't get an opportunity to express myself on this decision! You're leading us the wrong direction, and I feel helpless!" The situation beckoned the Core Group to reflect and change our methods.

A big detriment to creating loving, compassionate community lies in arrangements in which people feel victimized, with no power to change their environment. When people resent decisions, it becomes part of the life of the community. Resentments stem from not being heard when they believe leadership makes unfair decisions. They perceive leadership as stuck and rigid, with no opportunity for creativity, challenge or growth.

Hearing people's concerns, we changed the dynamic of agreements between the Core Group and the rest of the community. The new policy gave every member the power to question Core Group decisions. The final agreement stands only after every voice in the community is heard. If the Core Group makes a decision that any member of the community believes is detrimental to the good of the whole, then the issue must be heard and discussed in a general community meeting. We might discuss a topic at length so the Core Group can understand why the original decision is seen as detrimental. The topic will be discussed as long as necessary for everyone's concerns to be addressed. At the end of that discussion, the Core Group must go back and reconsider its decision based on the feedback received. After that, the decision becomes permanent.

Usually in the process of reflecting and understanding the situation more fully, people drop their opposition. The new process opened an avenue of empowerment because no one lives powerless under hierarchical decisions any longer. With the changes, everyone in the community was welcomed and encouraged to come to the meetings. Members felt empowered with more say in the community.

When interpersonal issues arise, we cannot ignore them in fear of stepping on someone's toes. Most of us in leadership are used to our toes regularly getting stepped on. Sharing discordant feelings is normal and everyone has them. But when we hold onto them and they fester, they can perpetuate other people's anger and resentment. To address the issue head-on is better, even if people get angry.

Growth opportunities always arise with power and leadership. We're building a cooperative atmosphere, more than just a place to get things done, so we lovingly accept feelings of resentment and anger.

When people want to end a marriage, they blame the other person, because if they tell themselves they don't love or care about their partner, the pain lessens. We blame others and objectify our problems, particularly in a one-on-one relationship. We might claim, "You're so screwed up I can't get along with you. You're always going to be the same, so our problems will never change!"

You lose your power when you make yourself the victim. This often happens in community. People make external accusations, "I hate what the community out there is doing!" But what is the community? Nothing more than all the people who live here. We distance ourselves from the problem, insisting, "It's the community's fault!" rather than exploring the ways we can work together. To talk more as a community about how this dynamic arises helps us work through our challenges better.

Issues of leadership, power and authority remain as key factors that fractionate group consciousness and often blow groups apart. Leaders must recognize that just because they hold leadership positions doesn't mean they are always right. We can be wrong like anyone else. I may have wisdom and understanding because I've been "doing community" for a long time, but not every word that comes out of my mouth is correct.

We all move through plenty of distortions. As we grow spiritually and evolve, the distortions lessen. We gain the ability to divest ourselves from our illusions and witness other people in their processes. The resolution may require several lifetimes to be realized, even extending beyond when we die.

Contemplating Departures

While I don't fully understand it, over and over again the cycles of the ebb and flow of the community have been dictated by waves of people choosing to leave the community, followed by many new people who arrive at the same time. Perhaps they come here to work out karma with other individuals, learn important lessons and continue on their spiritual journey.

We recently experienced a big exodus of people who lived in the community for years and years before a huge wave of young people came in. We mused, "Whoa, this is great!" Watching a big group of people leave disheartened me, but the new excitement renewed my interest in community and rejuvenated me to keep going. Witnessing marvels of instantaneous shifts in our young arrivals' consciousness restored my faith in the necessity of the latest transition.

When people leave we consider if people experience disillusionment from an inability to fulfill themselves in this environment. When we look at the departures, we sometimes recognize, "Oh yeah, we didn't respond the best to that situation." But rather than beating ourselves up over our mistakes, we acknowledge, "We learned lessons from that experience, and hopefully we learned them well." We are growing as we continue to change and evolve, and when we face significant upheaval in the community, we make fundamental changes.

The universe is mysterious, but I believe that as our evolution and consciousness evolves, all kinds of interconnected changes result. Similarly, when consciousness shifts in community, every member is impacted, though not everyone changes at that rate or in the same manner. Perhaps the discord prompts rearrangements in our membership.

People left for many different reasons, and quite a few went on to fulfill amazing projects on the planet. Some people who left wanted to live in a different kind of environment, while others stayed, deeply called by our spiritual group work. Other people simply needed more time for their families and couldn't devote as much time to the community as they wanted. Raising children in community can be a powerful experience, but it demands great focus. No situation stays the same forever and people must follow their calling.

The Outside Community

Our goals, beliefs and perception of reality at Sirius have generally differentiated from the mainstream. People often fear what they don't understand, and sometimes people feel threatened that we dance to a different drum. Our society defines what is considered important to most people, maintaining certain thoughts and beliefs around what constitutes a good, healthy, vibrant life. In contrast, here we choose not to follow the status quo because we deemphasize materialism and wealth, and many of the goals that society upholds matter little to us. We agree not to break any laws, but our inspiration lies apart from cultural norms.

Beyond the bubble and support of the immediate neighborhood, other people have come through here who disapproved of what we were doing. As a young fledgling organization we didn't exert great efforts to bridge gaps or attempt to create understanding from others. When we first arrived on the land, we were insular and did not interact or seek out our neighbors, and the local town of Shutesbury directed plenty of hostility toward us.

Over time we've improved our external relationships, breaking down barriers so that everyone can feel welcome. We especially went out of our way to cultivate relationships with the town, working on municipal projects. We joined town committees and volunteered with the fire department. As a nonprofit, we make a yearly contribution in lieu of taxes because some of the children attend the local school. Now we've been here a long time and, as people have gotten to know us, they feel less threatened. They know that we're not a cult and that many kind, loving people live here. They still don't align with all of our values and beliefs, but overall most people accept us and that creates harmony in our interactions. Despite this mutual respect, some individuals still feel intimidated by who we are and what we represent, and they refuse to come visit.

Even in the early years, before members left to buy property in the neighborhood, Sirius already existed in the context of a larger neighborhood. Our relationship has evolved through different eras and many people with a sense of spiritual connection in their life and a desire for a sense of belonging have been attracted to the area, not just because of Sirius Community, but the larger community called Hearthstone Village.

Because we were always in so many houses, and nobody locked their doors, the kids felt comfortable to roam the neighborhood on their bikes. We never feared for the children's safety because we all knew each other and the familiarity and shared living brought us a sense of trust.

Through the years other homesteads and projects emerged along Baker Road and in the area around Sirius. Without being directly involved, many families moved here because of the feeling of community Sirius brought to the neighborhood. They enjoyed walking on the land, swimming in the pond and sometimes joining in community meals.

In the 1980s the community cooking rotation systems involved most of the neighborhood. It moved from house to house each night and everyone joined in. Some nights we crammed into a small house across the street with ten kids running around, adults trying to maintain conversations, while cooks bustled in a kitchen so small that the host ran out of serving dishes and plates. But when cooks started raiding the Sirius kitchen for pots and pans to use, which often never returned, we decided to host community meals in one location.

The Hearthstone Village started printing a newsletter called the Cricket about events and opportunities in the neighborhood. Now it has gone online as eCricket, with about 340 people exchanging information. It includes apartments for rent, political events and happenings and local recommendations for business. When people need help, they ask, and oftentimes they receive good advice from neighbors and friends.

The Ark

One neighboring collective household project was the Ark. It was a four-story building built right at the end of our driveway, with a cupola on top pointing skyward. The ark held a chaotic beauty with the character of the residents visibly displayed on every windowsill. Children's toys jumbled together in corners loaded with musical instruments and cushions. The interior protruded with unfinished railings and exposed beams, decorated with colorful cloth and unfinished floors covered in layers of carpet. The kitchen was stocked with unmatching pots and pans and several refrigerators. Often as many as 15 people including kids, babies, adolescents, parents and single people all shared communal living space with one kitchen and two bathrooms.

The Ark's relationship with Sirius was mostly amicable. We were friends with people at the Ark and sometimes Sirius Community members rented space there when our rooms filled up. Their mission differed from Sirius's in some ways and while they understood spiritual principles, they focused more on cooperative living, managing interpersonal relationships between families and coming together in one common living space. They operated as a cooperative household, sharing meals, buying bulk food, and raising children.

Many members of the Ark engaged in our projects and shared meals with us. They participated in the garden share, accessing the food we grew, and donated time and energy, stacking wood, working in the garden and helping us run our programs.

They also exhibited behaviors that some of us at Sirius didn't necessarily condone or believe in. They hosted more parties, did more drugs and engaged more in the late night dance scene than we did.

It was not our business to tell them how to live, so we ignored the activities that didn't resonate with us and embraced our commonalities. We were always open to a mutually beneficial relationship and through the years many spiritual people who lived at the Ark stayed connected to Sirius. We practiced mutual support toward each other and tried to make the membrane of Sirius permeable so people could enter and be involved in the capacity that worked best for them.

In general, we avoided insulating ourselves from the neighborhood around us, trying to make the community feel accessible so that anyone has the opportunity to experience our spiritual, communal, and sustainable work here on the land. People could get involved directly by living and working here and becoming members, or more peripherally by being our neighbors, walking the land and attending events in the hall.

We especially succeeded for several years when we hosted a village-wide dinner once a week, usually with a speaker or event afterward. At one period as many as 30 to 50 people attended. Other times, however, the larger community is not so present and needs more encouragement to come visit. Currently it works well as people can get involved or ignore us as they please.

Extending Perspectives

Over the years many people lived at Sirius and then moved on to travel or raise families. Some bought their own homes in the neighborhood or in nearby towns. Though I am not motivated by the pursuit of property ownership, the opportunity to invest in land offers a worthwhile path for others, and we want people to be able to choose their own path.

I understand why individuals and families choose other paths. People are busy and caught up with daily life including work, children and relationships, which can be all-consuming. They don't often have much time to fully participate in community. They have to give more and often work extra hours on community projects. The pioneering experimental model takes more commitment and energy than simply living with one's own family.

People often come to community thinking, *Oh I'm going to come to Sirius! It's going to make my workload so much easier; I'll be taken care of.* Instead more difficulties arise with a certain level of energy needed to support and relate to the community. The lifestyle takes a certain kind of personality. To live in community and maintain focus and creativity requires a tremendous amount of internal and external work. You must hold your personal life together, while maintaining more relationships and handling more drama.

In trying on a great experiment, while pioneering new living methods, the process demands tenacity and vision and some people aren't ready for the intensity that community living brings. To be in so many relationships on a daily basis requires perseverance and stamina. Good people, growing spiritually, need to experience it through their own method at their own pace. This might mean living in a nuclear family and visiting a community occasionally.

While some past members left and never returned, others wanted to maintain a connection with us. Most past members respect and appreciate the community and value our continued existence. Even though they are no longer involved, they understand and appreciate how our work changes people's lives. They come back with their children to remember and admire which nail and board they installed, or reminisce about a workshop that helped transform their life. Sometimes old friends return to tell me, "Even though I'm not really involved, I truly appreciate the fact that Sirius is here!"

To have been a part of our work stimulates feelings of importance for people. If they lived here in the past, they feel a powerful energetic connection to the community. They say, "How is it going? Is there anything you need? How can we be helpful?" They know our work is powerful and appreciate it, even without active involvement.

While challenging, the investment proves immensely rewarding. When you strive to live a more spiritual life with others who share our ideals and beliefs about the world, a deeper space for sharing your authentic self also emerges. Space opens to ask, "*What's going on in your life? Let me share my current challenges and how I'm dealing with them.*" You see the strategies that don't work and where other people learned from failing. Some strategies work well and result in a more successful relationship or better family dynamics.

People overcome limitations and the pool of knowledge is larger and more diverse than interacting only with your own nuclear family. In an average American life situation, you don't interact with the same vast array of individuals. You have your immediate and extended family, and some friends who you may not see very often. You're busy working and driving from school to soccer practice or dance lessons, for example. If you plunk yourself down in a community setting instead of a single family household, you now see others quite often. You're dealing with others' emotions and triggers as well as your own. You learn not only from your own life experience, but from the challenges and decisions that other people face, and you feel the shared human journey we are all walking.

You see others dealing with habits, shadows and stresses and it expands your awareness as you witness how others may deal or react to similar issues you might face. You expand your life experience by 30 people who have different ideas and methods to deal with their finances, interact with their children or handle conflict. People who act differently than you, beyond your close family or friends, give you new perspectives. Personal growth accelerates when you live with others committed to spiritual growth and your connection deepens as your learning expands and you witness others' life experience.

I respect all methods and one is not better or worse. When people live on their own homesteads, learning at their own pace, the experience provides its own diversity. In the early days we didn't imagine we would reach an audience who would create a wider neighborhood, yet it's been a wonderfully positive development. When people outside Sirius form relationships with us, we experience more depth and breadth in our lives. The relationships enhance and stabilize our work, providing interaction with a larger audience beyond the people who live on the land.

Every individual chooses a path that works for them to grow. As long as they commit themselves to grow and learn, many methods are appropriate.

Guiding Role

As our group consciousness evolved, we attracted people at our present level of evolution, or even higher. As seasoned community members, we played a guiding role in the newcomers' processes, yet were blown away as they shifted so quickly.

We felt as though we were merely reminding the new people of concepts they already knew, rather than teaching them. As if their souls had temporarily forgotten, with a small reminder they would say, "Oh yeah, I know that!" I was shocked to see how much wisdom was already present in their minds. I didn't need to teach, all I needed to do was help bring into sharper focus the awareness that already existed. We helped open the door for understanding to emerge as we catalyzed the process, but they learned lessons without direct teaching.

Those who left were not less evolved; they contributed to our evolution at important stages, but each time the next wave of people rolled in, they raised the consciousness of the community even more. I feel uplifted as more love and compassion pours forth.

A young woman, Kira, who arrived in the newest group of young people, reflected on the process, "As pioneers you created emotional, mental and spiritual pathways to realize change, like forming a synapse in the brain. Once the synapse exists, the earth as a whole understands such realizations so much more easily."

To think that our realizations are creating the whole planet's ability to understand certain concepts feels a bit grandiose, but we do understand the importance of subjective work and the possibilities to help open pathways in the collective mind. In the collective consciousness of humanity on the planet, we can work with intuitive levels of thought as our expanding awareness and new thought patterns make it easier for others to awaken to inherent truths.

Limiting Thought Forms

Limiting thought forms, held collectively by millions of people, are extremely potent and keep human consciousness stuck in self-destructive patterns. But we can break free through our intuitive work. Either people play out these belief systems until their soul grows strong enough to gain autonomy, or they eventually feel so shut off, frustrated and unfulfilled that they burst through their limitation. Without the burden of limited thought forms, we become conscious about who we are and how we treat each other.

Creating an atmosphere where collective thought forms can be seen and understood allows the space to open for creative, spiritual and expansive thoughts to come in. Expanding that energetic, the subjective field powerfully affects the whole.

People often choose to stay here because they feel free. A visitor once remarked, "On this land I don't feel weighed down by the collective thought forms of humanity. I can just be me!" New thinking, and a lighter way of being emerges. While some thought forms persist here, they are not bogged down or layered heavily with the collective thought forms about who we are and how we should act. People don't usually realize the powerful energy force of thought forms. We need to find ways to free ourselves from their grasp. As individuals it's easy to be influenced until we reach a very high level of spiritual development, because the thought forms are so strongly held by so many people. I consciously work to open the atmosphere with others in the community.

A certain amount of transmutation and purification needs to break through all those thought forms and feelings. Human beings can raise their awareness about what is real, and what is fake. We have been trained or programmed to believe what is real, and we can break these limitations.

My part in changing thought forms is to work on myself. I don't judge it, I simply ask what part do I play, and how conscious am I being? Though our actions as a small group may seem insignificant compared to the mindless destruction happening on the planet, our impact has *great* significance to change the collective thought forms and we *are* creating a pathway of new thinking, while countless groups all over the planet are doing the same.

Clearing the limiting beliefs proved essential to our power of manifestation. Had we succumbed to certain defeatist attitudes, relying our manifestation on basic principles of logic, we never would have found the power within ourselves to fulfill our vision here. And yet opening the space in our minds to allow for the principles of manifestation is astonishingly simple.

Physical Manifestation
BUILDING THE COMMUNITY CENTER

7

Energy Flow

Sirius benefited tremendously over the years from the principles of manifestation. Because we created for the greater good of others on the planet, not just for ourselves, the universal energy forces supported our powerful intention. Intent carries weight and attracts more energy, which allows immense abundance to flood the systems we created. When we put ourselves into the stream of higher universal intention, energy flows toward us.

Energy flows in many forms, from dollars to a truckload of windows...enthusiastic volunteers to a limitless selection of tiles. If you follow the principle, you will experience energy entering in to fill your needs. You might not get everything you want but certainly everything you need. We don't need to be perfect in our process of manifestation. Pure intentions carry us far, but if we ground and align our intentions and soul forces, the manifested universe supports us even more powerfully.

Great teachers and founders of Findhorn taught us these principles. David Spangler described how unimaginable miracles arise when we work with the Laws of Manifestation. Peter and Eileen demonstrated that when we attune to God's will, we receive exactly what we need to move forward.

Living at Findhorn and understanding these powers of manifestation enabled us at Sirius to work with the same levels of consciousness. With acceptance and grace, as we follow the basic principles and ideals, abundance flows. As we practice personal transformational processes we connect deeper and deeper to the innermost parts of our being, not just in spiritual consciousness, but also in physical reality. Manifestation translates down into physicality because we *are* physical beings, living in a physical universe.

We explore how to interface between the spiritual and the material realms to meet our needs. Led by great spiritual ideals and intentions, we feel the spiritual presence and power growing stronger within us as we build in the physical realm.

The energies of the manifested universe actually exist within us. They don't reside somewhere off in the distance. We need not go somewhere to find them. Deep within our inner realms of spiritual connection lives the power of manifestation.

We ask, *How do we apply the spiritual understanding to material ambition? How do we bridge those two realities? How do we bring recognition deep down into the physical manifestation of everyday life?*

When we carry out a vision for the greater good, the universe supports and helps manifest that vision. When we invest our entire resources and energy into creating our vision, the universe responds dramatically.

Many people come here with all kinds of ideas, and then they try to start living it, but to actually manifest the ideas into reality requires of them and everyone here to anchor deep spiritual understandings in the physical forms that we all inhabit. That recognition makes Sirius a little different, a little special.

We took on this project not merely for our own personal interests; we felt it was an act of service, educating people and demonstrating new hope for the world. Absolutely convinced that we were making correct choices, we put all of our energy, resources and time into the project, and the reciprocal flow of the universe followed.

We explored several important elements of the Principle of Manifestation:

- *Manifestation happens in the right timing.*
- *All existence is sacred and interconnected.*
- *The universe supports efforts for the greater good.*
- *The quality of energy invested becomes permanently imbued in its manifestation.*
- *Conflict reduces the resources of manifestation, while resolution and harmony attracts resources and facilitates the flow of manifestation.*

We manifested what we needed more often than we thought possible over the years and these ideas proved indispensable when we set out to build the Community Center.

The Community Center

One project that demanded our attention to every element of the principle of manifestation proved to be the construction of the Community Center. The tremendous project occupied much of our resources for ten years, but we approached it with a conscious intention in a fun, relaxed pace.

Manifestation happens in the right timing.

As a group we had tried to start building the Community Center soon after we formed the community, but our efforts fell flat. The money, design and resources did not emerge. We realized later we weren't ready because we didn't have the skills or experience yet.

Ten years later we learned of a grant for such a project in the amount of $12,000. Seeing an opportunity, we meditated and received a clear yes to go ahead and build the Community Center.

With our second attempt, when the timing was better, we didn't have total consensus on where to build it and walked the land countless times. Some individuals thought we should put it further up the hill at the top, but others disagreed, and after a long process of meditation together, we decided to construct it in its current location.

We applied for and won the grant, so we drew up the plans for the whole building with no idea where the rest of the resources would come from. We had absolute faith that we would succeed and we started building. We were driven by irrational intuition and were ready to pour our whole heart and soul into our work. We attained a building permit, called in an excavator, and poured the foundation for the first section.

All existence is sacred and interconnected.

Most houses that are built out of standard building materials are ecological disasters, as the ecology of the land is completely ignored in the name of profit. A high percentage of landfill waste comes from the building industry. When old buildings are torn down, they contain toxic materials such as asbestos, lead paint and fiberglass insulation. The materials don't return to the earth, and they create a huge problem as the landfills overflow.

The products used harm both installers and occupants. Carpets and paints offgas, affecting the indoor air quality. Lead paint seeps into the soil and hurts the development of young children. Painted wood and old concrete are dumped in overflowing landfills. Fortunately, with growing awareness of the toxic waste stream of the building industry, new practices have been developed. We applied our spiritual value to construction of the building itself, integrating the sacred interconnected concepts. We chose materials in the building that were the least toxic, local and most environmentally friendly materials available.

While our construction has some impact on ecological systems, it is far greener than most of the houses built in the area. Most of the wood used to build houses is shipped thousands of miles across the country from locations such as Washington state or northern Canada. The amount of construction waste we produced was minimal compared to normal construction. Scraps became firewood or were used for other projects. We were constructing a beautiful, energy-efficient center, built with plenty of love, care and compassion.

When we built here, we strove for a different model and practiced ecological methods. We looked at local timbers and local materials and examined the source of every product used in our buildings. We assessed the embodied energy, a concept that takes into account every resource used to get the product from its place in nature to our doorstep. This includes the time for the resources to grow and the fuel used in cutting, hauling, storing, cooling and shipping products.

We asked, "How much embodied energy does this product have? How toxic is it?" We searched for alternatives. At times we made compromises in order to look at long-term impacts. Sometimes we used a longer lasting material, knowing it would save energy through the lifetime of the building. With our experience building the Community Center and a few of the other residences, we experimented with some less well known techniques.

Because one of the great resources in the Northeast is an abundance of trees, we saw them as a great local nontoxic resource, and 90% of the wood we used came from local sources. We tore down old abandoned barns nearby and used the old chestnut beams for our framing. Just as with the Longhouse, neighbors donated the trees to us. We cut them ourselves after we meditated with them and waited a few weeks for permission. We appreciated the offering of their lives before planing and drying them. People helped out, donating time, materials, and money, and offering loans when we really needed them. We weren't just slapping together a structure, but building in consciousness, intentionally learning to work with Spirit while becoming more compassionate and whole in ourselves.

I started a building apprenticeship program which ran for years, sometimes working with up to eight apprentices, many of them women. We constructed in a relaxed way, and much of the building was built by inexperienced people under my guidance.

We built the first wing without stopping, and when we finished, residents occupied the space, providing more income for our project. But the new income alone was not enough; when we were ready to start the next big section, we realized we had completely run out of money and resources! We believed wholeheartedly in the good nature of our mission and put our full trust in the powers of manifestation.

The universe supports efforts for the greater good.

A woman who had attended one of our programs came to visit and asked what we were working on. We showed her the new Community Center and told her we were out of funds to start the next wing. Without blinking, she offered us $10,000 a year for three years to keep going, which helped tremendously!

We never actually stopped working on the building when we ran out of money. We focused on other aspects like cutting trees to keep the construction going. A couple times we stopped in the winter when the weather became impassable, but we never stopped due to a lack of resources.

The quality of energy invested becomes permanently imbued in its manifestation.

In our designs and building projects, we strive to create sacred space. Whenever I'm constructing a house, building a wall, or designing a garden bed I ask, *How do I make this an endeavor of sacredness?*

I want to protect and care for what's already present on my site. When we work in gratitude, with care as our guiding principle, the original energy of the site stays. Whenever I work with the land in any way, I am making a connection to divine energy radiating through me.

Working with joy and enthusiasm is incredibly important to me. If the inspiration disappears, the situation needs to change. When we were building another house, I had apprentices who didn't really want to be at Sirius working with me. Distracted by their own life issues, their heart was not in the carpentry. Instead they brought negative energy every day to the job site. It felt miserable! Eventually I told them, "I don't want to work with you anymore! Something needs to change."

I gave them the opportunity to shift, but they were bogged down by such personal crisis and turmoil they could not make the leap. The negative energy continued and so I decided to stop working with them, even though I had no one else to work with me at that time. I knew

I made the right decision, and in time other people showed up full of excitement for the project. They wanted to put good energy into the carpentry.

When I enter a room after someone cleans, I can sense the mood they were in while they worked. I can tell if someone toiled in anger and frustration or if they sweated away in love and gratitude. They leave their energy behind, which can be a powerful healing energy or disturbing negativity. Although apparent in the physical cleanliness and organization of a space, before I even open the door I can feel the quality of energy. I sense it in common areas, in personal dwellings, and on the land because the disharmonious energy lingers heavily, while the energy of love illuminates in lightness.

This resonance is as tangible as turning on a hose and spraying water everywhere. When you spray out water it doesn't immediately disappear. It seeps into the soil and affects the plants. Nourishing water provides life the ability to grow, while poisoned water withers them in dread.

When you construct a birdhouse, lay tile or build a home, the positive or negative energy stays in the materials. When I look at an object, I pick it up and feel it. I can see the mindset used in its creation.

My friend Klaus built a shelf for my mother. He had a great time crafting it and put a lot of love into it. From a carpentry point of view, it has imperfections, but from an energetic perspective, it radiates out love. He made the shelf for Jo as a gift, and it holds a beautifully loving energy. Such are the lessons that inform our work and run deep in our lives here.

Our visitors love the Community Center. From a carpenter's perspective, it reveals many flaws and imperfections, but people walk through the doorway and exclaim, "Oh, what a beautiful space! I love this place." Because it was built in a non-stressful, loving, compassionate way, it emanates a beautiful energetic quality, which doesn't just go away. Guests feel the love in every beam and countertop that stays in permanence.

Though not everybody who lives here fully embodies this perspective, we all have a responsibility to pay attention to our mindset and watch the energy we create. We should approach the whole land with this sensibility in mind. When we built the Stone Circle, we created a sacred space, full of uplifted energy. When we clean the buildings with positive energy, people experience uplifting joy.

It's an important tool not just for our community, but for the planet and humanity. We must be aware that what we create here is sacred. Our actions and feelings create an energy field, and when we live our lives with a sense of love and gratitude, we leave trails of positive resonance.

It would be an illusion to expect ourselves to do everything perfectly, and Sirius is no exception. We must embrace the fact that people are going to show up grumpy, even angry sometimes. We bring our issues and baggage, but we are growing all the time. People work in unhappy moods sometimes, but if it changes from day to day, rather than consistently dominating the energy field, then we can work with it.

Yet if we are coordinators of the project, and we can't focus because of major distractions in our lives, our attitude more greatly impacts the field. We must pay attention and change our circumstance or our perspective in order to lead with presence.

Generally we do the best we can with our imperfections. Even when we try our best, our process might come out negatively. We learn to practice acceptance of ourselves and work with each other on our journey together.

As the builder, working on the Community Center often racing against winter, exploring the spiritual principles and our attitudes became imperative. We didn't anxiously drive ourselves insane, frantically exclaiming, *"We've got to get it done!"* We calmly approached each project with, *"Let's build this place as consciously and environmentally sound as possible."*

I received the guidance that it didn't matter how long it took to complete the building. When some people would anxiously ask me, *"How long until the Community Center is done?"*

I would always answer, "Two years." No matter how much work was finished, whenever I heard the inquiry, I dropped the line, "Two years." Two years became a running joke, because everybody knew it wasn't going to happen. Eventually people stopped asking, unless they were looking for a laugh.

The process transcended the mere construction of a building; it embodied our spiritual growth as a community in connection. We attuned every morning, and gave our best effort to bring good energy into our work. The process was more than an attitude of *"Oh, we're just building a building, and it's taking us forever to do it."* Rather we held the inspiration of, *"We are intentionally building consciousness here."*

It wasn't always perfect. Life is messy, and holding all of our various intentions and limitations simultaneously caused conflict. Yet we realized the beautiful profundity of the whole process. Because we remained conscious, working with Spirit on different levels of awareness, we're still manifesting here forty years later and the Community Center stands imbued with a loving, spiritual energy.

As a builder, I understood the direct link between who we are and what we create in the physical realms. The spiritual energy flows through us into our hands and tools and embeds itself in the wood, anchoring in the nails and the physical substances and forms we create. I've seen how when we build a material creation through the pathway of love, we embed our creation with love forever. As a builder I maintain a responsibility to create with a sensitivity to the environment with a mindset of love, compassion and caring.

In our work, we admittedly lost the connection to love and compassion at times. We didn't always follow through perfectly because we also were evolving, yet we would always come back to this intention that we need to act with love and compassion.

We are not just dreamily or selfishly creating a place to live for ourselves, we intend to imbue this land and community with spiritual energy so that it can help facilitate the transformation of consciousness. When we truly honor, love and send that loving energy to the planet, it makes a huge, lasting impact.

Conflict reduces the resources of manifestation, while resolution and harmony attracts resources and facilitates the flow of manifestation.

Over the ten years of building the Community Center, I observed a fascinating phenomenon. When our relationships harmonized and everybody was working well together, happily inspired, the finances flowed. When unresolved inner conflict between people dominated the community, the whole process of manifestation and flow in the community slowed down. But as soon as the conflict resolved, everything would flow again!

I watched the ebb and flow of resources and money come and go, *directly* related to the quality of the relationships we experienced. We witnessed this phenomenon repeatedly, with plenty of people coming and going and it was a powerful lesson. Our process reflected our current consciousness. Here we were constructing this building, but we were also working out how to live together and be more compassionate, loving and understanding of the world around us.

This phenomenon provides greater understanding to the spiritual principle of manifestation. While the universe supports us when we create for the greater good, that alone is not enough. Our relationship dynamic must also be loving and supportive as we envision together. When we set the intention, we invoke all the challenges to overcome those blocks. The struggle proves valuable eventually, and as a community we could see this because we had a commitment to the spiritual unfolding of life and all that comes with it.

We worked very consciously with the harmony of our relationships when we were constructing the building. We wanted to create with as little stress as possible, and we wanted to do it with plenty of love, compassion, and goodwill. We wanted to have fun with it, making joyfulness a priority in the whole process.

Certain aspects of the construction I had never attempted before, so I was learning and growing as well, as I learned how to supervise people. The process was a spiritual expression, and the building represented our deep soul aspirations. To build a structure that was environmentally friendly, beautiful and serviceful allowed us to express our spiritual values in concrete form.

It is not always smooth going because, as we all know, when we come up against our own limitations and blocks, we struggle, especially in our relationships. Even when I think, *I'm going to be a loving, light filled being*, oftentimes with the invocation to expand consciousness I have to confront everything that stands in the way of creating that dynamic within my being.

People who come here may bring challenging personalities, and we consciously work with them using love, compassion and humor. The compassion and lightness dissipates some of the unresolved challenges. One particular young man presented an interesting conundrum, and we worked through it in a very humorous and healing way.

The young man joined the crew and immediately upon arrival took everything anybody said personally. Every time we encountered a problem in our work, he thought we were blaming him. To communicate without upsetting him became quite a challenge, as he started to fulfill his own expectations of himself. Unsure how to proceed, one day we tried an idea. We all agreed to choose a scapegoat for the day, and each day we would rotate who played scapegoat. On my day, everybody blamed me for everything that went wrong, even if it had nothing to do with me, and we all burst into laughter.

"Bruce! You cut all the boards the wrong size!"
"Oh, sorry!"
"Stop making it rain so hard, Bruce! We can't work in the rain!"
"I won't do it again…"
"The porcupine ate all the raspberries! *Why did you invite the porcupine to the party?*"

We had a blast, rotating the victim and coming up with ridiculous, nonsensical stories. The young man joyfully joined in the fray, teasing the next person, until the final day, when his name was called. I was nervous. *Would he able to handle the onslaught?*

We went ahead and set out blaming him, bracing for his response. He had the time of his life! He rolled with every punch, laughing gleefully as we slung the mud. The quality of energy in the man shifted in that moment and completely lightened up. From that day on, the issue dissolved and the man never again interpreted our dialogue as blame. The whole crew relaxed into a rejuvenated, harmonious flow.

Our experience exemplified how lightly working more consciously can actually bring healing into a situation that might otherwise be extremely difficult. It's one of the more inspirational stories of how transformation can manifest in a collaborative project.

I try to think of a time when we had no conflict and all our endeavors flowed perfectly, but it never happened. Conflict always bubbles about in the community; sometimes it settles down, and sometimes it reaches a fever pitch, affecting everyone's energy.

The conflictual elements of the community are always present, laying out our work, the sandpaper, where the rubber meets the road. While internal challenges get smoothed out, without the tension, something would be missing. The conflict is essential to the transformation of human consciousness.

Once we transform our consciousness completely, we will no longer need the conflict, but presently the conflict adds an important ingredient for conscious evolution. Perhaps we invoke the conflict to help us transform, which may be the reason why some form of conflict continues endlessly.

Some days when we were building the Community Center, the money and resources almost completely dried up. I looked around and saw conflicts exploding all over the community, tension pulling from every direction. But as soon as interpersonal issues resolved, the money and resources poured forth in abundance. After about the third or fourth time I witnessed the pattern in absolute clarity, I became decisively convinced that one directly affected the other.

I shared my observations with the rest of the community, and the community responded, working to improve the conflict. At times we faltered, but the knowledge that our relationships affected our manifestation inspired us to introspect and find greater success. Esoterically, we shifted our consciousness and plugged into a stream of energy that leads to manifestation. We attuned to the guidance we received and focused our full intention behind it.

We all agreed to the vision of the Community Center and pulled together to make it happen, which created great times full of high energy and excitement. Everybody recognized the enjoyment of the process, the whole community felt engaged beyond just me and the apprentices. Despite working outside jobs and busy with activities that occupied their time, everyone in the community volunteered in service. The vision unified the community as we created a tangible building that, once finished, would enhance our outreach and spiritual work. The new building allowed us to do the work that we had envisioned from day one.

Miraculous events occurred throughout the construction of the building. When we started to drag along, in need of a boost of energy, instantly new people showed up to help, providing an amazingly powerful, cohesive experience for the community. As the center unfolded, people saw the emerging beauty and became inspired to enhance it further. We all wanted to be a part of this beautiful, purposeful creation of communal connection, energy efficiency and spiritual embodiment.

We hit road bumps along the way; by no means did we exemplify a picture of utopia, but our willingness to address conflicts helped the process. We confronted significant challenges in the construction, but we also enjoyed incredible fun and inspiration along the way.

Nobody was too concerned that it took 10 years to build. It became a huge inspiration for the community to fulfill this magnificent vision together. Even in the final days when it was almost finished I still told everyone, "Well, it looks like it's going to be another two years…"

Though we still invested about three or four hundred thousand dollars, with the end result, we erected an immensely valuable building at a fraction of the cost of paid labor and store-bought materials. The construction lasted a long time, but we ended up with a building with no mortgage, debt-free except for some borrowed money from friends and associates, whom we paid back in a short amount of time.

Our methods to operate with limited funds, at the fate of the universe, and trusting manifestation is not always the best way. Manifestation takes many forms. In our case, to work extremely hard, without much money proved to be a challenge that strengthened us. If someone just walked up at that time and gave us a million dollars to build our Community Center, it would not have strengthened the community in the same way.

When we aspire toward a goal of the evolution of consciousness, we evolve and mature into a deeper, stronger place with our spiritual practices through devotion to our work. The unfolding of the building provided a perfect catalyst for our maturation. Every step of the way we had to be conscious and certain we were making the correct choices. Our task required a great deal of faith, tenacity and perseverance in order to make it happen. The Community Center became the esoteric teaching of those powerful spiritual qualities that we all need to develop.

Events unfolded in the right timing and at the time, and we utilized our limitations and lack of resources to learn fundamental lessons. Whether we need to continue on a similar path going forward, I don't know. Money and affluence may get in the way of that growth, but not necessarily.

We should accept the possibility to receive large manifestations of money if that is what is offered. I believe the community is at a place in strength and consciousness that it could handle a large amount of money coming in for its development without losing our ability to grow.

Humans learn some lessons from manifesting from limited resources, and we learn another set of lessons from consciously working with lots of money. Both challenges can stimulate spiritual growth in different ways.

Particularly in the west and specifically in this country, for a long time we have been learning important lessons about how material abundance affects our consciousness. People who live in less developed countries encounter different lessons. We all receive the lessons that we need to learn at the appropriate time.

In the development of the community we needed to learn about grounding, strengthening and all the lessons that come along with how we erected that building. It became the perfect spiritual teaching. Every day, life is a spiritual teacher.

Now complete, the Community Center fulfills many roles and functions. Apartments provide homes for members, while the rest of the building features guest accommodations, offices, laundry facilities, a commercial kitchen and a dining hall, as composting toilets reinvest the nutrients back into the land.

A massive ash tree trunk cut from a neighbor's land stands sturdily in the center of the expansive dining hall, holding up the second floor. Sun floods through enormous windows and skylights into a spacious, octagonal gathering room built without posts. A five pointed star inlays the maple floor inside a circle with rays radiating out to the eight corners.

The greenhouse on the front of the Community Center heats and insulates the building, while simultaneously sprouting vibrant greens and providing a warm, sunny, nourishing place to eat amidst several feet of snow stacked outside. The center's beauty and grace is a direct reminder of the beautiful consciousness that went into creating it.

Sustainability:

building and infrastructure

8

Straw-Bale and Cob

Over the course of 40 years, we experimented on the land with many different types of housing. In order to construct our buildings with positive energy, we always consider toxicity and try to avoid creating ecological disasters. We want our structures to be as nontoxic and low impact as possible, and as new techniques emerge, we study and practice new methods of natural building.

In response to a toxic, commercial building industry, the natural building movement has grown, gaining popularity around the world. Natural building uses a few simple ingredients. Sand, clay and straw are often the main building blocks. Other materials, depending on the part of the building under construction, include wood framing, wheat paste, powdered milk, linseed oil, beeswax, bamboo poles and rocks.

Straw-bale construction has gained traction in the last 20 years. Now, with great effort from straw-bale builders who lobbied hard for legal recognition, practices and techniques are written into most of the building codes around the country.

Straw-bale construction utilizes two main methods. In one method, the structure of the house is built using wood and usually a post and beam frame is erected to hold the weight of the roof. The straw-bales are stacked, cut and trimmed to make the walls. They tuck in and around the post and beams and create a wall about two feet thick, and

because straw is hollow and creates air pockets, the insulation value of straw is incredibly high, with minimal toxicity levels. The straw-bales are covered with a mixture of clay as a base layer and often finished with a lime plaster in both the interior and exterior of the building. The design creates deep, wide window sills and works well with a passive solar model.

The other method, less accepted by the building industry, involves stacking bales directly in a circle or rectangles, and the bales themselves hold up the roof. While this method works, building inspectors are more hesitant to sign off on the design because it lacks structural analysis. At Sirius we used the first method and built a small house using post and beam construction with straw-bale walls.

Cob, another form of natural building using a mixture made of sand, clay and straw, is the most environmentally friendly building technique that exists. Unfortunately the building codes for cob lag far behind because its lower popularity has generated fewer legal campaigns for approval. However there are movements and organizations that are currently working to change the laws. If it gains approval in other locations, attaining regulations in Massachusetts becomes more likely. A local building inspector and an architect or engineer who is willing to stamp the permits makes all the difference. They approve the structure with their knowledge that the structure is safe, and it will not fall down and kill somebody.

People in England and Britain occupy cob houses built over 500 years ago that still stand today. They never had structural problems, and the technique is popular in so-called third world countries the world over. Cob is used every day around the planet, not only to build houses, but in commercial and personal pizza ovens, cook stoves, information boards and benches.

Currently nothing is written into the incredibly dense American building code books about cob construction. Because of this, most building inspectors are reluctant to embrace it as a valid building technique, despite its proven use for thousands of years.

Cob House Artistry

Jan Sterman, originally from South Africa and a former member of Sirius, constructed a cob house here on the land. In his travels he lived and worked at the Cob Cottage Company in Eugene, Oregon and learned all the details on how to build cob houses. From an ecological sustainability viewpoint, it's a wonderful method of construction. After his work in Oregon he said, "I want to build a cob house here at Sirius as a demonstration project!" He didn't initially consider occupying it, but intended to use it as an educational teaching model.

He got a permit to build a shed out of cob and as the project evolved, people grew especially interested. Jan ran workshops on the techniques and strategies of cob. Participants gained hands-on, educational experience with a new set of skills. Because it was a new technique not widely practiced on the east coast, people felt inspired and intrigued to volunteer all the time. People saw that the construction of a house could be simple and doable without extensive carpentry expertise.

Jan had the eye of an artist; he applied his creativity to every step of the design process. He dismissed the line and square for natural curves and round corners and windows. He incorporated woody, spiraling grape vines as railings and framed the windows in wood slabs featuring marbled grain patterns. He kept the second floor ceiling low, which provided coziness and comfort.

In the foundation he dug a trench below the frost line and filled it with small stones. On top of this he added a two-foot-high wall using rocks and cement. He erected the walls with a mix of sand, clay and straw.

As the structure grew, he realized he was building more than just a simple shed and considered living in it. He went to the building inspector to apply for a change of use permit. The local building inspector had never heard about cob as it was completely foreign and not written into any of the building codes in the country.

In some locations, people have received approval to live in them, but Jan was not so lucky. Because the plans were not stamped by an architect or engineer, the building inspector of Shutesbury demanded an extensive structural analysis of the material from a laboratory, with calculations of the insulating value. The red tape requirements in order to approve the building as a residential structure were vast and added 20 to 30 thousand dollars to the project cost.

To meet code requirements, he needed to enlarge the windows, add a driveway, a well and a septic system. Jan at first tried to meet the requirements, but they were so complicated and expensive. As a young person, he did not like all rules and regulations of the power dynamic, and he abandoned the idea of living inside as the structure remained listed in the town record as a shed. No one lives there now, but with a $20 to $30 thousand dollar investment and some energy, it would be possible.

The building is beautiful with a low ceiling, curves, arches and an overhead walkway. Shelves are built right into the cob walls, and from the outside, the back entryway forms an imaginative face. The artistic expression shines through and visitors feel its magic and unique character. The love and good energy radiate from the walls and windows. The building is used for meetings, afterhours hangouts and campfire gatherings. It demonstrates a structure built without any negative ecological impact on the earth.

Cob Oven

Another natural building project that caught our inspiration is the cob oven. We wanted to demonstrate sustainable methods while simultaneously creating a central gathering point for social events.

Our former member, Will Stark, grew excited about the idea and conducted some thorough research. He read all about cob ovens and visited other people's wood-fired baking ovens. As a master craftsman, he had earned a reputation for installing meticulous, beautiful work.

When he proposed the idea, the community was swept up in his excitement and immediately gave a consensus agreement to move forward. The community paid for the minimal cost of material which included clay, sand, straw and metal for the roof. The rocks came from the land for free and when he started construction, he piqued people's interest. The public location at the Community Center enticed any passerby to stop and ask questions, quickly drawn in to lay some cob.

The cob oven boasts many parts. Will dug a four-foot hole in the ground, and he wanted a stable base to sit below or near the frost line. A strong, deep foundation would prevent the oven from cracking over time. He filled the hole with fist-sized rocks in layers and packed them together without mortar so they would not shift or wiggle. The ground in New England repeatedly freezes and thaws with the presence of water, destabilizing the foundation through expansion and contraction, but when you remove all the soil, the amount of water is reduced, and the upheaval in the ground created by water lessens, stabilizing the structure.

The rock foundation rises up about three feet above the ground. On top of this came two feet of cob, laid on in layers and poked full of holes to allow even drying. As the height climbed, a stove door was added as a trap to clean out the ash.

Once the cob foundation was in place, the crew installed a flat layer of firebrick, which forms the base of the oven where the dough bakes. On top of the flat firebricks, the builder used a mound of wet, compacted sand. The sand created the inner chamber for the fire. Once the structure was finished, the sand was removed, forming the inside of the oven. In order to differentiate between the sand and not dig into the first layer of the oven, Will placed wet newspaper on top of the dome.

Above the dome Will added many layers. Some were a mix of clay and sand without straw. Others layers were clay and perlite—puffed up mica sold as attic insulation—above layers of tinfoil. The outer layer was finished off with a fine clay plaster, which included decoration with seashells and rocks. The form included a vent for the chimney and Will added a meter to record the temperature in each layer. The data collected about the oven's efficiency gives feedback to the builder to improve the design over time. The whole structure was covered in a metal roof since cob is not waterproof. The final result is a well-made, efficient oven in the center of the community.

When it was finished, many visitors specifically came to see it, and Will was hired to build other cob ovens in the area.

The oven plays a central role in community events and celebrations; pizza parties draw people in and lots of people show up. When people get motivated, we heat up the oven and bake pizza. You can burn any kind of wood in the cob oven, usually smaller pieces, and pine works fine.

When the cob oven reaches peak temperature it cooks a pizza in a minute and a half! I baked my entire open house lunch in it once, which included potatoes and cornbread. It takes an hour to bake the potatoes in a gas oven but in the cob oven it's done in half an hour. The food cooks so much faster without burning it because the radiant heat works much better than a conventional oven.

Alternative Fuel Systems

Another innovative project we decided to explore was to create a waste oil car cooperative. I learned about the brilliant idea to convert diesel vehicles to run on vegetable oil through a student project at Hampshire College. The conversion is possible with any diesel engine if you install

an extra tank for the oil. The car runs both on waste vegetable oil and diesel and one system supports the other. Any diesel engine could run on vegetable oil except that it gels at lower temperatures. If it's too cold, you use diesel but once the vehicle warms up, just flip a switch and the engine changes to the other tank.

The idea innovatively fulfills our mission by reducing the burning of fossil fuels. It uses a waste product restaurants pay to have hauled away and the oil pollutes less without releasing sulfur dioxide into the air. Some pollution still comes out of burning vegetable oil but it is considered CO2 neutral because when the plants grow and oxidize, they offset the carbon dioxide produced when they are burned.

Our oldest resident, my 90-year-old mother, volunteered to be the first candidate to buy a diesel car to run on vegetable oil. We bought the kit and converted her car successfully, so I bought two diesel trucks; one was a dump truck to run my tree business, and we converted both of them. We went to Chinese restaurants and to the universities and got permission to collect their oil, and since they had to pay to get rid of it, they were happy to give it to us. The grease made excellent gasoline after we filtered and cleaned it.

Other people in the neighborhood were interested in buying fuel, so we started a small cooperative. The mini co-op included a pumping station in the basement of the Community Center and when we needed to fill up, members drove up to the pumping station, wrote down how much they used and away they went with filtered, clean vegetable oil.

Unfortunately the federal government has rules and regulations that make it difficult to run such an operation. But one of the members of the co-op was a CPA, and he came up with a brilliant solution. He said, "The way to avoid legal hassles is to create a club." The members buy into the club and pay membership dues rather than buy fuel. We called it Club Recycle, and everybody interested bought a membership. The nonrefundable membership fee enabled participants to get vegetable oil at the pumping station and with each use we each paid an extra fee for the oil, which covered costs for the space that we were using, the pumps, repairs and general maintenance of the operation.

When I collected the grease, I received free fuel and a salary. My pay was about $12 to $15 an hour, and the system worked well because everyone was honest and accountable. People wrote down how much they used and we employed a bookkeeper who sat down once every two or three months, calculated the use and sent a bill out. People would pay the bills to our business account, and with the extra money we bought new equipment, pumps and barrels.

During our operation, an official heard about us and warned that burning waste oil in vehicles was illegal. The EPA issued a declaration and the law existed not because the fuel was dirtier or unsafe, but because alternative fuels had not been studied and approved. Millions of dollars are required to get new fuel oil approved for sale commercially so the long process to regulate its use in vehicles had not happened yet. Their statement read, "Anybody caught running vegetable oil will be fined $1800." They also mentioned they had no plans to enforce the mandate, so everybody ignored it and used the fuel anyway, and no one received a fine. The law existed simply to placate the fuel distributors who were concerned the innovation would cut into their profits.

Unfortunately picking up the grease, cleaning and filtering it proved to be labor intensive, dirty work. When the oil spilled in the back of the truck, the barrel pump malfunctioned or a barrel tipped over, I came home covered in oil, and I got burned out spending a whole day every week dealing with it. We wanted the fuel but needed another option to process it. At one point we had 14 members using the co-op regularly, so it became a considerable amount of work.

We met a guy who wanted to start a biofuel business on a larger scale so we gave him our contacts and our collection sites and loaned him money to get the business started.

He filled up a giant truck, picked up the oil, filtered it, and dewatered it to sell it under the company name, Reenergizer. They had better equipment and warehouse space to filter on a large scale which was more effective. Currently we buy grease from them, clean and ready to use so we all benefit from the new arrangement. They deliver the fuel here and the extra cost spares us the effort of collecting it ourselves.

Converting a vehicle to use vegetable oil is not a matter of changing the engine but rather heating the oil before it goes into the engine. When it's too cold it congeals and clogs up the fuel lines. In systems with a separate tank for the vegetable and diesel fuel, a heating oil from the antifreeze in the engine runs through and heats up the vegetable oil.

One time we met a trucker who ran a 16 wheeler semi trailer truck on straight vegetable oil. The exhaust system from his truck sat right over the diesel tank and warmed it up so it didn't congeal. He didn't convert the truck; he just poured vegetable oil directly into his diesel tank. He could drive all over the country without the lines congealing.

Every once in a while this big truck came rolling up our winding little gravel driveway to fill up with waste vegetable oil and we enjoyed talking with him. He drove the cab of his massive tractor trailer truck up to the Community Center. A few times we filled his tank with hundreds of gallons of fuel, and he drove away. He was from Ohio, so he would contact us ahead of time to receive his fill-up.

He was a cool guy, living with an environmentally conscious mentality, and we gave him a tour of the community, as he appreciated us and our mission. We also saved him money because the cost of the oil at the time was significantly less than diesel fuel. While he appreciated the financial break, he was mostly concerned about the environment, and it pained him to burn so much diesel.

In each trip he learned more about the filtering process from us. Eventually he returned to Ohio and set up a system for his truck to collect and filter the oil himself. We educated him and passed our learning forward.

For a while we also offered a biodiesel pumping station. Biodiesel is *supposedly* made from waste vegetable oil. Instead of converting the car, you convert and change the oil. The process happens through a chemical reaction, and the waste product left over is benign.

We bought the biodiesel in bulk and stored it in big plastic tanks. Biodiesel works in any diesel engine vehicle without a conversion kit but the viscosity changes with the time of year and the outside temperatures. In the summer, cars use 100% biodiesel, and in the winter 30% diesel is mixed with the biofuel.

The biodiesel station lasted until I discovered the product was from virgin oil. Originally the biodiesel we received was being made from waste oil, but we were shocked to learn that the industry was taking farmland out of food production in order to fuel vehicles, which did not align with our ethics. We couldn't find biodiesel made from waste vegetable oil, so we stopped running the pumping station. In recent years, a biodiesel plant developed in Greenfield that exclusively uses waste vegetable oil, so it *is* possible to obtain biodiesel that meets a higher green standard.

Transportation is an important need and fossil fuel is harming the planet, so alternative systems are important for the future. Unfortunately, converting your car is a commitment, the work is messy and the location is out of the way for most people. Fifteen years later, we still buy the grease from Reenergizer and still have the co-op which anybody can sign up to use.

The hardcore environmentalists among us still use waste vegetable oil. It's not the perfect solution, but it's cleaner than burning fossil fuels. New methods may be developed in the future that surpass our current experiments.

Permaculture in Action
Growing Food in Connection

9

A Visit from Permaculture's Founder

Bill Mollison, considered the father and founder of the permaculture movement, inspired much of our sustainable vision. An Australian who studied with the aboriginal people, he started writing books as he worked with agriculture, using harmony with nature to create balanced systems. He used the natural flow of the land while creating fascinating energy systems.

We planted the orchard after reading Mollison's books and invited him to come visit in the '80s, with no expectation that this prominent figure would oblige. To our amazement, he agreed, and we prepared for his workshop with excitement.

Already well known, he piqued participants' interest and enthusiasm about using agriculture and energy systems in a new way. During the workshop, he made suggestions for our land and gardens. Since he was from a warmer a climate with little understanding for New England winters, some of the suggestions weren't very practical for this climate, such as installing pipes under the driveway to heat water, which honestly would not have been helpful for us. But he also encouraged us to dig little ponds in all the gardens to invite frogs and toads to eat the insect pests. We implemented his suggestions that made the most sense and ignored the rest.

Mollison was conscious of the natural rhythms of life, yet was quite a character. He acted like a cowboy, smoking, drinking and hitting on all the women, which was unusual for us, but he was brilliant. He presented the wisdom he learned from the aboriginal people in a language that people in the West could understand and developed it further. Permaculture has become a global movement, inspiring a huge impetus for change that spread all over the world. As one person, he made a tremendous impact.

Permaculturists use the most ecological and environmentally friendly practices possible. Mollison's ideas expanded outward and developed even further beyond his original vision. The movement became more sophisticated as it took off, its ideas and methods continuing to evolve. As more and more books are written about the subject, the movement impacts many people's lives for the better. Permaculture fits in well with the work that we're doing here, so we started teaching permaculture training courses founded and implemented by local designers.

Web of Interconnectedness

At Sirius in all the work we do, we honor the sacred in all aspects of life, feeling our divine connection. We pay attention when we practice permaculture, clear land and construct our buildings. When we consider the ideas that people propose for various projects, we bring awareness into people's consciousness. We often implement the projects using meditation and conscious awareness, so that our method regenerates rather than harms.

Sometimes in the process I have contact with devas and nature spirits. Even if many of the people who live here don't relate to nature spirits, they can understand that all life is sacred and everything is interconnected. They can practice this in all aspects of our work on the land.

As a little boy I felt the strength of the web of energy in nature. I felt deeply at peace in the woods and in nature. I spent most of my childhood in the fields and the forests, often by myself. Feeling the presence of nature spirits, I never felt alone. Without being given any knowledge about nature beings or devas, I didn't have the vocabulary to identify the beings I interacted with. No one told me they were real, but while in nature, I sensed their company and presence, and I called them my good friends. I felt them deeply but I never shared my experience as a child.

I always felt happy under the trees. In other parts of my life I was socially inept, but I never felt loneliness because of my nature connection. As an adult with more wisdom, I recognized and reflected on the connection from my childhood, and as Sirius grew, we learned more about Permaculture ideas, striving to put them into practice while communicating and working with nonhuman life forms.

When we work in the vegetable garden, we talk to the plants and express our intent to work with them. We listen deeply and ask, "How can we best support you? What do you need to grow better?" We establish a relationship between the plant and the human kingdoms. The accepted cultural norm in relation to nonhuman life is dominance rather than cooperation, taking for our own benefit in whatever manner suits us. But the mindset that we can just dominate and do whatever we want is causing a great catastrophe on our planet.

Here, our vision moves toward a new model in which we ask, "How do we cooperate together?"

We can still cut down trees and use resources, but we must focus our efforts on meeting our basic needs in harmony rather than exclusively satiating our rampant desire for more. We do the work in a way that's cooperative and honors life and consciousness without being so destructive.

Every space on the planet contains a humming, living web. To go on a rampage and kill trees, plants or animals creates massive imbalance because all these beings exist as part of a larger entity. Instead we try to keep the web intact and when we start a new project like cutting trees or construction, we always tune in to the environment and notice the energetic feeling present there.

When humans cut trees, pull plants or bulldoze, some of the lifeforce energy in the web withdraws. But we can prevent this withdrawal if we use the right methods. When we cleared the forest to build an orchard, we honored and expressed our appreciation to the forest. We acted consciously and meditated with the trees. We communicated, "We're building an orchard here for growing food, with respect for all life. The new orchard will create more diversity, and we need to cut you down. We thank you for being here, for your presence, for the lumber that we will receive from you, the wood chips, the firewood."

In my meditation, the trees told me, "We don't mind being cut down; part of our purpose here on the planet is to serve humanity. But we don't like being cut down with total disregard. We don't like the ecological imbalance that ensues when people engage with ignorance in a ruthless and destructive process. We want appreciation and acknowledgement for who we are and what we give. If you can practice this, we are here to serve you."

Trees offer vast resources for us. We receive food and shelter, clothing, heat and paper, and if we give a tremendous amount of respect, in return the trees give us tremendous wealth. If the work is done with deep gratitude and appreciation, without causing ecological or environmental unbalance, when the harvest is done consciously and respectfully, the web stays intact.

As we built the orchard, we began cutting, first with the little trees and then bigger ones. During the process we never felt the web tear apart. When we shut off our saws and chippers at the end of the day and quiet returns, the site integrates and new energy emerges. It weaves itself back into beauty and harmony.

The Lakshmi Garden

Pretty early on we recognized we didn't have enough space in the Shanti garden to grow the amount of produce we consumed. We contacted the agricultural extension service and were advised that our land was completely unsuitable for any kind of agricultural endeavor, but we decided that would not stop us. We believed we could create gardens anywhere if we invested the right energy.

We decided to create more garden space and a small group of us looked at the land to determine the best location. We walked the land looking for a relatively flat place, which brought us through the woods to the lower part of the property. We all agreed it looked like the ideal spot, facing south and relatively flat. Growing a garden requires full sun, and despite the whole land being covered with forest, we believed we could work with it. We wanted to preserve the large trees on the land, and the trees in this part of the forest grew relatively thin and small.

So we decided to clear this part of the forest and engaged in our usual process. We sat with the trees and meditated on them for a couple weeks before we started working. We explained what we were doing and why. We gave them gratitude as we thanked each tree individually. I felt a sensation of reciprocal acknowledgement and connection. A feeling of acceptance was present because we acted consciously. Already alive, present, and pulsing, the nature energy continued to vibrate, undisturbed. The consciousness of the nature beings was willing to create cooperatively with us because we were approaching our task with sensitivity and appreciation.

We were redirecting the energy into garden space, enhancing the nature energy already present. When we add another ecosystem to the forest, we actually expand the diversity of the bird and animal life. The number of species that mingle together multiply exponentially on the edges where different ecosystems intersect.

Some days when we went out to work, we knew that on an etheric level it was not a good day to go out cutting. We gave the forest space and allowed gentleness in the process, as the energy changed. We allowed that reorientation and redistribution of the energy that was already there on a more etheric level. It wasn't a harsh ripping of the etheric web that happens with clearcut forests. The energy passed within the nature kingdoms among the trees. They readjusted, and a repatterning of the energy took place which allowed us to return on a different day and resume our work.

When we finally finished clearing the land, you could feel no sense of disruption. Everybody who walked in there said, "Wow, this feels so nice!" They did not feel that we had done something terrible to the etheric web and the web of life; instead it felt perfectly balanced and in harmony with the already existing land. When we first started working on the land we learned a lot from that process. It is a beautiful, balanced, natural process, and the end result is remarkable. Even when we use tractors and machinery, the feeling of intrusion doesn't exist; harmony is present in the forest, and everyone's happy.

Once we had the trees cleared, we dug our hands in the ground to find only an inch and a half of topsoil, full of stones and gravel, in addition to some enormous boulders. Because the conditions were so poor, we decided to hire a machine. We mapped out a design and they came in with a backhoe and dug beds that were about three feet wide and two feet deep and long, following the contour of the land. The amount of rocks and glacial till that we hauled out of the ground was unbelievable.

When they left, we had huge piles of dirt and rocks from the ditches, with humongous boulders strewn about. The site was a mess and looked like an absolute war zone. I was concerned about the energetics of it, but it felt okay. With the big pile of rocks, which did not have much function in the garden, we built a massive stone wall but still we had more boulders. We hauled away at least half of the rocks to use in various building projects.

Originally a hundred-year-old small wall existed across the middle of the garden from the time of grazing sheep. We roped the unearthed boulders with a chain, tied them to the tractor and dragged them into piles in a haphazard line on top of the old grazing wall.

The large wall created a microclimate for a smaller garden we call

Parvati. The beds planted right next to the rocks warm up and stay warmer longer. The rocks suck in the heat during the day and release it slowly after dark to create warmer nighttime temperatures. We use the beds for hot weather crops like corn and melons and benefit from all those rocks. Unfortunately they also provide perfect habitat for woodchucks, who come out at night and lay on their bellies, eating every broccoli and green bean plant in sight.

One year a family of foxes moved in and we saw the mom with her babies for a few weeks sitting and playing on the wall. They tolerated us and it was magical to be so close to the animal kingdom.

We backfilled the ditches with organic matter but due to a limited amount of topsoil, we used decomposing wood chips mixed with urine to break them down. We used any kind of organic matter we had to fill up the two-foot-deep ditches. We needed to fill an enormous volume.

I worked for five years on that garden, removing the rocks and gravel and filling up the beds. I loved it! I felt a beautiful sense of connection to be out doing work on the land, digging the earth and just being in this process.

Building the beds took a long time because I was primarily the only one working on it. We didn't designate it as a community project because people were so busy with other important needs in the community. We constructed other buildings at the time, so I mainly worked on the garden in my free time. By the end of the project, the beds became amazingly fertile because over those years we added manure, compost, wood chips and urine. Right now we have two feet of good rich soil, perfect for planting.

Because the forest completely surrounds it on all sides, the unusual garden creates an interesting feeling. It's as if you are more a part of nature with the forest surrounding you. It has good energy and produces a great quantity of delicious vegetables and berries.

Sheet Mulching

When we finished the Lakshmi Garden, we decided to build another garden we call Parvati. Right before Y2K, we expanded our food production even further in preparation for the worst, and we opened up the forest on the far side of the rock wall created from building the Lakshmi Garden. This time we decided not to excavate with heavy machinery in order to keep from tearing up the ground. While we didn't feel there was anything terribly wrong with the ditches we dug for the first garden, the work and energy the task demanded was too much.

We found a better way to design our soil base when we learned about sheet mulching, which creates garden beds without disturbing the soil. Sheet mulching is a process developed through the permaculture model, which benefits the soil because it uses no rototilling and maintains the interconnected soil web already in place. The soil is loosened over time by insects and deep taproots rather than machines.

When building a new garden bed, the method consists of a layer usually made of overlapping cardboard sheets that smothers any grass and weeds, which is then covered in whatever materials are available to build the soil. In a lawn setting, particularly in the spring, the cardboard is laid directly on the grass. On top of this comes a mixture of compost, soil and amendments ready to plant in immediately.

The implementation can be done more slowly, which reduces the cost of materials. When we want to build a new bed, we select an area to develop and over the course of the growing season we dump leaves, weeds, grass clippings and old plant stalks in the area. In the fall before the snow arrives, we add a thick layer of cardboard to the top of the pile, throw in some kind of animal manure and top the area with leaves. By the next spring, the grass underneath dies and the buried weeds and their seeds are smothered by the cardboard. The bed is still rough, so a hearty first year crop like squash or potatoes works well. The following year, the soil will be beautiful. If the soil is exceptionally compacted, we poke holes with a garden fork to aerate before we lay down the cardboard. Planting a first year crop with deep taproots can loosen compaction, especially in heavy clay soils or areas that have been driven on with vehicles like a power riding mower.

We noticed that this garden becomes much wetter because of its location, with poor drainage. By the middle of the summer, it produces well, but at times early crops like garlic or planted potato chunks rot before they mature. Some of the boulders below the beds emerged when the ground would repeatedly freeze, melt and dry out. They pose a hazard to the lawn mower when we mow the grassy paths.

Initially the first garden was more productive and the plants grew better, while the second garden struggled. But over the years we added more and more organic matter. After a couple years, the sheet mulch garden caught up, and we haven't noticed a huge difference between the two gardens since. Both gardens are equally productive now. We built the second garden without disturbing the earth, so sheet mulching is a better method in the long run.

Permaculture Orchard

When we designed and implemented the orchard, we left some ferns which grew three or four feet tall. We incorporated into the design many wild highbush blueberries already on the land.

We also used the sheet mulching method with some modifications. When planting a perennial bush or tree, we always dug a planting hole, added amendments with a bit of compost and water and snuggled the bush into its new home. Around the bush, we laid down cardboard in a ring overlapping the edges and adding more compost and a good layer of hardwood chips on top. The tree roots have time to develop without being choked by the grass. In the second phase, we add supportive understory plants that help the tree and either bring in nitrogen or attract pollinators in the spring.

Because we did not need to plant every square inch, we left many wild plants, which added diversity to the orchard ecosystem. Many plants from the original forest such as wild blueberries began to flourish because of the added sunlight. An interesting dynamic emerged between the interface of the original wild plants and the cultivars we added. The energetic relationship powerfully develops into a diverse ecosystem that mimics the layers of the forest, which include tree shrubs, ground cover and vines. They interact in a symbiotic relationship while providing food, medicine, beauty and biomass for compost building.

The whole process of building those gardens taught us many valuable lessons and we embraced the permaculture ideas. With the permaculture method, the solutions are simple and less labor intensive. When we built the Lakshmi Garden we didn't know about sheet mulching, but since then all the beds that we've made use sheet mulching. We built up on top of the earth rather than trying to dig it out and our crops are successful. In a few exceptions we dug down by hand deep into the soil using the double digging technique, but only on a small scale.

Greenhouses

We constantly ask ourselves, "How can we live more sustainably?" Most of the food consumed here is shipped 3,000 miles across the country from California or from other countries altogether. Cutting the cycle of fossil fuel consumption is a worthy endeavor and growing food creates sustainable culture and systems. The local food concept invites us to examine our life. Regeneration motivates us to create these gardens not solely for the yield we receive; we want to grow our own organic food to lessen our impact in a more simple and sustainable lifestyle. It's healthy for us and good for our planet.

But what about the wintertime when ice and snow cover the New England farmland? New Zealand ships food all over the planet in the winter because their seasons are opposite from all of us in the northern hemisphere. In order to extend our season and keep growing our food when production ends, we built a couple greenhouses. They allow us to start plants early while the ground is covered in several feet of snow and the temperature drops below freezing. We can harvest winter greens like kale, chard, spinach and radishes in the middle of February and eat early hot season crops like tomatoes, eggplants and peppers.

The first greenhouse we erected was an eight-foot plastic hoop house. It wasn't designed for heavy snow loads and for many years, during big snow storms we cleaned off the snow every few hours when it snowed heavily. We went with brushes, gloves and shovels to keep it from overloading and bending the metal hoops. Sometimes we went out at three or four in the morning, trudging through the storm, up to our knees in the dark, to knock the snow off.

This worked for many years and we had good yields until one year Linda and I went away to India for most of the winter. We couldn't expect others to clean off the hoop house while we were gone. When we returned, we found the hoop house collapsed and buckled inward from the weight of the snow.

The plastic was getting old, and every three to five years it needed replacing anyway from the sunlight stops filtering in. So we knew if it collapsed, the loss would be minimal. Nobody had the same devotion and we let our attachment go before we left. We repaired it once after that, but when it collapsed again, we decided we needed to plan a more permanent greenhouse of glass and wood.

When we first envisioned the Community Center, we designed an attached greenhouse on the south side as part of the original plan. We constructed the whole building, but we had no money for the greenhouse, which we knew would be the most expensive part of the building, per square foot. All the glass, the metal tracks and the post and beam were quite expensive materials so we laid the foundation but left it as an empty cement slab for a couple years.

A woman visited from South Africa and saw the empty foundation. She asked, "What's going on here? You've got a foundation but there's nothing here!"

I told her, "Well, we will build a greenhouse here eventually, but we don't have the money right now."

And she replied, "Oh, I can give you some money." She pulled out her travelers checks, while sitting at the picnic tables, and she wrote out $10,000. She handed them to me and said, "Go ahead and build your greenhouse!"

I was floored. *What spontaneous generosity!*

Even with money, the greenhouse took several years to build, because we were in the midst of several other projects, such as the reconstruction of the Phoenix House, but eventually we put her money to good use.

All we had designed was the basic shape. The unfolding greenhouse design became a process in itself. We erected it using post and beam framing and angled glass windows before considering the interior design. We sat inside the space and asked ourselves, "What can we do here, and how can we do it well?"

We started work on the design, then we built the first section before going back to design the next part. We designed each step of the way after we constructed the previous section. With each new element, the inspiration came in the moment. Brilliant ideas emerged as we went. We added a frog pond, which increased the biodiversity, reducing the pests and inviting people with a natural ambiance. We built a ramp for wheel barrows and added a cistern to store water, none of which we had originally placed in our plan. The final result pleased us delightfully.

We worked with the permaculture principle stating that each element of the design should include at least three functions. Because buildings take massive amounts of energy to create, as a designer you want to get maximum return from your energy investment. Our greenhouse has five functions, which are food production, heat for the dining room, hangout space, water catchment and habitat. The wall between the greenhouse and the dining room is uninsulated and the excess heat created during the day, when the sun shines full blast, radiates into the dining room at night.

The little dining area inside the greenhouse has become a popular place to gather for a meal, particularly in the winter. Being surrounded by green plants illuminated by natural light while the snow drifts from the sky outside is a remarkable experience. The sun provides a welcoming warmth when it shines through the wintry clouds.

The pond and the plants offer spaces for frogs, spiders and a variety of pollinators. They are admired by visitors to the greenhouse while they feed on the pests that would otherwise disturb the people *and* the garden. The lower windows open up, welcoming pollinators into the greenhouse who are essential for the plants' growth.

A water collection system helps, especially in the super dry months. A cistern that we built beneath the garden beds collects water from the roof of the greenhouse and the entire Octagon meeting space above. A large amount of the water from the roof is collected to water the plants.

Since the cistern is partly underground, it raises the height of the beds so the plants receive the maximum amount of light, while providing the most ergonomic access to gardeners. We water the plants in the greenhouse from the cistern using a small attached pump. Pumping water up from out of the ground would require a much bigger pump and a lot more energy than just pumping it out of the cistern.

The greenhouse moderates the temperature quite well so it rarely threatens to freeze inside. In the coldest nights of winter, we prevent the rare freeze by lighting a fire in the wood stove, perhaps three times a year. Wood panels, doors and windows open to cool off when it gets too hot and close to keep the warmth in during the cold.

We also created a system to insulate the plants by covering them in a double layer of plastic on cold nights, a design that Eliot Coleman introduced to us. Bamboo hoops curve over each bed to hold the insulating material. The warmth not only helps the plants survive the coldest months, it increases their growth and production and we grow food all winter long.

We wanted a growing system that uses less heat and energy input especially during the winter. Thermal mass in the form of rocks helps heat and cool as well. The sun shines through, optimally heating up the thermal mass.

A few flaws provide some challenges, such as the danger of

forgetting to open the panels or if a door is left open by accident in winter, which can destroy much of the garden overnight. But as long as we pay attention to such details, the greenhouse works amazingly well.

We pushed the potential of our climate zone, planting a fig tree, which has grown enormously and offers delicious figs! Every year we cut it back but it grows right back up to the ceiling. Everyone enjoys the fresh fruit that would otherwise be impossible to grow in New England.

We applied the experiences and lessons we learned with this project to design and build the new greenhouse. In 2009 we decided to build the more permanent greenhouse currently under construction. We wanted to grow more food locally and demonstrate it's possible, even in New England, to grow a high percentage of your food.

Fire

DESTRUCTION AS REBIRTH

10

Community Center

In the middle of winter during a raging blizzard, we almost lost our Community Center. The Octagon upstairs was under construction and the roof was on, but the building was not yet fully enclosed as we had not installed the doors and windows. What is now the community kitchen was set up as the woodworking shop. Though half finished, with plastic over the openings, we occasionally used the space for events. Old couches and chairs sat along one wall and rolls of carpets were piled up out of the way of the construction.

Trudging through the sparkling snow, I walked up the steps and immediately smelled the lighter fluid. I looked around and thought *"Oh God! Oh my God! What is this?"* I saw a trail of burn marks in the first landing, leading up the stairs. Knowing people had gone to sleep upstairs, I ran up the stairs shaking. The burn marks ended two feet below the second floor. I walked over to the rugs and the smell intensified. The stench of lighter fluid burned my nose and saturated the air.

As the enormity of the close call sank in, I had to sit down. Somehow by the grace of God, it didn't catch on fire and everyone was okay. We had spent years working on the building, expending so much of our time, work and money, but none of that even mattered considering the lives of the people sleeping in the East Wing. I ran and called Linda and all she could say over and over was, "Oh my God. Oh my God, we are so lucky."

As others heard about it, everyone wondered who was creeping around in the shadows late at night and why they wanted to harm us. Some of us went on higher alert after this incident, but it didn't last as the day-to-day work consumed us and the fear faded. I thanked God for putting out the fire and felt the protection of the Divine with us. The second time we weren't so lucky.

Phoenix House

During this era of the community around 1994, Gordon and Corinne spent six months of the year living in Washington, DC and the other six at Sirius. They moved away from the "hands on the ground" aspect of community to focus on teaching and spiritual education. They wrote books and toured, offering lectures and workshops, directing their energy toward the public awareness of spiritual community. They pursued the intersection of politics and spirituality, and their influence held an angle of importance distinguished from the hands-on community work.

After living in Washington, DC halftime for a few years, the pace felt too hectic and chaotic and they wanted a quieter location without all the traffic, commotion and intense political energy. They decided to move back to Sirius fulltime, and that spring they returned and settled back into their house at Sirius.

Apparently God had other plans for them.

During the summer, Gordon left the Thursday night meeting and walked home in the dark following the small path through the woods to the front door. He opened the door and his eyes widened as he saw red, angry, hot flames shooting across his tile floor. He turned and yelled in a state of panic, *"Our house is on fire!"*

Corinne, right behind him, turned and ran down the path, stumbling and tripping in the dark, searching for water and a hose. Without any emergency fire systems in place, we were helpless as the fire burned fast, hot and vicious. By the time they ran back, armed with hoses, the whole building was blazing, waves of heat radiating outward as the flames shot into the black sky above the roof!

Members also leaving the meeting ran up the hill and gathered, milling about helplessly, moving the cars and wondering if their cats were dead, as the fire department finally arrived. But it was too late for the house.

Linda, the kids and I were away from the property on vacation in my mother's cabin in the Berkshires. When we got a call the next day, I stood there holding the phone thinking, *"Oh my god. Oh my god."* My whole family, noisy in the background, kept asking *"What? What is it? What happened?"* Once I hung up and shared the news, we quickly and silently packed up all our stuff. During the hour and a half drive home, we wondered what awaited us and if Gordon and Corinne were okay.

We drove up and saw the blackened timbers outlined against the deep blue sky, burnt splinters hanging at odd angles and smoking window holes. The plastic picnic table outside was melted into an abstract sculpture and the glass that used to be windows merged and melted into lava piles of plastic glass and metal. Slowly, not wanting to face the reality in front of us, we got out of the car.

Walking up the driveway, I saw a surprisingly touching image emerge from the rubble. A concrete Buddha from the living room table sat serenely, silently meditating among the ashes, ruined timbers and chaos. The black timbers smoked and the frenzied people paced about, but the Buddha, amid the rubble and the ashes and the chaos, remained as still as could be. It was such a huge loss and such devastation, but I

looked at the Buddha sitting there, and I knew in that moment that we were going to be okay, that we could to get through this and new positive outcomes would emerge.

Over the next few days, the loss settled heavily on all of us. Gordon and Corinne lost everything except for their cars. All their important work files, cherished wedding photos, their entire wardrobe, computers, dishes, toothbrushes, shoes and most tragically, their beloved cat, had all perished. They were scheduled to go on a book tour in Europe and the new suitcases were all burned up. We dug slowly through the debris all covered in soot and ash until we managed to recover a few precious items. Corinne looked for a set of heirloom silverware and tokens from the bedroom, but the fire was so hot that very little remained.

Fire is the great destroyer, yet in some ways it brings freedom. It leaves you raw, exposed and empty-handed. Any physical items with past life baggage, stuff we carted around for years, are gone. It cleanses and refreshes, yet leaves you raw and disoriented. Just as in the forest, new growth and life emerge after fire. After the shock wears off, with the right mindset, the experience can be liberating.

Because flames leapt on the tiles, which typically don't burn unless doused in gasoline, we suspected arson. To have your house burn down by accident is always a tragedy. Deliberate intention and an element of being attacked instills a much more terrifying feeling. Accusations flew as unfortunate names were tossed around. Anyone not attending the meeting was under suspicion. Names of the teenagers in the community surfaced, much to the anger of their parents. Rumors about a kid that lived in the neighborhood and kids at high school bragging about the fire came back to us. But none of us found the truth as tension rippled and neighbors called us, urging us to determine who was responsible so it would not happen to their home.

At the time, only two people worked on arson cases in the whole state of Massachusetts. They were busy investigating another recent fire where people had died. Eventually they came to collect all the information and data from the burnt building, but the case was never pursued further. Corinne wondered about it for years. I bet that person still carries some emotion and guilt about it, as it's a big weight to carry in one's soul. We'll never know, unless someday they come forward.

After all the anger, fear and loss, Gordon and Corinne took the long view and examined their loss from a spiritual context. To straighten everything out and get their affairs in order, to rebuild their lives from nothing, reflected a huge tragedy but also an important message. In meditation they decided they had made the wrong choice in coming back to Sirius full-time. Their work in the world needed to continue elsewhere, and so they left to return to Washington and take stock.

As we figured out how to respond to this catastrophe, we learned and grew. The neighborhood around Sirius was thriving and the sense of the village was strong. When this incident occurred, we were afraid to lose our closeness in our community as people closed themselves off.

We had freedom in our neighborhood that did not exist in other places, and we wanted to protect it. The kids ran in and out of houses all over the property and were welcomed in most places. Many of the buildings had no locks on the doors. We had created a space with a different paradigm, one that was more free, open and accepting, and we did not want the fire to change this. After the fire, some people wanted to lock everything and protect themselves with guard dogs.

I did not want to live in a culture of fear but tried to hear all perspectives and figure out the best strategy going forward. For the first time ever, we started locking the Community Center and someone was assigned to do a lock up each night. They were on duty to watch for suspicious activity and catch anyone sneaking around late at night. Others chose individually if they wanted to lock their doors. In my house, I just couldn't do it with my dedication to cultivating openness and love. Though I understand why it reassured others, I was unwilling to close myself off and live in fear. Locking up lasted for a while, but with time it faded as the fear lessened.

Gordon and Corinne, after spending a few years back in Washington,

DC, eventually moved to California to continue writing books and teaching seminars. The organization they founded, the Center for Visionary Leadership, continued, and they traveled extensively, giving talks and lectures around the world. They contributed many teachings through seminars and books and worked with many people over the years. Without the fire, they may not have had such a big impact.

In the aftermath of the fire, we wanted to rebuild on the empty foundation. The entire infrastructure still present included a well, a driveway and a foundational slab. We always needed more housing but didn't have the money to rebuild as we were also in the middle of other projects and could not immediately switch gears.

At the time, my mother was living in a big house all alone where I grew up in Plymouth, Massachusetts. She was widowed for the last five years and Gordon and I were concerned about her, wondering if she needed some kind of change. She was living in isolation for the first time in her life, but as she was still relatively young and independent, we did not want to tell her what to do. She often came to visit us and was always open and supportive of our work here. My father was the one who always resisted our ideas, and in the course of his life he never once spent a night at the community as it pushed too far past his edges.

The next time my mother came to visit the community, we walked the empty space where the house had once stood, the ashes settling into the earth. "What are we going to do here now?" someone pondered. As though a foreign voice moved through her vocal cords, Josephine blurted out, "I'm going to build a house!" She seemed taken aback by her own declaration. Yet of her own desire and volition, Josephine suggested she put up the money to rebuild and join the community.

Slowly the idea took hold. Learning from our past housing mistakes, we created a formal legal agreement to finance the project. Three years after the fire, we started rebuilding the renamed Phoenix House. We expanded the foundation and turned the structure into a multiple person dwelling and Josephine received half the space while the rest was used for other community members. A sculpture of a rising phoenix adorns the top of the front door.

Josephine moved here while her new home was being built. She lived below the kitchen in the Community Center. Often with the isolation in our culture, elders are not put in a role of being valued or honored for their life experience and what they bring. Being here was good for her and the community. She always says her time at Sirius marks some of the happiest years of her life and as an elder, her many friends of all ages like and admire her. She is needed and valued for what she offers, with a chance to shine. She doesn't go out shoveling every day, but she brings in the mail and hangs out with the children. I think this has contributed to her longevity well into the ripe age of 97.

After Gordon and Corinne's house burned down, the only remaining structure was one shed that housed all the wind and solar equipment. About nine years later a second fire occurred. The events were not likely connected but some long-term members remembered and wondered about a connection, because the fire also happened on a Thursday night during our meeting. Again people came back from a meeting and noticed flames. We ran up the hill, and the shed was fully blazing. I remember just standing there frozen, thinking, *Oh shit, this is not good, this is really not good! What are we going to do?* The shock was so intense, it paralyzed me.

All the electricity and power in the building were tied into the shed with the solar equipment currently on fire. There was no water and no way we could immediately think of to put it out. The shed was so close to the rebuilt Phoenix House that the flames were licking the side of the building.

Before the fire department arrived, we tried to figure out what to do. I remembered that the straw-bale building under construction next door had a cistern underneath, likely filled with water. We grabbed the clay mixing buckets, ran over and flung off the cover. It was full and about 20 people passed water along a bucket brigade to try to stop the flames. The shed was already so engulfed in flames, we could not save it, but we were mostly concerned about keeping the Phoenix House from burning down again.

The fire crew investigated and tried to determine the cause. They looked at the charred remains and were able to assess where it started by where it burned the hottest. They decided someone probably put ashes in a bin or trash can and that it caught something else on fire but the source remained uncertain.

We learned a lot from both of these fires. It is easy to get really angry and blame whoever we think lit the fire. But whoever is responsible is still human, with some form of their own suffering. It was important to me to try and respond with understanding and compassion. Many people did not find it easy at the time, but our work is to try to create a world filled with more understanding and compassion. Responding in any other way is not in alignment with our values; our purpose would lose its meaning.

Peace Pagoda

It's amazingly common that spiritual centers with powerful energy emanating from them have at least one huge fire over the course of their existence. I know many places where this occurred and I'm unsure why this happens. Perhaps the high concentration of spiritual energy attracts such sparks of transformation.

The Peace Pagoda, another local organization near here lost their temple to arson. They are an order of Buddhist monks who live in Leverett. They created a sacred temple open to the public to honor the Buddha and the spiritual life in all things. I worked with them for many years and helped build their temple. We constructed it from old barn beams in the valley.

Unfortunately someone burned down the temple weeks after it was finished. It was a great tragedy, but the way we respond to an event always shapes how it affects us. I visited the monks shortly after the incident and in conversation with the leader, Gyoway Kato, he clearly said to me, "We must respond with compassion, for all our work here is meaningless if we cannot continue to live our values in the face of tragedy." When asked what he would to do prevent someone from doing it again, he smiled wryly and said, "The new one we build, it will be completely out of concrete. No one can burn it down."

So despite the tragedy and all Gordon and Corinne lost, in the long run good came out of losing the Phoenix House. As we try to see the situation from a negative or positive light, we may not understand the messages until later. I believe there is always a divine plan. If we can pay attention, surrender and put some of our own strong feelings aside, we learn a lot. We grow as we come closer to our true calling and mission in the world.

Garden Magic

DEVAS, NATURE SPIRITS AND ELEMENTALS

11

Editor's note: While recording the stories for this book, a stranger came knocking at Bruce's door and they spoke about the nature kingdom. Bruce thought Spirit stepped up and wanted this conversation to be part of the book. The text is preserved in dialogue form to portray Steven's strong and clear messages.

Fairy Games

Steven: The fairy folk and nature spirits have been telling me for a year to come and talk with you, and today they insisted that I come visit immediately! They've always been part of my life, though I never shared about them. I called and made an appointment for a different day, but they insisted I had to come here today. They told me, "No, go with what you have now and stop protesting!"

They told me to send an email and make two calls. One would be answered and I was supposed to leave a message with cryptic language at the end. I should depart my house at four minutes of 11. And I got in the car at 11:11 to come see you. I was instructed to go past the parking lot and stand there to look, and wait for directions. I protested their demands, but went anyway. I arrived at 11:58 since they said I needed to arrive at your house by 12:04. They said I would find your wife working in the garden and she would locate you, as she did. Usually their guidance is not so specific but today it was, and here I am.

Bruce: Your presence is synchronistic. You're not intruding, in fact you're very welcome here! You arrived in divine timing. When my wife said you were here, I had a sense that our conversation will be important. If your guidance is right, which I am sure it is, then you are here for an important reason.

Steven: All my life I've had experiences with nature. I had no context for them. Instead I thought, *Well maybe I'm just a little weird.* This increased the hours of my childhood time spent in the woods alone by streams, and I felt the best company with me in the forest!

People questioned, "How could you walk in the woods alone, aren't you afraid!" I thought, *No, I'm afraid when I'm with you!*

I was sensitive to others' energies and often didn't understand myself. I could walk into a room, and instantly feel physically ill from the people around me. Everything is apparent about a person when you first meet them, you don't even have to greet them. You lock eyes, and you see their full truth. As a child, with little protection, it's overwhelming. No one else seemed to experience this, so I believed there was something wrong with me. With time, instead of blocking it, I let it move through me. I didn't internalize it, I just let it go.

As I have grown, I gained a better understanding. I work with my sensitivity, and I developed a language with the nature kingdoms. Now the spirits are with me all the time, but merciless in their requests, they refuse to leave me alone! Their energy is demanding, but always arrives with incredible humor and joy. They laugh as I tell them in frustration, "I don't want to do this!" I receive urgent messages that I don't often talk about. Reading *The Magic of Findhorn* helped me understand this relationship.

I work at our organic community garden and on the other side of the street, the city installed playing fields. Last year they chose to spray the fields with Roundup and the town agreed to warn us before they sprayed. The long garden hours were demanding and I needed some time off because I have health issues that require me to rest. One day the spirits arrived in my room and urgently stated, "Come now!"

I answered, "No, I'm not going." Despite this, I got up and dressed myself, surrendering to the fairy folk's urgency.

When I arrived, the tractor across the street was spraying chemicals and the wind blew the chemicals wafting toward the garden. Though I couldn't stop it, I alerted people, and the fairy folk were happy with my actions.

They call me often in this manner. I welcome new members in the garden and I arrange plots for them to use. Before a new person arrives, the spirits call from the garden and ask me to meet the new visitors. Once I get there, the devas direct me to a specific plot and I ask, "What now?" Shortly someone will come walking in. They are mystified at my constant presence. They say, "Every time I come to the garden, you're here!" They don't understand I arrive five minutes earlier at the fairies' summoning.

I feel the fairies right behind me, orchestrating the interaction. It's a magical experience, as I come open up the space for them.

Sometimes I enjoy the dialogue, and other times I find it challenging. I tried not to come here today, because I felt sick and didn't want to show up, but they kept pestering me. Finally I sat down and accepted, "Okay, guide me. I surrender."

The garden lives just one turn from my house, so when I drive home they tell me, "We're going to the garden now!"

I answer, "No, I'm busy." But at the same time I find myself turning toward the garden.

In our garden space, the fairies have clear plans for the next 150 years, which spans the next seven generations. They express interest in the land and want to see it developed with certain goals. While their energy is not desperate or fatalistic, they insist that I take certain actions and want me to consult them on all aspects of our project. They want input on infrastructure, the garden, everything that our organization does with the land.

Bruce: The fairies you describe sound like they are only playing with you. Very clear boundaries will help them understand you. You don't need to react to their sense of urgency. You're part of the divine cosmos, and your balance also matters. In each moment, decide how much you give in. You can check in with yourself and consider, *Is their request going to affect my wellbeing? Am I resisting because I don't want to go?*

Is there something that I'm not understanding here? If you follow their lead, even if it doesn't feel like your decision, ultimately you choose it. Clearly say to them, "I hear what you're saying, I *will* act on it, but not right now. In order to maintain a sense of wellbeing and balance in my own life, you must respect my boundaries. I love and respect you, and this is what I need in this moment."

Making this assertion is perfectly okay and they'll back down! These spirits are fun loving yet you are allowed to set clear boundaries. They may keep asking for a little while as they are mischievous. If you seem ambiguous, they will keep asking, but if you make yourself clear, they will listen. They will not withdraw simply because you assert yourself, and they will not force anything on you. But if you fear them, they may leave you, never to return, or they might just keep asking.

To ignore your request would deviate from spiritual principles. As an independent, divine being, you have free will, which you should never give up. All spiritual teachers I've studied agree. Anyone who interferes with your free will is not acting of the light and for them to demand something that throws you out of balance would not be right.

Steven: By default I was pushed into a leadership position. People come to me for counsel, and I just wanted to grow some vegetables. I wasn't planning on take on a leadership role, but people keep asking for direction. I've been gardening for years, but I'm not an expert. A woman came up and asked, "What should I plant in the late season?"

Off the top of my head I suggested whatever came out of my mouth. The next day, she told me, "I did what you recommended. I dug everything up from my 20 by 20 plot full of weeds, bought all the seeds and planted everything you mentioned."

The information I spewed off the top of my head is considered the answer. Sometimes I don't want the responsibility that leadership brings.

People come to me for gardening advice and the advice comes from the fairies. As I speak, I feel the light coming through. Other gardeners think my advice is excellent. I think to myself, *This advice does sound good doesn't it? I must know what I'm talking about!*

People thank me, and I tell them, "I'm just the transmitter," which sounds better than, "The voices in my head are talking to me." The fairies try to keep accolades of me and without my desire, the fairies call me the mayor of the garden. I keep telling them no. I resist the title and while I don't mind taking on this role, I try to be careful with my ego.

For years I thought, *Ego is evil, it has to stay behind!* Three years ago, ego was bothering me, so I said, *Okay fine! We do this together but you have to behave.* Ego laughed at me and said, like a three-year-old, *"I will!"* The child then starts throwing food. I've struggled to find balance. While I must allow the ego to express itself, I cannot get caught up in unconscious ego dramas. I struggle to give myself permission to embrace success. Fortunately when I speak for the garden and see success, I can celebrate, "Yes! We did it!"

I struggle with the messages I receive and ask myself often if I am delusional. The fairies want me to fix the problem and frequently I don't know how. I try and fail miserably. I am an imperfect vessel to address their concerns. The fairies and nature spirits ask me to speak for them, and even as I tell them I don't have the right words, they say, "Speak!"

Sometimes I get unclear, diluted perceptions somehow. Though I face frustrations with my experience, I conclude that I am sane. When the spirits call and I respond, I see how appropriate my call to the situation is, such as the spraying of Roundup near the garden.

Now that I'm involved in a community garden in the area, I have a place to share about my experience. The spirits insist that I declare these interactions openly, and I want to, but I also feel reluctance. I fear being dismissed as "the guy who talks to fairies." Most people don't understand. At the meetings of the steering committee, sometimes the spirits ask me to declare myself when I speak for events that involve them. They want me to come out of the closet and talk about our relationship.

This resistance in being a spokesperson is connected to my past. In 7th grade I had insight and saw a path open up for me to speak and to teach. I was in Roman Catholic Church when this vision came to me. Sitting there, I looked up at the crucifix and remarked, "That's what they do to people who teach!" Because of this fear, I have resisted the path to teach and speak.

I start with neutral language and tell others I am concerned about the unseen garden. Even this makes them back away. I need language to bridge the request from the nature spirits to the gardeners. I need people to understand the importance of leaving a wild corner in the garden.

We have some areas in the garden that are wild, but they keep diminishing. In a 20 by 20 plot everyone should leave a corner. For example let oregano grow wild without harvesting it, let it be, and that's where the spirits live. They like to be honored and considered. I don't know how to communicate this without mentioning fairies, nature spirits and devas. I struggle with how to respond and I know other members of the committee will only see my big ego.

Bruce: You truly understand the dance we all have with our ego. The ego never goes away completely, thus we make friends with it. Your personality can have likes and dislikes, as long as they don't rule the nest. Honor and embrace your power of spiritual connection and don't fear it. You understand the ego/soul relationship well enough to accept power without getting carried away by it. Your fear might stem from past life trauma. Maybe you experienced circumstances where you stepped out to speak and you got squished. This happens to all of us, and I've gone through a similar struggle within myself when I faced fears and doubts about speaking out.

Sometimes power is thrust upon us because we're the right person to fix the problem. If the words resonate from your deepest innermost truth, speak from your heart even if you don't know all the answers. Sometimes I speak without knowing what I want to say. When I speak to a group, Spirit moves through me; when I hear the words I muse, *Wow, this sounds pretty good!*

When those words come out and make sense, I know I am aligning with my core essence. People ask where my wisdom comes from, so I acknowledge I am a vessel. The light of Spirit is everywhere and I am simply connecting to its presence.

You possess spiritual connection and energy with the nature kingdoms and in my experience, you have a responsibility to represent them. If you don't take responsibility, act on it and work with it, then it doesn't grow or get stronger. Some us have spiritual connection and are guided to share it. If we don't respond to this request, it's irresponsible. To refrain limits the message to the world and also limits our own ability to grow spiritually and expand consciousness.

You must also have criteria for inner guidance. When you hear voices, analyze and discriminate, because being delusional is possible. I meet people who claim, "I hear the direct voice of God!" Often their messages come through blurry and unclear. Look at the message received and ask, "Is this being harmful to anyone in any way? Does it meet the criteria of harmlessness on the deepest level?" If the message you receive benefits the greater good and helps people, it's not fanatical or crazy. Trust your own discriminating powers and believe in the message if it passes these criteria.

Hundreds of people I met do channeling and have inner connections. I always evaluate their message. Some people's egos take over when the message becomes an aggrandizement of their personality. People attach to the message and its results. Their energy veers away from pure hearted, clear intentions. On my bad days when I am psychologically and emotionally off, the messages I receive are not clear at all. They come through clear when I am in a state of joy, so if I find myself in a negative emotional space, I must acknowledge the messages and change my energy before I can receive an accurate message.

Even with a clear heart we might receive messages from our inner space, filled with static. Despite the static, if our intentions are altruistic, the message is pure enough to be true. Sometimes when I'm not feeling good I can meditate and bring my alignment up to hear a clear message. I've learned this over years and years; I must watch my own distorted perceptions and find my pure intention.

The fairies are asking you to be deeply involved. They see something in you that resonates with them. You can present the information they bring to you in a way that doesn't block your communication with other people. You have enough sensitivity and inner connection to find the right words. When you surrender to a request, filter it, and express it in language people understand. Tune in to consider, *How do I communicate this message to people so they won't dismiss me as some kind of nutcase?*

When you see and recognize spirits or energy in the natural world, work with them. Your presence enhances the line of communication. Put your experience into words in a way that expands rather than limits people's consciousness and creates interested curiosity rather than reaction. Rather than talking about fairies, nature spirits, elementals and devas, speak about energy in nature.

Rather than stating, "The fairies don't like that," name the scientifically proven consciousness of interconnection in the natural world. Approach your listener with love and respect, and describe and illuminate the ensouling spiritual presence in nature. People will respond well to a general idea as opposed to when you start talking about fairies, which induces stronger negative reactions.

Most people are open to the idea that all life is sacred and everything is interconnected. This term is used often enough to be familiar so that it doesn't immediately alienate people. People understand it makes sense to honor this web of life that exists.

When I meet someone new, I tune in to who they are and how open they seem. Some people can deal with socially unaccepted norms. I ask inwardly, "How can I communicate to this person? What words will help them hear and understand my ideas?" I start with general concepts such as life is sacred, and we are all interconnected. If they are listening, the gateway opens to express more. The language can be as simple as, "My sense of the sacred interconnectedness in this garden requires us to do this," or, "We are disrupting the sacredness of the garden if we don't leave a corner wild." You don't have to say the fairies told you. Most people will hear you as they recognize and relate to the concepts.

Dance Vision

Steven: Sometimes I have incredible experiences and visions in the garden. Often I walk at night in the city where I live. One particular night I walked and walked, over five miles, until I came to the garden. Sitting in the garden, an intense supermoon rose directly behind me, full and enormous. I started chanting and singing, which centers and grounds me. Slowly I danced what I imagined to be some form of indigenous dance. I started chanting, and the nature spirits and fairies emerged and joined me from all corners of the garden. I was in the center as we danced and I saw women holding hands in a ring dancing clockwise. The chanting held a continuous background rhythm as it ebbed and flowed, with three or four voices emerging in harmony. I could hear the other voices clearly as I sang.

I saw a circle of men facing forward, moving counter-clockwise. They chanted the lower notes while the women chanted the higher melody. I stood in the center, reciting verse. The spoken word moved through me and the children came and joined the circle. In freeform movement, they wiggled and spun in the center of the circle as they danced with wild abandon. Other beings simply held space with their presence, working in the shadows. I danced over to a tuft of long grass reflecting the moonlight, and then I danced over to the shrub full of crickets, chirping loudly in unison. Their chirping grew louder and louder. The dance extended into timelessness while a voice from a deep recessed corner of my brain, kept wondering faintly, "Maybe I'm nuts!"

This night sticks with me. It is as real as any event I've ever experienced. It eclipses any other moment I've ever experienced on this planet in its healing upliftment.

The Girl in the Yellow Dress

Steven: Most beliefs I hold about the garden align with what the fairies want, for example a space with no cars. The management team, which includes me, is turning the space into a drive-in garden. The fairies don't like cars because they smell bad and disrupt the space. They attract the wrong kind of people who want to drive in all the time, even though rules only permit people to drive in to drop off big heavy materials and equipment. People don't respect the rules because they are addicted to driving.

When the cars drive in, they interrupt the space, and the fairies disperse and draw back. I walk in and I feel so lonely in the garden until they return. I feel the absence in my soul rather than see it with my eyes. I see disruption emerge when the desires are ignored. People who violate the parking rule are clouded and dishonest with themselves, as the garden allies draw away. One woman drives to her plot daily. All the nature spirits and fairies leave and don't return for a while. Her lingering presence dissipates slowly and eventually the spirits return.

A play structure sits right by the road, where kids play without any traffic mitigation. People think the 5 MPH speed limit sign solves the problem, yet people drive much faster and I feel concerned for the children's safety.

I keep receiving a horrifying, persistent vision of a young girl crushed under the wheels of a truck by the play structure. The image wrenches at my heart, and I'm terrified of what might happen if people keep driving in by the play structure.

Solving the problem is complicated. The land is owned by the town, which leases to us and the traffic patterns are not enforced due to a parking lot and overflow situations. The committee did not want to enforce the policy, but simply add an additional sign.

Upset by this errant decision, my sensitivities reemerged. I was emotionally invested and angry because of everybody's selfishness and imbalance.

The only way we can know if the problem still exists is if someone gets hurt. Since no one else in the group sees or understands what I experience, I can't say to our committee, "There's a small girl in a yellow sun dress with sandals and dirty blonde hair lying crushed near the play structure." My current challenge is to put the agreement in legal language, and I will know if the solution works, because the vision will go away. But if the vision doesn't go away, I've done what I can. I have to be able to let it go.

Other people in the garden share my awareness. With encouragement, they meditate with me, and maybe we can get somewhere.

Bruce: Change is a process. When new ideas are suggested that are for the higher good, the subjective realm comes to your assistance. All thought forms of humanity exist in this dimension. In your mind when you propose new methods, others will tap into them on an energetic level. When forward thinking individuals start projecting new concepts and beliefs, the space allows greater positive thought forms for everyone. If someone is at all open they are affected by a new way of being, a new way of thinking.

Our collective personality of the mental realm exists and everyone can access this. Many thought forms and ideas hanging out in this realm are garbage as they are antiquated, outdated, destructive and harmful. This collective mind with all its thoughts affects people's decisions, and how they perceive themselves and the world.

Interjecting these new changes and positive ideas ultimately affects people's behavior. As soon as you start vibrating on the energy level of another, resonance occurs and the feeling magnifies. In your concern about the garden, hold a positive outcome and others will tap into the energy you create.

Sometimes we have an idea of what we think the best outcome is. Maybe we don't have the whole picture or all the information. Maybe there's another outcome you can't currently imagine that will emerge. If you're meditating on it, hold it and say, "This seems to be a problem, what is the highest possible solution? Is there something I'm not considering?" To ask Spirit for help is very powerful.

Anastasia

Bruce: Another set of teachings influenced me that might lend insight into your experience in the garden. *Anastasia* and the *Ringing Cedar Series* offers a powerful message. Anastasia is a Russian mystic who lives in Siberia alone without a house, or any kind of structure, deep in the forest, even through the freezing winter. The story is true and the woman actually exists! She portrays and exemplifies the depth possible with interspecies connections. The series of books portray her consciousness and they describe how she communicates with nature. She maintains a symbiotic relationship with animals who take care of her.

A very rigid businessman heard about the valuable cedar trees and brought a crew to harvest the pine cones. He encountered Anastasia, and thought he could exploit her knowledge for personal financial gain but instead he experienced an unimaginable transformation of consciousness. When they met, he was a millionaire, and she told him he would lose every cent, that he would write a book about their encounter and sell millions of copies. He said, "I can't write, I'm a businessman!" So he left, and his business immediately went under.

He lost everything, penniless and homeless on the street before he remembered what she told him. He was so desperate, with no other options he submitted, "I guess I'll try writing this book."

He wrote the book and became her voice to the world. The first book was filled with terrible writing. While the wisdom it contains is indisputable, you read it, and think, *Oh my God, they actually published this book?*

In fact, no one would publish the book because it was so poorly written, so he printed up a few copies and he went on the street selling them cheap, while living in a flop house with no money. He sold a few copies, and readers came back. They wanted to know more about the mysterious lady in the forest. He sold a few more and people wanted more and more even though they were terribly written. The story was so compelling, and the energy behind it was so intense.

He started selling the books, and eventually the first one was published. The momentum grew and Anastasia became known throughout Russia. Over time he sold millions of copies. After the first book, he took a writing course and learned to write properly. With each new book, the writing gets better and better.

He went back to Anastasia to relay his experience and in seven more books he wrote the unfolding story about their lives. She had a child with the author, whom she raises in the wild. He documents her lifestyle and records the spiritual components, living embedded in nature, with interspecies communication with all the beings, describing her interactions with animals.

With millions of copies in print, hundreds of thousands of people in Russia now who are following her guidance and practicing her principles. It's become an amazing movement in Russia.

Some of her messages go far beyond most people's comfort zones as she communicates with alien beings, yet nothing that I read in those books is impossible in my experience. I have a good bullshit meter and am very skeptical; I discriminate when I hear new ideas and stories, I don't automatically accept them and I look deeply on a spiritual level at the information presented. Many people are skeptical about Anastasia. After I read the first book or two, I experienced her energy in the pages and I felt the beautiful spiritual presence of her soul.

I've recommended the books to others. Some people think the author is nuts, while others find truth and wisdom in the vision.

INDIA

LESSONS FROM A SPIRITUAL CULTURE

12

Chaos

I had been meaning to go to India for many decades and I knew a profound experience would be waiting for me when I finally made it. I was on my way to India and Nepal in the '70s when I visited Findhorn Community for a short visit. Instead I stayed at Findhorn for four years, which completely changed my life.

Twenty-five years later the International Meditation Group I participate in scheduled its next meeting in India. Linda and I decided to travel in India after the meeting in order to learn about the culture, an entire system that embraces spiritual reality. In India spirituality dominates the people's consciousness, while materialism takes a back seat. They believe the spiritual realm underlies everything, whereas in our culture materialism dominates and spiritual principles are left on the margins. I have always been fascinated with this culture as many spiritual teachings brought to the west originated in India, Nepal and Tibet.

Together Linda and I felt this trip was a spiritual journey. During our stay, we arranged to visit different ashrams and holy places including Auroville, a massive intentional community. Being immersed in a culture that is so infused with spirituality was a total culture shock to us. I had visited other third world countries but never felt the same level of spiritual intensity. It deepened my spiritual connection in ways

I could not have imagined.

For two weeks we walked around in disbelief thinking, *Oh my god!* It's a different kind of experience and the initial adjustment was hard, but once we got used to the poverty, the chaos and the filth, I really enjoyed being there. For any westerner who hasn't experienced this level of poverty before, it's a huge shock. We saw kids sleeping in the streets, poverty on every corner, disheveled beggars, crazy chaos and so many people.

Cars roar back and forth and no space exists that isn't filled with people. In America you drive down the road without seeing people for 15 minutes at a time. In India people occupy every corner. In remote areas travelling by train, we never drove more than two minutes without seeing more people. The streets chaotically overflow with people, cows, chickens, everything you can imagine, passing through the streets.

Underneath the crime and theft, we saw the spiritual aspect of life still present. India has a strong relationship to nature, with a deep respect for animals. No one will kill a cow in India, no matter how old or sick it is. In one city, everyone agrees the rats are sacred and refuses to kill them. They feed the rats milk and eat out of the same bowls with them. Nobody has ever died of disease from a rat in this place and the rats are extremely healthy because they are so well fed.

In another city the monkeys are considered sacred and run around everywhere as they overtake the city. People feed them and take care of them. They believe these animals are part of divine nature.

The whole country in India is filled with poverty. Materialism and greed lives strong right alongside sickness, destitution and poverty. People will steal everything possible. If it isn't nailed down they will find a way to take it, but because they are so impoverished I can't blame them. I would do the same in their situation if I were hungry with no resources to meet my basic needs. All the time, the children steal books, pens, backpacks, necklaces, watches—anything they can get their hands on. We kept our guard with constant vigilance but they were clever. The westerners come along, dressing nice, loaded with money and if you steal then you can feed yourself perhaps for the first time in days.

One day in the ashram, we were sitting in the meditation hall. The westerners had their possessions lying all around. A little kid came in and *Fwoosh!* He snatched a purse and was out the door again and gone.

He was so fast, nobody caught him. They tried but he had the trick down; obviously he had done it before.

Jagannathan and Krishnammal's Orphanage

Some of the ashrams we visited emanated an energy so beautiful, it was different from anything I had ever felt. I was amazed. We went to one ashram run by a couple, Jagannathan and Krishnammal, direct disciples of Mahatma Gandhi. They had worked with Gandhi and his spiritual teacher, Vinoba Bhave. Vinoba Bhave is known for traveling around India, convincing rich people to give land back to the poor people with no land. The leader of this ashram had joined the effort and at one point was imprisoned in jail with Gandhi. The people who ran the ashram were remarkable.

This was the most amazing experience during our trip. The ashram that Jagannathan and Krishnammal ran, with the assistance of others, served as an orphanage for 40 boys made up of untouchables off the streets. They fed them, gave them clothes and took care of them, and these kids were so happy, so joyful; something I did not expect from street kids who are orphans, and probably mistreated for much of their lives.

We heard of this place and asked for a visit, and as they rarely had visitors, they weren't prepared to host us, but they said, "Yes, please, be

our guest!" Jagannathan was in his late eighties and Krishnammal was in her late seventies. He was mostly blind, but he still worked hard and took on many tasks.

Their house, a tiny concrete block structure, boasted no doors or windows, just a simple bed, and a few clothes and personal items. When we arrived, they moved out of their little house, and *insisted* we sleep in their beds while they slept outside! They would not let us object.

We got to know everyone there quite well, playing and hanging out together every day. We brought them to the temple and spent time sharing fun games and activities. Most of them had never seen a white person before and they would rub our skin and stare at it.

The boys expressed such joy and gratitude to be in this ashram even as they each had one change of clothes and all slept in one room on a concrete floor on little thin mats and nothing else. When they played, they were completely joyful and happy, and I felt the juxtaposition to the young people in the United States who, despite extreme wealth, often sink into depression. The irony completely overwhelmed us, as we hung out with these content kids.

Every action in Jagannathan and Krishnammal's lives comes from spiritual connection. The orphanage is well respected in the local area as people come to them for advice. They are the wise elders in the whole region, yet live unbelievably simply with almost no possessions. They are amazing, deeply spiritual people.

Besides running the ashram they work with local poor people. They obtain land, help them assert their rights and protested the shrimp farmers who kill the land with their chemical saline pools. They are fiercely dedicated and support justice for people everywhere. We stayed for a week and left by train, as it is the only way to get to this remote place. Of a tiny town that never sees any tourists or guests, people stared at us, wondering who we were.

When we left, the 40 boys from the ashram walked half a mile to the train station and stood on the platform as the train departed, waving like crazy. It was just an incredible experience and it moves me to tears even now.

After I left India, I thought about them often as years went by and I sent money to support their work. Many years later I received a phone call from a woman in Northampton.

She told me, "I know about your spiritual community. There's a woman from India who's coming to America. She won an award for $100,000 and she's coming to receive it. She wants to stay in your community." And it was Krishnammal! She won two awards, one called the Right Livelihood Award, and another was an award that came with $100,000. The synchronicity blew my mind when she came here to Sirius to stay for a few days.

We set up a public event in the Octagon and many people attended to hear Krishnammal talk about her experiences and her time with Gandhi and Vinoba Bhave. I was amazed and moved as I never thought I would ever see her again and here she was at my home in our community!

She returned home and started a brick factory with the money she received and also used the money to build houses for the poor people, putting every penny into service for people who have nothing. She kept not a penny for herself. She is an amazing woman and gained some fame when Who's Who of India wrote up an article about her. She is considered by some to be the next Gandhi of India. Her life's work is a huge inspiration and I am incredibly grateful for our experience together.

Karma and Reincarnation

I think the east and the west have something to teach each other. There is a balance between what they offer as a culture and where they failed. In the United States and much of the world, chasing wealth and finding material gain is the most important goal. We lose sight of everything else, even if our health, happiness and families suffer. We have no spiritual base for our lives and we feel hollow on the inside.

Being in India was refreshing because the focus is so different. In India the attention lies completely opposite of material wealth. Unfortunately they have trouble taking care of their own people *because* they are so spiritual and their physical wellbeing is often compromised.

It was sometimes terrifying, because there it caused extreme poverty. In India the basic belief revolves around reincarnation, so your lot in life is based on your karma. Unlike this country, death loses its power because if you die it's not a big deal; it's part of a bigger cycle of your soul. Because of this belief, very little effort goes into improving the plight of the most impoverished. Culturally, rich people refuse to give money to the poor people. It simply isn't done.

In the United States, the systems admit their many flaws, but the care for the impoverished is better than in India. There, poor people receive no support from the government. There is no welfare, no social security, no homeless shelters, no food aid. The food distribution that does happen comes from the ashrams and spiritual communities. One ashram I witnessed offers a soup kitchen two or three times a week, and the poor people gather to receive food, as the kitchen feeds as many people as possible. Unfortunately the need is endless. It's never enough. The suffering has increased in recent times with the onset of rampant capitalism.

We walked out in the street and twenty people mobbed us pleading, "Rupees! Rupees!" Little deformed kids came and tugged on our sleeves, as very young children slept on the streets. It wrenches your heart, the need is so huge. I could not feed or give money to everyone. I did give money when I could but then twenty more people would show up and I saw I couldn't alleviate a systemic problem with a few rupees.

In Darjeeling I saw a man who couldn't walk. He sat on a little rolling platform and I walked by him on the street every day. One day, I gave him a huge amount of money, about twenty bucks, which was not an exorbitant amount of money to me, but in India it was a fortune, particularly for a beggar! When I handed him the money, his expression was one of complete shock. I walked by him many more times after that, but he never asked for money again. Instead every time he saw me coming, he would express his gratitude. It was a profound experience to help him out, to give wealth to somebody who so desperately needed it.

So we need balance. We must meet our physical needs and take care of the less fortunate, but also have strong enough spiritual beliefs so that rampant consumerism doesn't take over our lives. When we find a balance between the two, we will create a beautiful society.

Ganges: The Sacred River

Most Indians, at some point in their life, take a spiritual journey to the Ganges. It's considered the most sacred river in India and microorganisms thrive in the Ganges that don't exist anywhere else in the world. Of all the rivers on the planet, the Ganges has more oxygen in the water than any other and the origins come right from the snowmelt of the Himalayas, directly from the glaciers. In the river exists a living process where microorganisms eat all the toxic bacteria, such as feces and other kinds of waste. The more pollution in the water, the more the positive microorganisms grow! The high levels of oxygen and other microorganisms neutralize all the pathogens.

The Ganges flows through the town of Varanasi. The people who live there bathe in the river and drink the water regularly despite the fact that it receives the most pollution of any river in the world. It's filled with feces and garbage but nobody gets sick from it.

Linda and I thought about bathing in the water since no one else refrained, so we rented a boat and rowed around the river. Then we saw dead bodies floating next to our boat and in our utter shock we decided jumping in the water would be a bad idea. The bodies were too much—that was over the top!

To send out the cremated ashes of loved ones into the river is a sacred honor. The people carry the dead bodies through the town and bring them to the burning ghats. The burning ghats ignite into huge fires, sitting right on the banks of the river. The bodies are cast into the fire, right out in the open. Everyone witnesses burning bodies regularly.

Once the bodies have incinerated, they are sprinkled in the river.

Unfortunately for many people, the wood to burn up the bodies is very expensive, so often people just throw the bodies in the river directly without cremating them! The dead bodies float around and eventually wash up on shore. What a different culture! It's a huge shock to see this other reality.

I went to Rishikesh, a town upriver on the Ganges. There are about 30 ashrams and the river is full of fish. Nobody eats meat or eggs so you can't even buy them in the town. No one eats the fish or touches them but consider them sacred and feed them instead. In Rishikesh the water isn't as polluted, because it's closer to the source.

One day I felt very sick. I had a headache, tired and nauseated. In India with so much contamination, it's easy to get sick. People tell about the healing qualities of the river, so I figured I might as well test it since I was by cleaner water. I jumped in the river and to my astonishment I immediately felt better! I got out of the river and was completely healed. I felt the power of the Ganges!

The water has intense purifying properties and so people even drink the water in Rishikesh where it still receives a fair amount of pollution. They swear that it heals them and this has been the culture for thousands of years. In Rishikesh on the side of the river, big steps lead out of the town down to the riverbank. Everybody bathes in the water with all the dead bodies and the feces. They brush their teeth with it and drink it. I could not believe it, as, astonished, I asked myself why these people don't get sick. The people said no one died or became ill from the water. Perhaps the oxygen and the microorganisms protect us and create perfect balance. I swam in it daily despite some of the disconcerting debris floating around.

Temples and Refugees

Nepal felt quite different from India. The poverty was even worse, but as farmers they root into more of an earth connection. Often shrouded in clouds, the mountains are usually invisible. For a few days after we arrived, we looked for the mountains, to no avail. One day the clouds lifted and the mountains came into full view higher and higher, with snowcapped peaks, radiating a beauty beyond imagination. They hovered into the blue sky way above. They are the tallest mountains in the world. Their presence and astonishing beauty absolutely floored us.

We rented a motorcycle and drove it up into the foothills. Only one road connects the country, with few cars on it. The meandering road is full of people, potholes and perilously steep ravines.

While in Nepal we also visited a Tibetan refugee community. We met many Tibetan women, people who had fled their homeland. Their remarkable spiritual strength struck us powerfully. The women especially hold so much beauty and power, while they weave enchantingly beautiful Tibetan carpets as their livelihood.

They build ashrams in refugee communities which included enormous Tibetan prayer wheels wrapped with scrolls of thousands of mantras. Often the same prayer is written over and over again, and the wheels spin on an axle, many as large as an entire room! Everyone walks around spinning them as part of the daily rhythm. I felt humbly honored to be with them in their presence.

After Linda left to go home, I also visited another Tibetan refugee community in Darjeeling, India. Here they also come together in a temple. I approached the temple and peaked in, unaware they were in the middle of a service, singing prayers. When they saw me, they grabbed me and pulled me into the temple and sat me down right in the middle of the service without missing a beat.

They blew 12-foot-long trumpets and prayed and chanted. The service was completely relaxed, the kids were so sweet as they ran around, talking and laughing. They exuded this sense of joy and happiness. At the end of the ceremony, they fed and welcomed me so completely and treated me like an honored guest even though I interrupted their service when I poked my head in. I felt the rich presence of these Tibetan people and the Buddhists amazed me as I enjoyed sitting with them.

In Darjeeling where we stayed, we looked out over the mountains and could see Tibet. We saw lights, movement and events happening on the other side of the border. The refugees could not return there without persecution and death while they wistfully looked often at their country from where they were in the ashram.

The refugee community was so strong. When the Chinese invaded and took control of Tibet, many people were forced out of their homes, and a lot of them went through hell in order to escape to India. They climbed over the mountains and many froze to death as the challenges they faced were incredibly difficult, but they demonstrated no resentment or hatred toward the Chinese. They took life as it came and believed they were living their karma from past lifetimes and could not hate their persecutors. In talking with them, they told us they wished the Chinese better understood the importance of compassion in one's life.

Auroville

Of all the ecovillages in the world, the biggest, most well-known of all is Auroville. It is an amazing place, with an intentional community made up of little communities inside a bigger community. People from all over the world constitute a grand diversity as they come to live in and experience the community.

The community is founded on the teachings of Sri Aurobindo. He taught participants how to connect to the Divine, and shared a vision to create a new culture. The Mother, a French woman, also one of the community's great spiritual leaders, was deeply involved with him, and they strived to create a city of light. Indeed, they created an international community founded on the principles of spiritual reality. The beautiful community is thriving, filled with all kinds of amazing people. We knew we must visit this unique place on the planet during our trip to India.

When they first obtained the land, they came upon a complete desert. Nothing grew from the dry, cracked earth; it was just a washed out, degraded wasteland. Despite this, they started their community. For ten years they planted trees and protected them from destruction in the harsh climate. They meditated together and practiced their spiritual work.

The trees represented the sole focus to revitalize the land. Even as rains poured off the dry dirt, they persisted. Eventually the trees the community nurtured broke their roots into the soil, catching the water and holding the decent soil in place. Plants began to spring up in the ground held by the tree roots, and slowly an ecosystem took form. Over time the land revived. It's now made of 1,700 acres, completely restored to lush forest. The water table came back, the plants diversified and the land turned green again. It was so successful that the government of India copied the model. Reforestation projects in other parts of the country use the same format as Auroville.

The people of Auroville reflect an extreme amount of diversity. Each small community operates with its own intention. Some of them focus on ecology while others work on agricultural endeavors. Some dedicate themselves to spirituality. They all exist under the umbrella of Auroville, which honors the spiritual teachings of Sri Aurobindo and The Mother. Each neighborhood embraces the idea that all life is sacred.

Auroville creates an international place of peace and goodwill, and the United Nations recognizes it as a place of great importance for humanity. People from all over the world come for huge international gatherings. Sirius Community maintains ongoing connections with Auroville over the years. Many people who travel to spiritual ecovillages go to both Sirius and Auroville. Findhorn also has had deep connections with Auroville as it is a place of great power and light radiating in the world.

Most of the ashrams in India are connected to one particular teacher or religion. But Auroville breaks the mould with more openness. The approach is eclectic, without devotion to one particular teacher or teaching. Despite its salutation to Sri Aurobindo and the mother, the community honors all religions.

When I arrived I sat and meditated for a long time, tuning into a uniquely powerful consciousness. One can learn and experience deeply from the presence that exists there.

I felt like I merely touched the surface of it; I could have spent years diving into the depths of the energy alive there. Much of the wisdom extended way beyond any understanding I could barely grasp.

The giant spherical dome meditation temples are incredible. The main temple, Matrimandir, stands as the biggest meditation temple, a huge spherical dome with a 150 foot diameter. The meditation chamber contains at its top a pure white sphere, with giant pillars coming out.

Below the chamber rests a huge glass crystal ball, the biggest crystal ball that's ever been made. Light from the skylight shines down onto the glass, breaking it down into colors. The colors radiate out over everyone in prayer. They only allow silence in the hall. People sit and meditate for hours and spiritual vibration radiates at an incredibly high level.

Outside, the temple is covered with real gold. I asked them why they didn't you use the gold to feed the poor people. It seemed a waste to use is as art on the big temple. They explained to me how part of the culture in India maintains that wealthy people will not give money to the poor people. However they're happy to give money for a temple, so using the money to cover the temple in gold made the most sense.

In the construction, they used paper thin sheets of gold. The gold is encased and melted in glass. The metal loses all its value, because you can never remove it from the glass. The gold creates a remarkable energy and beauty in the temple; its radiance flows through the temple itself. I came home with a piece of it, because I met the guy who was doing the process of encasing the gold and he offered me a souvenir.

Tamil Visitors

In the late '80s, four Tamil Indians from Auroville came to Sirius to stay with us. When we built the Octagon, they came for a couple months and worked as apprentices. They were really sweet younger guys and we got along great with them; they got very involved in the community and everybody loved them. We had a good connection. When we poured the foundation of the Community Center, they placed several Indian coins in the cement.

Coming from India, they were always cold in New England. When we were out sweating in our tee shirts and shorts, they bundled up in heavy jackets. They cooked us Indian food a few times that was so incredibly spicy we could barely eat it.

They went with me to a nearby farm to cut beams for the dining room. We needed to climb the trees in order to tie a rope that we would use to safely direct the falling tree. I climbed the trees with big spiked spurs, hanging from a harness.

The next tree I was ready to climb had no limbs. One of Indians asked, "What do you need those tools for? You don't need those spikes to climb the trees."

I said, "What do you mean? How else would you get up the tree?"

He said, "You want me to climb the tree?"

Intrigued, I said, "Yeah, sure," as I handed him the rope.

He took a kerchief rag and tied it around his ankles. Grabbing onto the tree, he climbed right up, tied the rope and zipped back down! I was impressed.

"See," he said with a grin. "You don't need those tools!"

At the end of their stay, their wives came to visit, and we ate one last Indian meal together. We had not seen each other when we arrived in Auroville almost 20 years later and we decided not to tell them we were coming but surprise them instead.

We were standing in line to receive a pass to a garden school and the woman there giving out the passes stopped and stared at us. She looked again in disbelief and cried, *"Bruce and Linda, is that really you?"* She went berserk, jumping up and down, she was so happy to see us. We had met four men and four women in the '80s and we had the good fortune to see every one of them again.

After the first encounter, we kept running into them. Every time, they took us to their home, introduced us to their family and cooked for us. They showed us all around the community and brought us out to the countryside. With their presence, our whole experience at Auroville became so uniquely personal. It was an amazingly blessed experience to be there.

Enlightened Children

It's common in India to teach young children about quieting the mind through meditation, as it is part of the culture. They learn Sanskrit and how to maintain a spiritual practice. The mind is a tool and it's the soul that should occupy the mind. The mind should not be the master. In countries like India, you quiet the mind and you use the mind in the way that your soul wants to use it. The impressions from the soul guide the mind.

In America, developing your mind by gaining knowledge and building intelligence is most important. It is seen as a power tool. Little is taught about disciplining our minds, so we never learn how to achieve a quiet state. Instead we cram the physical brain with information. Almost all the universities and academia teach us this viewpoint.

In India, meditation permeates the culture, even in young children. The kids practice stillness and emanate a strong vibrating light! With their big, open eyes, they radiate Spirit because they have learned the practice. You look at them and you feel and see it. They've been taught God is everywhere and it's so strong, you look at them and you just want to bow down and touch their feet because they radiate the God presence.

It's not like this with all the kids. Many are street kids who behave in crazy ways, but some are enlightened, with saintly qualities. This awareness is ingrained in the principles of the culture, and the ideas start with the children.

You're taught to fine-tune the mind, and to listen beyond the rational brain. This is where a lot of knowledge and wisdom comes from. You develop an intuition, quietness and pointed focus of the mind. The intuition of the non-rational mind helps us receive the information we need.

Rabies

One day as I was walking down the street, a rabid dog ambushed me and sunk its teeth into my flesh. For fear of my life, I went to the hospital to get some rabies shots. The hospital was unbelievable beyond imagination. Any image of what you might think a hospital should look like, you can throw right out the window. Outside the entrance, a huge line of people waiting to get in stretched out of sight. The building looked like a rundown house covered in dirt, but this was the public hospital, so I had to go in.

I joined the line but as a Westerner, people from the crowd grabbed me and put me in the front of the line. I felt unconformable, but they insisted. I entered the building to see that even on the inside, dirt and grime covered the surfaces.

I talked to the doctor and she exclaimed, "You've got to have rabies shots, or you'll die!"

They took me into a room and sat me down on a table caked with dried blood. They picked up a giant package containing a massive syringe off the shelf. It looked like it had been collecting dust and grime for twenty years. Fortunately the syringe was wrapped in a sealed container; otherwise there's no way I would have let them touch me with it! They pulled out the massive needle, stuck it deep into my belly, and slowly depressed the syringe. I cringed in incredible pain.

They pulled the needle out and nonchalantly declared, "You'll have to come back for nine more of these." Aghast I went back to my hotel room in excruciating pain. All alone, I spent the entire night in agony; I couldn't move from this shot in the belly. I decided I would rather die of rabies than go back in and be subjected to those shots.

The next day I found out about a private hospital run by British doctors, so I went there instead. Even in the private hospital, the conditions were not much better, adorned with filth and dirt, as dried blood splattered the exam table. This was the private hospital that cared for the wealthy people. Unbelievable! The cost was almost nothing, only about six dollars. Here the doctors told me, "Oh no, you don't have to take those shots, they are completely outdated. We'll give you six little shots; much less painful." He gave me a shot in the arm, and instructed, "You need to come back for the next six days to get your shots, or you're going to be in bad shape. You've got to take all six, or you'll die from rabies." It's a very serious illness, but I was about to come back to America and I couldn't change my flight, so I received three shots and flew home.

In the hospital in the United States I said, "I need rabies shots; I got bit by a rabid dog," and they ushered me in. Fortunately I was at the income level that if I didn't have insurance, I didn't have to pay for my stay. The medicine in India that I got at the first hospital cost about 25 cents. At the second hospital the price was six dollars. Here I received the exact same shot, with the same package for $900, which opened my eyes to capitalism and the inequality of the world. Fortunately I didn't have to pay the $900 for my final three shots.

Return to Isolation

When I returned to the United States after two months, I fell into complete culture shock. At the airport, people talked about the most trivial nonsense. I thought to myself in disgust, *Oh my God, such superficial absurdity!* In India, I often saw situations where life and death smacks you right in your face; there's no time for superficiality when famished children plead for help in the street and burning bodies drift down the river. The immediacy of the situation holds such a raw potency.

I drove back from the airport in desolation, and wondered, *Where is everybody?* America is such an isolated society. Everybody's stuck in their own little box. People hardly communicate or relate with each other. *What the heck!* What used to seem normal felt impossibly strange. I drove for miles and miles and saw nobody. Houses lined the street, with not a soul in sight.

Nobody talked, nobody communicated. The interaction I witnessed 24 hours a day in the streets was gone. In total shock, it took a while for me to acclimate back to a culture of separation. I realized how isolating our society feels. You have your own little house, only interacting with your nuclear family. You might have friends, and be social and outgoing, but it ends there. In India everybody visits the watering hole, chatting and laughing, roaming the street all the time.

I felt safer in many Indian cities despite the petty theft. Major violent crime was almost nonexistent because the society is not violent. In the United states, if you go in the slums in some cities, you could get shot. I traversed through the slums of Calcutta at night, and I felt completely safe. People in destitution would steal stuff from me if I was not aware, but I never feared for my life. There were so many people everywhere that if you harm someone, ten people would see what happened.

After being in India, I understood in a new way how deeply we need community. Social interaction brings people together and promotes spiritual growth, and breaking out of an isolated existence changes us for the better. Many people in our society live narrow lives, and while they might connect with their family members, that's where the communion ends! If a family is small, they might live their life, go to work and never break out of the narrow mould.

Interacting with lots of people creates an evolution of consciousness. Exposing ourselves to other people's lessons, struggles and heartbreaks helps us grow. We evolve faster when we share spiritual life and growth. To learn the struggle is part of our growth and to be in the presence of others who struggle, our whole world broadens. We're exposed to the difficulties that we go through in life. We see how people learn and cope and what mechanisms people find within themselves to create spiritual strength.

I was shocked by the isolation here with everyone in their separate little boxes. In other cultures, you socialize and interact all the time. India practiced this every day. Everybody knows what's going on in the village. Everybody knows everybody's business. Everybody has shared experiences.

When I was in Darjeeling I went to a little village and a little boy had run away from home and he came to this other village. Every person in the whole village gathered to discuss what to do with this child. The boy was crying, insisting that he couldn't go back and two hundred people gathered to determine what to do with one child. Everybody knew about the deliberation, everyone cared, and not a single member of the village lay hidden away in their house. The contrast struck me. The difference is so great. Here isolation carves such despair and depression into our lives. That just doesn't happen in communal cultures like in India.

We returned fired up by our realizations. We presented to the community, and people were powerfully affected by our experiences. The two and a half months in India opened up an amazing spiritual experience. When a westerner goes to that land, eyes open, but you have to be prepared for plenty of challenges and unusual or even shocking happenings. I've been in a some intense situations in my life, but none of it prepared me for some of the scenes I witnessed. Truly amazed, I gained a deep appreciation for the Indian people's perspectives and values.

We work here with many of the same spiritual principles and ideals of the Indian culture. The lessons I brought back to Sirius continue. I fostered a deeper commitment to practice spiritual connection. The journey helped me with my own spiritual growth and inner work. The whole experience reinforced my beliefs of the vital importance of spiritual life. It provides profound richness and depth on our path. In India everyone meditated regularly and believed in reincarnation and karma. It was fundamental to their practice and personalities.

Daily rhythms of spiritual communion affect the basis of our world view. I brought this in as part of our daily lives here. In India it was ingrained in the culture itself.

Lawsuits

SIRIUS IN JEOPARDY

13

In community, where we constantly work together to create new systems, we want to believe all people involved align with our values and everything will always work out in the end, but the reality is sometimes different. Since joining community back to the early days at Findhorn, I learned how conflict happens and its integral role in any community experience. Our shadows and past wounds linger right below the surface, and in community when others hold up the mirror we are forced to deal with ourselves. It's not a matter of *if* we get in conflict but when and how severe the lasting impact is on everyone involved.

Community often attracts colorful and eccentric individuals. People who have a hard time in mainstream culture gravitate toward some kind of alternative, often hanging out on the fringes of society. When new individuals come to Sirius and participate, though they may seem a bit odd, we let them be who they are. They find more love, acceptance and tolerance in places like Sirius. Sometimes they thrive and heal old societal wounds that come with the labels, hurt and misunderstanding they receive and Sirius provides healing for them. The spiritual change is part of our work here and we try to counteract negative societal messages.

Other times people come in and make life challenging and difficult for everyone else here. We dance a line in allowing an opportunity for people to change and, in rare instances, asking them to leave when their unchanging behavior becomes unacceptable. When they grow angry, deny the issue, stop communicating and flatly refuse to compromise, we learned to take more aggressive steps. If their behavior is challenging, we encourage them to change and grow as we hold back from limiting them to past patterns. When they step out of integrity with their agreements, we often check in with them to see why and put into place some clear action steps to correct the problems. When people are clear and honest with a willingness to grow, we are more lenient and willing to work with them.

In the course of our time here we have asked no more than a handful of people to leave. We want to see the good in all people and allow them to change and make different choices, yet this approach over the years left us with many unpaid debts and lots of hindsight. The individuals we did ask to leave needed to go as they jeopardized the stability of the whole community. Some of them refused multiple times until we found ourselves in court with a judge or facing lawsuits.

Perhaps there are some people we should have never let live on the land in the first place. When people contact us to live here they often visit as guests and participate in community work so people can get to know them. Because we cannot assess their entire character with a few visits, we use our intuition to guide us in determining if they might be a good fit for Sirius.

Confronted with a Stubborn Hoarder

One of our residents, Joe, came to live at Sirius, and we experienced him with a decent personality. He stood tall and thin with sloping shoulders and wore thick glasses. He moved to Sirius at the recommendation of a counselor who thought being here might help him with his psychiatric problems. He remained quiet and private and didn't speak much in groups but came across as nice, while a little mysterious.

Over time he stopped doing his community work, stopped paying his residence fee for many months and disappeared from the community sphere. We repeatedly approached him and asked for communication, trying to work with him and give him clear boundaries about his behavior. Over the months, he stopped communicating and responding to emails, phone calls and in-person visits.

He lived in a small one room apartment consisting of a studio with a tiny kitchen tucked under a sleeping loft, a wood stove in the middle with room for a couch and a hall leading to the bathroom. As the situation deteriorated, he changed the locks on his door to prevent all access to his apartment. When we went to his space to communicate with him, every window was blocked with stacks of cardboard boxes and we couldn't see inside the house.

One day I received a letter in the mail from a lawyer. The letter spelled out in five neatly typed pages of legalese that Joe was suing us for the following infractions: We did not provide adequate housing in regard to clean drinking water, the ability to heat his space, etc. The letter stated that on these grounds the client would not pay the residency fee and refused to leave, demanding that we report to the lawyer and take immediate action to remedy the situation. Infuriated, I almost tore up the piece of paper so filled with lies. I knew we faced a long, expensive and stressful process to resolve the issue.

Forced to hire a lawyer to defend ourselves, we watched the issue drag on for many more months while the lawyers engaged in their slow process and Joe's unpaid bill increased.

In response to his lawyer's demands, we needed more evidence to prove the falsity of his claims. We called a locksmith and, at a time we knew he was home, gathered a handful of people. Armed with a video camera running, we knocked on the door, and I called to him, "I know you're in there. Please open the door. We are here with the locksmith and will take apart and dismantle the door if you don't let us in." The locksmith backed away, raising his hands in the air stating he wasn't here to get into the middle of a messy situation, and this was outside of his job description. We convinced him we were legally justified in our actions.

We cued up the video camera and opened the door and were confronted by walls of boxes stretching to the ceiling. His apartment, one of the smaller spaces on the property, was packed absolutely full, not just a little, but entirely crowded and crammed with boxes, junk, debris and old food. One narrow aisle ran down the center of the room from the bathroom to the bedroom. Four boxes spilling over with papers, cups and towels covered the sink and stove. Buried six feet under the chaos stood the woodstove.

Joe climbed up onto the loft as five or six of us marched in with video cameras and started filming. He climbed into the loft and kept telling us, "You can't do this! I am going to call my lawyer. You can't be here." We clearly informed him we were in our legal rights and were here to collect evidence to justify or dispel his claims. We clamored over the stacks of stuff and reached down behind piles covering the kitchen sink to turn on the water and show that potable water did indeed come out of it. We filmed the wood stove along with all the piles and we left knowing his case held no weight.

His lawyer, realizing he would be unable to win based on our collected video evidence, chose not to concede, but instead make the process hard, time consuming and expensive for us to win as it dragged on for several more weeks.

In the end we lost on a minute technicality built into the Massachusetts building codes. Because all of our residents live here in service to the nonprofit, we officially do not act as landlords, but apparently in this case the judge saw us as such, and we are required to meter the electricity for each apartment separately so each tenant has separate, clearly defined electric bills. When we learned this, we settled and were unable to collect any back rent. When asked, we were required to tell everyone that he left of his own accord and not to give him a bad reference.

Determined not to go through such a situation again, we put new systems in place to prevent people like Joe taking advantage of us. Unfortunately we faced a similar confrontation sooner than we expected.

All Assets at Risk

Sirius has many buildings and while some were built by Sirius, others were built by individuals and Sirius acquired them when they left, paying back over time any assets invested in the structure. We recently acquired one of the houses that a private couple was managing, maintaining and inspecting for years. All of our buildings constructed must meet all legal requirements, including fire alarms, legal window size, septic needs and zoning restrictions.

The house was a three story brown duplex and the guy who built it was truly not a finish carpenter. He used to live on a ship and was familiar with tight confined spaces and overhead bins. The house he built featured the same personality, inundated with cubby holes, poorly cut joints and plenty of wood putty. While out of the ordinary, the house provided a quirky intrigue with big picture windows looking out into forest, and it added essential space for new members.

The recently acquired house boasted unusually high heating bills as one of the few spaces on the property without a woodstove. The couple who built it complained for many years that the space smelled of gas. Each time the gas company came out to look at the heater, they told the owners everything was fine and there was no need to be concerned.

As we took over the building and the space came up for rent, we advertised for new residents. A woman named Christie came to visit and many people were excited about her. She came with her daughter to an open house and started visiting the community and interacting so others would get to know her and sense if she was a fit for our needs. An eager talker, she claimed a long list of skills working for nonprofits. She went through the residency interview process and many people liked her and believed her skill sets would be valuable. She moved into the house with her nine-year-old daughter and another woman moved into the other side of the duplex.

From first meeting Christie, I had a hit that something was a little off and I did not like the energy I sensed from her. But because others were enthusiastic, I ignored my hesitation and refrained from voicing my concern, which I regretted often in the years to come, when I would lie awake at night, thinking how her behavior almost ruined us.

From all first appearances, Christie seemed okay. She came across as a little forceful and needy, but she showed up for community work and attended meetings. People chatted with her at meals and liked her company. I thought maybe I misread her and my hesitation was unfounded.

One day she smelled smoke in her house and called up the fire department. They arrived with fully loaded fire trucks, poked around and found nothing about a fire. They clomped down the bulkhead into the basement, looked around and pulled out their instruments to measure carbon monoxide levels in the house. They ran upstairs and warned her, "The carbon monoxide levels are unsafe! Grab your necessities and leave immediately; do not return until further notice." She started yelling, grabbed her kid, ran across the property, picked up the phone and called my number, yelling, screaming and cursing at me, *"I've been poisoned and my health is ruined because of you!"*

Within a few days, I was knee deep in inspections, phone calls, and official letters from different branches of the local town government coming out daily to assess the situation. The board of health, the fire chief, the police commissioner, and the gas company called daily.

I called the couple who used to own the house to retrieve all the paperwork documents and history of the place. I called the fire chief. I called the state. I called the gas company. I got the incident report and I pored over the details.

The gas company came out and inspected the heater and again kept assuring us there was no problem and did not know why their heater was malfunctioning or why the fire department found such alarming carbon monoxide rates. After getting nowhere but completely frustrated, we decided to call someone else so we could get to the bottom of the problem. Every time we hired another person, it cost more money. Every time we thought we were getting somewhere, we found ourselves tied up in greater complexity.

A technician from another gas company came out in his big utility van to look and walked down the stairs. He stood there and opened his tool box and in less than five minutes stated, "Of course your heater has problems! It's never been properly set up to convert the system from propane to natural gas."

I looked at him and shook my head. "But it passed inspection for the last ten years!"

We had a big mess on our hands that I had to fix. The gas company was at fault for inspecting the heater and passing it every year for over a decade. We later learned Sirius was legally at fault because Massachusetts recently implemented a law requiring a carbon monoxide detector within ten feet of every bedroom door. We thought the law only applied to the Community Center. During the next few weeks, we invested over $1,000 for the work crew to install detectors on all our buildings.

We did all we could to accommodate both the women who lived in the house. We paid for treatments to mitigate their health damage and gave them free rent and asked them to sign a release form agreeing they would not sue us. One of the women, though upset and worried that her health was compromised, agreed.

Christie flew into a rage. She called me three times a day, yelling and cursing into my answering machine, telling me she would have me arrested because I ruined her life and the health of her and her daughter. She called back to apologize and take back her words, only to call again a few hours later yelling, screaming and crying. I almost unplugged my phone to stop her diatribes.

I told Linda, "This woman is nuts! I am doing everything I can to care for her, but she keeps berating me. And she has a strong case against us, which she could probably win. If she wants to pursue this, we're in big trouble. She can ruin this place and take us for every penny. We might have to sell the land and give up the community, and that will be the end of us!" I couldn't sleep at night and started taking long walks so I didn't have to hear the phone ringing.

I knew we faced a difficult road ahead, so we started recording every bit of information, including reports from town inspectors, emails, phone calls and notes from our meetings to compile concrete data. Everyone, always looking to me to fix and manage these kinds of problems, wanted answers. They pestered me daily with questions and concerns. I went to meetings and at times sat in the chair looking at the floor with no words, only the sense that this process would be long and messy, and we had no way to protect ourselves. As the person in charge, in a role of leadership, even if you also don't have a clue, it's still your problem. Sometimes I wished all of this wasn't happening and I could just make it go away.

The situation dragged on for many months without resolve as we paid for health treatments and lost income from the property. Everyone tiptoed because we knew she held the power and the situation was delicate and precarious.

Christie became angry and manipulative. One day she would act sweet and apologize and ask for help, and the next day she would yell at us and tell me I was an awful person. We found out later she had a similar pattern in past housing situations. We packed up all her boxes, cleaned her house, drove her to appointments and helped her find another place to live. We had other renters waiting to move in and rented a U-Haul for one of the community members to drive it to New York to the new place.

Even after she left, I feared retaliation and imagined we had not seen the end of it because she never signed a release form. If she or the gas company sued us and won, we knew we would not have a lot of cash flow to defend ourselves by paying a lawyer and paying out whatever settlement was required. Our only option, if the amount was very large, was to close Sirius and sell off our assets in order to pay whatever demand was made of us.

The shadow of the unresolved conflict hung over our heads. Sure enough, about a year after she left, we received a letter from the gas company informing us we were being sued. We learned later she sued the gas company and they wanted compensation from us in response. The mandate demanded every receipt, documented transaction and decision about our organization for the last 20 years.

I read it over three times and thought, *Oh God. You've got to be kidding me. Are they even allowed to ask for all this? This is absolutely asinine! I don't think we even have half of the documents they are asking for.* We sat on the couches at lunch and imagined every scenario possible, all resulting in a complete loss of everything we worked so hard to build for decades.

I knew whatever lawyer we chose, we could get dragged through the mud for years. As much as I wished to, we couldn't just burn the letter and ignore it.

We brought the situation to the community meeting and once again I was at a loss for how to proceed. One of the young men living here at the time suggested we put together a video about our situation and start a crowdfunding campaign. His friend came and voluntarily interviewed members of the community. Without disclosing all the details, we explained the situation we found ourselves in and asked for support while acknowledging the value and the history of our work here on the land.

The video went to a final edit, but never reached the public. Many people were angry and afraid that we didn't understand the power of corporations and what we were up against. They refused to release the video for fear it would be used against us later. The video's creators were upset and felt powerless after wanting to make a contribution that would really help the situation.

For many months, we waited to hear what would become of all this mess. We worked with our bookkeeper and dug through old files, looking for documents to appease the courts. We cancelled all our accounts with the gas company and had all their tanks removed from the property as we did not want them to gain another penny from our organization.

We researched laws about nonprofits and learned that unless the suing party can prove "gross negligence" a nonprofit cannot be sued for more than $20,000, even that amount being more than what we had. Eventually the case was settled out of court. We had to pay all our lawyer fees and a settlement as we learned hard, expensive lessons from all of this.

Lessons Learned

When situations get messy and people get into conflict, no matter how many alternative systems we have put into place, in the end we are still beholden to the laws of the towns, states and governments in which we live. We had to meet the building codes, zoning laws and health code, and we learned the hard way that it also applies to interpersonal dynamics. We learned how much we must stay updated and informed on the nuance and details of state and federal laws as they are constantly changing.

The right lawyer is also essential for understanding tricky and complicated laws. We hired the lawyer who beat us in the previous case to defend us. And he showed up clever and good at winning.

We created more policies and procedures to protect against future incidents when people first arrived. When you first enter into agreements and spell out all the details clearly in writing, people know what is expected of them. You can more easily hold them accountable later when they get angry or disagree.

People are not renters, but come here to be in the program. There are very strict laws in the state about the rights of tenants and what is legally allowed and not allowed when conflict arises. We removed all language that put us in the position of being landlords. Every person that lives on the land is now subject to a background check. When applying in a written statement, they must sign that if conflict arises they must be willing to address it with others, using the systems we put in place.

I try to see the good in all people, but I learned not to ignore my intuition and that it's a powerful tool for discernment. Even if you are the lone voice of dissent, we must tune in and pay attention to our inner signal when something feels off. Often in life we try to do our best and be clear and accurate, but hindsight is a powerful tool and we are not able to guard against every possible incident and scenario. But when chaos ensues, we can learn from the damage, collect ourselves and gain insight for further spiritual growth.

Conflict

LEARNING HOW TO DANCE WITH EACH OTHER

14

Friction: A Recipe for Growth

Because I was so bothered by the social isolation in our country and the culture of the isolated box, with a desire to break it down, I felt motivated to start living in community. In the mainstream, when people find themselves in conflict and can't deal with the feelings that arise, they often walk away and say, "I'm never going to talk to you again," which society finds acceptable. Each person mows their own lawn with their own lawn mower, watching television, isolating from their neighbors, basically living a menial existence.

It's easier to stay in your own little world where you don't have to deal with other people. Community and close proximity forces you to develop those spiritual qualities if you want to live in relation to others. It offers opportunity for change within yourself faster than in society at large.

We are meant to be in proximity with others to share our life journey, our lessons and to understand what others are going through. In community others hold up a mirror for us, and we learn to look at ourselves. If we don't look inside ourselves, a constant state of conflict emerges. We have to choose another way and face the uncomfortable, abrasive parts of ourselves and find a place in our soul that embraces the messiness. We practice love, compassion and understanding as we work our spiritual muscle to hold the shadows without going ballistic and getting all bent out of shape.

When we join with others, the box disappears and we must deal with other people's drama, shadows and wounds. They all have their own unintegrated hurt patterns and triggers which create a much more challenging dynamic, yet it pushes our edges and forces us toward spiritual growth. We gain more tolerance as we tap into our own deep level of unconditional love, compassion, acceptance and forgiveness. We are forced to break down barriers and open to new thinking, which expands us spiritually. When we are committed to growth and to working through conflict, spiritual development increases rapidly.

Community and socialization offers great value to the evolution of consciousness. Some people come here unready for the stretch. They haven't reached the consciousness level to shift as they need to go a little slower.

Though community living does require more effort, once in community, I felt more healthy and vital. Living at Findhorn Community, I gained a foundation of spiritual practice and an understanding of how to lead a spiritual life. Findhorn integrates an international population with people from all over the world, which brings together many perspectives, and I learned what worked and what didn't. I saw the pitfalls, glamour and sidetrack illusions that people face.

Doing this work for many years has accelerated my spiritual growth by many lifetimes. By living in community so long, I always stretch myself. I broke through the years of cultural programming that surrounded me about how to act and feel. The war is waged within us and we need a warrior on the inside in order to break free of our societal limitations. The liberation can take many lifetimes but eventually it breaks old encrusted patterns. Culturally we are taught to act and be a certain way, and when we realize the status quo doesn't entirely work, we must find a whole new vocabulary and perspective to face the situations of life.

Speed and Consciousness

In working with group dynamics, conflict has power. While conflicts and tension can slow down the decision making process, they also provide impetus for growth and relationship through the friction.

Friction and tension change consciousness, which is an important reason we are here on earth. If we fixate solely on material development such as projects being completed, then tension and friction look like limitations. Instead if we see friction and tension as stimuli for change and growth, we can welcome them as tools to accomplish our goals. In this process, balance is key, because the process may take longer. We must not get so bogged down with each other in the group process, but we also must not fixate on physical growth and erect structures too hastily. With sloppy work, consciousness suffers and what we create lacks the same impact. The deep connectedness, love, compassion and goodwill among participants would be lacking.

Either the physical growth or the spiritual growth can teeter off balance. We can become so process oriented that the project never happens so we must remember that accomplishing our goals is important; we must move forward in physicality in order to expand consciousness and educate people.

Yet the friction process is needed in order to open up to the greater whole energy. We must allow for this relationship to exist to help us learn. The balancing act continues and we must keep the two parts in harmony. When friction rubs, consciousness expands. We often want to just get on with it, but this can only happen if consciousness expands as well. Both must occur: a dynamic tension and friction. The balance is not always easy to achieve or find. The interpersonal work, while temporarily slowing the process, helps bring the physical manifestation into fullness.

Once we start building on the physical level, consciousness expands as participants learn new skills and see their ideas realized. When that balance is reached, the end result of the project is more stable, more integrated into the landscape and lasts longer.

When I lived at the Findhorn Community, the community expanded rapidly on the physical plane. They acquired new properties, built houses and added new members. It was exciting and stimulating, but in my perception, it got out of hand. The layout was not thought through well and the attention to consciousness to do it well was lacking. The energetic field lacked balance, and correcting the field required a great deal of energy and time.

The fast pace of development created a lot of difficulties and challenges on the emotional, interpersonal level and in the backlash, the growth in consciousness did occur though it was slow and involved. It brought us back in line because we were capable of calling the process back into balance as we understood our core values. When we lost sight of them, we could return to them as a grounded starting point and hold the huge expansion on the physical plane. We tapped into the consciousness that was already present from all our past group work.

We dance on a razor's edge, trying to maintain our balance. Our society values and promotes unfettered growth. The economic system is based on this syndrome, which creates problems for the employees who constantly attempt to maximize production, causing internal stress and harming the environment as we cut down more trees and mine the earth. All growth is not inherently bad, but when it compromises interconnection and ignores the idea that all life is sacred, we have a problem.

With any endeavor we undertake, we must use conscious awareness. We must seek balance between growth and proceeding in a conscious manner. If our focus is only on expansion and physical growth, we lose this balance.

For many years, Sirius lacked physical resources such as secure housing, food, money, tools and lumber. Because of the urgency to meet our basic needs, we took rapid actions steps toward security. In recent years, with more abundance, new challenges emerged. We had to discuss how to use our resources well and in a creative manner, which expands our consciousness. With resources available, people say, "Let's just go ahead and take on this project!" While this mindset is useful, we must not act so hastily that we don't think it through. Every action has ramifications, so processing first is necessary. On the other hand we can overprocess, so again we must balance between the two.

Sirius comes up against the tension between processing and charging ahead regularly in our decision process. In some of the community meetings, so much processing occurs that we lack time to do the projects. Using consensus compared to a hierarchical leadership model is much slower. In a hierarchy, projects move rapidly, but the majority of participants may not like or support the work. Even though the processing is slow, the end result is more effective.

With consensus, the process moves more slowly. However, once the project does move, everyone is on board. No one complains, "I didn't vote for that, so I'm not supporting it!" Instead the sentiment is,

"We all agreed to the best course of action. While I may not completely believe with 100% certainty that the decision is in the right direction, I didn't vote against it, so I feel the obligation within me to support it." We break free from the culture of winners and losers and everyone feels more interested and invested in the work at hand. The full support exists much more than in a voting system. When everyone is on board, the project flows in sometimes unpredictable, amazing ways. We might receive help, time or money from sources we didn't imagine.

The group needs enough people to balance between, "Let's just get on with it!" and "Well, we need to talk about it." There are process oriented people, and there are action oriented people. A tension exists between those different personalities and the resulting process can be beneficial. While sometimes challenging, the friction brings out creativity and keeps the balance.

Trusting Our Intuition

Sometimes the consensus process doesn't work smoothly. There are individuals who don't agree with decisions being made, but they see the mood and sentiment of the group. They notice that most people are in favor of a project and may be too shy or feel unsupported to voice a dissident opinion, so they say nothing.

Sometimes a poor decision is made because someone was too afraid to speak their dissent, ignoring their inner feelings. With any group process or any decision we try to make in our lives, paying attention to our inner intuition is always important.

Because we fear being wrong, we often remain silent. In group process, when you sense your intuition, it's important to share it and say, "I think there's something here that we need to look at." It takes a lot of courage to expose yourself. You must face the whole group and internally protect yourself from their reactions.

With certain decisions, I had visions or an intuition that the outcome would be a problem and didn't do anything or act on that intuition and I regretted it. At times, we had intensely excited people and their enthusiasm overtook the practical concern. Other people with concerns, including me, ignored our hesitations about the practicality of the proposal. In retrospect, we all cried, "Why didn't I speak up about that? I could see that coming!" Silence out of fear doesn't always benefit the process. Inside of us, we also each contain tension. We must check in with ourselves and ask, *Am I listening to my inner intuition? Am I ignoring my inner resistance because of group pressure?*

When the decisions turn out negatively, the process offers reflection. Even if you are wrong and act on your intuition, you can learn. We can recognize, "That didn't work well." We can examine the motivation that informed our decision and we figure out what took us in a certain direction. This time for personal reflection from individuals and the group is useful.

The action offers a lesson and we gain insight and wisdom. If you don't act on the stirrings in the depths of your soul, you won't examine whether it is coming from your ego or from higher guidance. We fear this process and don't often ask "Was I right?" or "Was I wrong?" We don't want to be wrong because in this culture we are often shamed for being wrong. But without examination, you never receive reflection.

Sometimes in a group, the opposite happens. The dissenter loudly and clearly states their position. Theirs is a lone voice standing in the way to reach consensus and the group gets frustrated. With more discussion and thought, this individual can change the outcome of the decision. It's a process, where one person's perception may be accurate or it may be false. When either of these dynamics arise, it creates tension and a powerful opportunity for learning and growth. This dynamic helps define the creative group process.

Even a lot of people on the planet who are not spiritually oriented often have a relationship with their intuition. A high-powered businessman who knew I was into spiritual reality once said, "I'm not very spiritual and oftentimes I get these moments where I can't solve a problem. It goes around and around. I think about it until my mind is ready to explode. And then I completely release it. I don't think about it anymore. When I do this, the answer just pops into my mind. It arrives from some other place! I don't understand it."

I said to him, "Your higher self is giving you information. If you quieted your mind from the very beginning, you would not suffer so much." He was open to my feedback even though he was a high-powered businessman.

He had realized the limitations of the thought process and that he wasn't going to get to a resolution with the rational mind. He let go completely and then could come back with solutions and answers to dilemmas.

In group dynamics, we can do the same using the tools of the higher mind to lead us to better outcomes. If we can monitor ourselves, even if our inner perceptions aren't always correct, we stimulate conscious evolution, greater reflection and awareness emerges. We must plumb the depths of our own soul to make decisions and our actions then reflect what is deeply within us. The dynamic tension becomes a learning opportunity. If we remain silent when we think something is incorrect, and we don't like the result, we receive feedback.

Self-actualization of participating individuals makes a very powerful and effective group. We cannot only be followers, we must pay attention to our inner landscape and trust our insights that will benefit the whole group. As we align to our true inner core, our mistakes become learning opportunities and they shape us as we grow into better alignment with ourselves.

Working with a conscious group using inner guidance is a new paradigm, and few role models exist. We draw our own roadmap with a new paradigm that honors the depth of spiritual wisdom within all of us.

Because it is so difficult, people often give up in frustration. But this cutting edge of consciousness forges a new way of being in the world. Though we don't decide perfectly every time, we still learn and grow. When situations get messy we must remember with compassion for ourselves, *We are dealing with uncommon challenges.* Despite the rarity of the consensus process, it *is* the future and needs further development. We must shift out of the old paradigm that we are enmeshed in that no longer serves.

The new model honors the collective consciousness and that we all hold a different piece of the truth. We might all be looking at a piece of money like a quarter. You see the edge that is bumpy and thin, I see the back, while someone else sees the front. We each have a different, equally valid perspective, and all are true. We each bring a different lens linked to our previous experience and our personalities. Only together can we see the whole to arrive at the best outcome.

The idea of working with collective consciousness is very powerful and expansive. Despite all the frustration with the process, the final result holds more power than one individual making decisions.

The process requires effort and self-reflection as we step out of our own ego. We must set our own wants and agendas aside and see what is best for the group. We gaze inward from a deep spiritual soul perspective and recognize the highest good for all. Our ego fights against this, which stimulates spiritual growth and awareness of our own shadows and limitations.

Ultimately our inner compass is our most powerful tool, if we work together and understand our own inner process. We mold our compass with the highest good and the clearest direction in mind.

Conflict and Abuse

Living in Community speeds up our evolution and creates rapid growth. Sometimes conflict brings out the worst in people and leads to ego trips full of physiological and emotional abuse. As a group, we learned new practices to deflect and handle situations when they arise.

I don't like conflict, yet it's a necessary tool. We ask, *What is peace? What is lack of conflict?* If the conflict is withheld for the sake of domination, we fail. Conflict is not the only way to resolve spiritual dilemmas, but you can either work *with* conflict or *for* conflict. Oftentimes people thrive on conflict, as it feeds their emotional state. When you are addicted to conflict, you work *for* the conflict itself, not the end result, and when conflict vanishes, you don't know how to behave, feeling empty and unsettled, as if something is wrong. But we can change that pattern.

Because people don't like conflict, this is a radical concept. I don't condone extreme conflict, such as genocide or oppression, but sometimes friction is a necessary component of growth. If you strive for peace only for the sake of peace, it's not really peace, it's avoidance, which only works for so long. I feel pain when people talk about peace on that level. Peace at the sacrifice of right relationship is *violence*.

During our years, we realized we needed to accept unconscious people who are just learning. We are each personally responsible for who we are, including how we act and how we feel about ourselves and others. Not just some parts, but every reaction, thought and feeling I have is mine to choose. To accept that I'm responsible for my life is challenging. For many people just learning about their own power is too much, so we work slowly. It's not about judging people as bad, which isn't true; it's about recognizing the evolutionary process with acceptance.

When people are so attached to their ego and ignorant behavior, with no openness or willingness to change, they prevent us from intervening and setting up clear boundaries. We don't allow people with such attitudes to stay here when they create unresolvable conflict in the community. But when they are willing to change, we can accept outrageous behavior and help them work on their own personal transformation.

When we join a community and participate in group process, many emotions and feelings are stirred up and revealed. We see and call forth the parts of ourselves that block us from the freedom of taking responsibility for ourselves. We can't hide from our own self-imposed limits and when we're no longer trapped by our own critical voice or the voices of others, we gain freedom from our own limiting stories about ourselves. We reach freedom and levity, and find ourselves in a space of love. The judgment, criticism and even self-righteousness hold less power over us.

When somebody acts abusive toward us, our judgmental, self-righteous attitude can emerge. With our own inner work, we can respond with compassion. We might recognize that person endured abuse as a child, or that their negativity toward us simply reveals patterns and habits they are working on and trying to break. In my experience, when someone exhibits abusive behavior patterns, the patterns are triggered by very traumatic events in the person's past. It is not one's true nature and if we don't react or judge the patterns, or hold the person in deep criticism, we give them a gift. As a witness, when we embrace the person, the individual gains the freedom to look at their own wounds and they are vulnerable and open. If we bring judgment instead, they close down and hide themselves.

This is an important role of community; we help accelerate each other's growth by bearing witness. While we don't condone abusive behavior, we see beyond the abhorrent acts and know this is just one part of who they are, not their whole personality. When I can focus on their whole self, I help them grow, I help them break old patterns and become a more loving, free person. If I see abusive behavior it is okay to say, "That's not right!" Yet we can do it without judgment, in the frame of love. Sometimes with abusive behavior, pure acceptance is appropriate, but to discern and intuit between the need for embracing someone or asserting boundaries is important. Some of us need a kick in the ass at times. Other times we need total acceptance. I've seen both methods have the power to change a person's behavior.

Once someone acted verbally abusive and attacked me in a negative way. I could tell they were on a rant, agitated, and nobody was sure what to do. One person in the room stood up and hugged them. It completely changed the energy and the aggressor broke down crying. The act of compassion completely changed their behavior pattern. And again in the group when the same issue came back again, they were less intense and changed more quickly.

In another instance, I've witnessed abusive behavior change. One person stood up and said, "Stop, you cannot do that anymore." The pattern completely changed too when the attacker had enough insight to look inward and say, "Oh, yeah, I *am* doing that. I will stop." One method is a kick in the ass and the other is total acceptance. I've seen both methods impact people when done with love and without judgment. Clear boundaries are set, but you don't make the other person bad or evil. You state what is unacceptable and not allowed and name that their behavior is not appropriate. The emotion of anger or criticism is withheld. The message is stronger and penetrates deeply.

But to me the world is imperfect, and through our growth process, we bring greater light, perfection, balance and harmony into the world, and the planet becomes a sacred planet. We are planet polishers, giving love and compassion as we allow the beauty to shine forth. Conflict is the polishing wax and without the wax, it is harder to shine.

Direct Experience as Daily Spiritual Practice

These lessons are often hard to remember. I don't always practice them because often it feels good to hold onto judgments and criticisms and get pissed off at people. I have to accept that I can still do this, but I embrace the experience, recognize it and work on it. I practice more love, compassion and understanding in the future. No one remembers to be compassionate *all* the time.

But we are kind to ourselves with our own learning process. We stretch and push ourselves when we need to, but with gentleness. Community helps us with all of this, as we practice it daily in our work. Deep open communication opens up doorways to more authentically know each other. You see the struggles and heartbreak of others and you fill with more love and compassion. Living the shift holds more power than reading it in a book. You can learn from a book, but the poignancy of the lessons are much greater when it comes through personal connection and direct experience. Practicing and seeing with other individuals puts the book learning into practice in a deeper way.

I've met people who studied esoteric and spiritual teachings for thirty years. Some had very little experience putting it into practiced interactions with others. Books have their place but when you don't work with their lessons in your daily life, they become less useful to you.

If you read how to build a house in a carpentry book, you have the theory, but when you get to the site and start digging and actually designing, you gain new information from the details and challenges that cannot be described on the pages of any book. The same is true when practicing spiritual teachings. Community is important as it grounds our knowledge of gardening, building, group process and sustainability in the practical everyday experience of being human.

When applied, more knowledge accumulates in your brain and you learn more by direct connection than all the books read over many years. I've seen people who are psychological disasters who studied this knowledge but never applied it. They held judgment and criticism and never integrated the teachings that stayed all in their head, rather than exploring the understanding on a practical level.

Thich Nhat Hanh, a famous monk, now 91 years old, runs a community called Plum Village in France. He said, "You don't need to live in a perfect community; an imperfect one will do just fine." He believed imperfection is necessary to an evolving state of consciousness, providing the stimulus for growth and change.

Sirius is not a perfect example in any of our work. We constantly change and evolve, which helps us grow. We always learn new techniques on the physical and interpersonal levels. It is an evolving, growing entity and an experiment in every category. We not only examine where our food and energy come from, but how to create relationships, practice conflict resolution, and run governance. We weigh our choices and use sustainability and consciousness as our measuring stick. We act in a practical manner, so we build on our book knowledge and attain greater understanding.

The Stone Circle

BIRTHING SACRED SPACE

15

A Vision

I heard of a peculiar man who taught the ways of the ancient druids, constructing magical stone circles around the world. A friend of mine knew the man well and invited me to his talk. I rarely attend talks, and this one lay on the other side of a long drive across wintry New England's icy roads…but a strong feeling inside prompted me to attend.

When we arrived I wanted to meet the man before his talk. I approached him and immediately noticed his strong character. He towered over me with broad thick shoulders and a protruding belly. A scruffy beard stretched across his face as wild, unkempt hair dyed bright orange danced atop his head. His nails painted green, I saw a large earring dangling from one ear.

I introduced myself and reached out my hand.

"Ivan MacBeth," he answered.

I was taken aback by him at first, unimpressed. I judged he outcast himself on the fringes of society. But when he spoke about building these stone structures all over the world, his power of manifestation blew my mind.

I reconvened with him after the talk and asked, "Is there any way you would help us build one of these stone circles at Sirius?"

He replied, "Yes, perhaps…" He told me he had read about Sirius and was interested in looking at our site and talking more.

I went to see one of the stone circles he built in Burlington, nestled on the edge of Lake Champlain. It sits in a small park along the bike path, overlooking the water. We arrived at sunset and gazed at the massive stones outlined against the orange sky, standing tall and erect. Their powerful, beautiful presence struck me, and although it seemed like a rather daunting task, I decided to think more seriously about building such a circle at Sirius, wondering, *Where might we find these giant stones, and how could we possibly move them?*

I asked the community about the idea of building this stone circle. Unsurprisingly, the people blasted me with strong opposition, exclaiming, "You want to do *what?* With all the things we need to do here, you want to build this gigantic circle out of stones? *Have you lost your mind?*"

I wasn't offended. I knew people would reject the idea mostly because the path to achieve this feat seemed totally overwhelming, even impossible. Yet I stayed unattached; I didn't push it, I simply brought it back up regularly and we continued to discuss the idea as a community. Slowly people started to change their opinion, and curiosity grew as I presented information about stone circles around the world, dazzling the people with fantastic pictures.

Over time some of the people with the most opposition began to speak up in support of the project. I was surprised. It seemed like it would never be accepted. After many months, excitement grew and everyone jumped on board. Finally, with enthusiasm reaching an all-time high, we reached consensus to explore the possibilities. Short of a full go ahead, the severe opposition disintegrated, as we explored how much the project might cost and other logistics.

I called up Ivan and told him, "The community's warming up to the idea of building the Stone Circle. Can you come see the land and share with the community how you build these circles?"

He agreed and came to walk the land. We wanted a relatively flat location, within short walking distance of the Community Center, but in its own energy field. We walked all over the 90-acre property, and as we climbed to the top of the hill, right before the peak slopes down into the sacred swamp, we both felt an energetic hit. We sensed we had found the right spot.

Overgrown with trees, the dense forest prompted an important debate. In this location, several large trees would stand inside the circle. Ivan had never before erected a circle among the trees, but I asserted my unwillingness to cut any down. Hesitant at first, he gradually warmed up as we talked about it and came to like the idea. He imagined the trees could enhance the spiritual presence of the stones themselves.

I brought the vision back to the community again, describing Ivan's visits and how the logistics would work. "We need to find the stones, but I'll raise the money and find people to help. Ivan has agreed to come teach us how to move the stones and build the circle." I cleverly added, "It won't cost a penny because we will conduct workshops on how to build stone circles, which will provide the money to pay him."

Because we presented a crystal-clear plan that demanded no financial investment from the community, we earned a consensus from the people to start the project. We still needed agreement on the location, so I led the whole community to the top of the hill and described the reasons why we selected that site. We meditated as a group, and everyone felt resonant that we had found the right place.

The site overlooks the swamp, enhancing the sacred space already present. With its rare placement just below the peak, the mossy swamp collects water in vernal pools. Oddly shaped roots twist around tunnels and cavernous fairy houses. Blueberries and hemlocks cover soft mounds, creating a shady grove along one edge.

The most sacred place on the land, the swamp attracts highly sensitive people, who, without us sharing any information, tell us they also feel the powerful energy. They say, "I'll walk around the land and see what I feel." Countless people have come back and told us about the sacred energy they felt while walking by the swamp.

We meditated and attuned with the trees, letting the land know which of the smaller trees we would remove. Three weeks later we slowly and very carefully cleared the land. We took out the small saplings over three Saturday workdays. Rather than depreciating the land, we felt an enhancement of the energy. We worked with care and love in attunement, which brought positive energy into the site.

One day I received clear guidance that I should design a path that begins at the Stone Circle site, wraps around the swamp and loops back to the Stone Circle. Before this, few people knew the way to the swamp and I felt hesitant to open the pathway to direct people to such a sacred energy, for fear that some might abuse it. But I received the clear message to open it up and allow more people to experience it. I had experienced many powerful spiritual moments at the swamp, and I hoped others would appreciate the presence in a similar manner. The path creates an energetic loop between the Stone Circle and the wetlands of the swamp area.

During the next five years, Ivan and I perused and purchased stones. We gathered them from a few different locations, but they all came from within an hour's drive of the land. We drove to the quarry in Goshen and walked all over the land to find the right selections. The owners agreed to use their heavy machinery to load our trailer.

The second quarry featured lower prices and the place opened much more recently. At one point in our search, as we climbed over the big boulders, I found a hidden stone in the quarry, already broken apart from its neighbors. Composed of pure granite in fascinating angles, the stone proclaimed its uniqueness from all the rest. Even the owners had not seen it. Extracting it took great effort because it lay buried by other stones.

At both locations, we found a couple stones that we especially liked, and we talked to the owners and agreed to buy them. Most were flat and thin, which made them easier to move and enabled us to acquire tremendously large stones.

Many of the stones are composed of schist from a 400 million-year-old sea bottom, which gives them their flatness. The stones from Goshen rose up with the shifting of the tectonic plates. When you look at the side of the stone broken out of its fossilized bed, you see the layers of sediment, compressed under immense pressure and heat over time. Most of the stones are excavated with dynamite. They blast stones out from the seabed and drill and chisel them into small pieces.

Many are adorned with shiny garnet crystals embedded in their surface. Garnet is revered as a sacred mineral element with healing properties. At night the garnets sparkle in the moonlight across smooth curves and multicolored facets.

Inspired by the idea as we drew up plans, several people donated money to purchase the stones, which cost $200 to $300 apiece. Whenever we needed to find a stone or we needed help, support would magically appear.

I had trepidation about hauling the big stones to the site. A small, dirt tractor path meanders around the trees. We couldn't drive a big truck or trailer up the hill, so we decided to haul the stones from the quarry in a big trailer and set them at the bottom of the hill. Then Ivan would teach us the way to move the stones up the hill.

Layout

Henry MacLean, my architect friend who helped design the Community Center, has acquired vast knowledge about sacred geometry and the earth's energetic meridian lines. He visited many of the ancient stone structures in Britain, studying the patterns in the landscape, and he helped us apply those patterns here.

We created an overlay of different alignments, including the four directions, the paths, the times of solstice and the equinoxes, using a dowsing rod to lay out the geometric alignments.

We based our proportions on the megalithic yard. All the stone circles in the world were laid out by the same proportion called the megalithic yard, or in multiples of that dimension, regardless of when they were erected. We wanted to follow the same pattern.

The stones aren't placed randomly in the circle, and they're not spaced evenly either. We decided to align them to celestial or planetary landmarks as part of the layout in order to generate energy and power. As we placed them, we thought about the gaps between the existing stones. We considered what lay in that direction and if it had spiritual significance to us. With GPS assistance, we lined up points easily. The alignment over a long distance changes with the curvature of the earth. Ivan calculated precise alignments using computer programs, unlike the ancients, who, even without computers, aligned the ancient stone circles perfectly.

We brought each new stone up the hill and dropped it in the circle with a location in mind. Then we gathered together to tune in and ask, "Where does this particular stone belong?" Several people received similar impressions about its location, which guided us to put the stone in its right place. We could tell when it didn't feel right, so we would move the stone to a different spot, but when it came into alignment, "Yes!" came through strongly.

I recognized the importance of this intuitive process in building the circle in its most clearly aligned power and presence. We did not know exactly why each stone needed to be in its particular place, but we felt a need to pay attention. Perhaps the stone has an energetic quality, which aligns to our goals in the project.

Each alignment holds its own significance to us as a community. We aligned them to the four directions and to the rising point of the star Sirius on the horizon, and the two Entrance Stones line up to the Community Center. One points to New York City for unity, another to the nearest mountain, Mt. Monadnock. Two stones mark the entrance, while one channels energy with the headwaters of the Amazon and another with the Hopi reservation. We directed one stone to Stonehenge near our roots at Findhorn, and one to Hiroshima for healing and finally completed the circle with the center stone.

North Stone: *Spiritual Power*

I advertised our vision to the local community of Hearthstone Village, and the idea of building a stone circle in the neighborhood excited people. They came out to learn and witness this great feat of engineering. Each time we needed to move a stone, people showed up from Sirius and all over Hearthstone Village and the local community. To move the stones requires quite a few people and the volunteer help was always an essential blessing.

When you raise up the huge monoliths using the proper method, it takes less people and energy than you would imagine. We used the laws of physics, balance, leverage and fulcrums. Ivan knew all the tricks and demonstrated them. We practiced and even when he wasn't here, managed to roll the first stone up the hill. We put the rock on a sled built with eight-by-eight inch wooden beams.

We put the sled on round wooden rollers, attached a rope to one end and pulled it with the tractor. We added pulleys for mechanical advantage. One person was in charge of grabbing rollers as they popped out the back and realigning them in the front as the sled moved forward. The rock moved very slowly but progressed one foot at a time.

We finally rolled the first stone up the hill and then Ivan came to start the workshop. While placing and moving the stones, Ivan asked everyone in the circle to touch the stones. We offered a meditation prayer and asked for the support of the stones. The silence and the power came out in our work.

He told us, "Stones will move for you, and you can ask for their help. They like to move extremely slowly and you can't rush this. Only move them very carefully and patiently."

If you're moving a stone that weighs about four tons, which was our biggest one, you *do* have to work carefully. When you raise them about five feet off the ground, safety becomes a serious concern and one person's job on site was always to look out for safety.

We always meditated and attuned before we started work and talked about the importance of moving slowly, at a careful and safe pace. When tension pulled at us and conflicting opinions flew around, Ivan would say, "Let's take a break. Let's have a little think." This helped us remember to breathe into the process.

We determined the center of the circle and laid it all out before the first stone went in. We considered the order of the placement and began with the north stone. North significantly represents guidance and alignment. It is used for navigation, and in spiritual traditions it holds the pure light of Spirit flowing in from the north. We felt this energy. As the project unfolded, we felt the presence of the guiding light and flowing energy in relation to significant events.

The energy of the south represents warmth and healing to balance out the north. We knew the north had to be first and south second. We dug the hole for the first stone using only shovels, pickaxes and strong arms. We used no machines, just simple tools and the power of the people.

This area of New England, particularly in the hill towns, is filled with huge boulders and ledge from the glaciers, and we hit a gigantic immovable boulder in the first hole. We had no way to continue. Our shovels helplessly clanged off the buried boulder, which lay precisely where we wanted to place the first stone.

We debated our dilemma. We had already laid out the whole plan. I scratched my head and mused, "Well, I guess we'll just have to move the circle over."

Ivan was concerned.

I said, "Can't we just shift the whole circle?"

From his stone circle building experience, Ivan told us stone circles could slightly alter the ley lines themselves, including different underground energetic fields. We meditated and concluded the shift would be okay.

The chosen site is a small plateau. One area in the middle is mostly flat, while all the sides slope up or down. We poked around and found a spot with less rocks three feet away. We moved the design three feet and the circle shifted slightly. Astonishingly, the circle moved from a slight hill to a much better location on flatter ground. Our shovels sank into the earth with little resistance.

We broke apart the soil with the pickaxe, pulling shovelful after shovelful of soil from the ground. Sweat poured off of us as we dug deeper and deeper. After several days of digging, our muscles sore from the pickaxe, the hole was ready.

On the morning that we would place the first stone, a big turkey came careening out of the forest and flew into one of the big windows at the Community Center. It fell to the ground, dead at our feet! We took the dead bird and buried it at the base of the stone as we felt a certain kind of magic already taking place right from the preparation of the first stone.

We raised up each end with long wooden poles and blocks of wood, one foot at a time, and slowly elevated the stone up in place to drop into its hole, with one end pointing to the sky. While we worked away, a Buddhist monk came to the site. He hung prayer flags in among the trees near the work site. He sat on the pine needles in his robes and chanted and meditated for hours while the first stone went up.

Another man showed up with Herkimer diamond crystals, and asked to put them at the base of the stone while a third man appeared carrying Scottish bagpipes. He played the pipes while we prepared to place the stone and it turned into this beautiful, magical celebration of placing the stone.

On one side a Buddhist monk is chanting and praying, on the other a guy is playing the bagpipes, all the while the rest of us are digging holes drenched in sweat. It turned into a sacred ritual. I felt the connection to Scotland, Britain and Wales, a place with over 3,000 stone circles, more than anywhere else in the world. In this beautiful ceremony, the north stone dropped perfectly into place. We worked hard to twist and align it with all the ropes and we pulled out the last block and let go of the last ropes and our stone sat upright!

Years later, the original dowsers would return. They said they noticed a shift and believed the change actually brought the whole energy field into greater alignment.

After the North Stone was placed, we stopped work for months. With one stone in, people started to come and meditate with the stone, as the magnetic energy already drew people in. Ivan taught us that when you place stones in a circle with a certain spiritual intention, you create a cosmic connection with prior divine presence in the earth.

A link manifests between the heavens and the earth, generating an energetic field.

South Stone: *Gaia*

One of our neighbors, Julie Rippich, approached us and said, "I heard you're building a stone circle. I have this big stone in my yard, would you like to have it?" I went over to her yard to look at it and was astounded to see how massive it was! I estimated it weighed about four tons. It was made of granite but looked very different from the Goshen stone.

I thought, *Oh my gosh, can we really move this thing? Is it even possible to load it onto the trailer?* We decided to try moving the stone even though Ivan wasn't there to help us. We used all the techniques we'd learned, and we finally got it off the ground with much patience and exertion. We had it raised up four feet in the air, and got the trailer ready. As we lowered the stone onto the wood frame, the entire structure collapsed, and the stone crashed back to the ground.

Luckily nobody was close enough to be crushed. But we had to start over. We said, "Well we'll just have to do it again and tie it better." With blocks, ramps, pry bars, levers, and long poles, we finally got it onto the trailer. Just to raise it up and load it on the trailer took us three days!

About to drive it over to Sirius, we noticed all the tires on the trailer were almost completely flat. We were stuck blocking the middle of the road with this stone on the trailer, and all the tires almost flat. What a scene!

The stone wasn't too heavy for the trailer; there just wasn't enough air in the tires. We had a compressor, but no electricity, no way to run it, so we ran to the shop and filled up the tank with air, carried it back to the truck, filled up one tire, and went back the shop to refill the tank. We hustled back and forth until we finally filled all the tires. Then we drove the stone back to Sirius and lowered it onto the wooden sled on short rollers. Getting it off the trailer was much easier! Here it rested for quite a while, moving only at rock speed.

Once we finally got back to it, it took two full days to move the stone halfway up the hill. We used our small Ford tractor, without four wheel drive. On the steepest part of the hill, the sled stopped. It wouldn't budge, even on the rollers. The rock was just too heavy. We were stuck with the stone tilted back on a big incline with the tractor refusing to pull it.

Oh my gosh, how are we going to move this stone? I wondered.

We added a block and tackle, a series of pulleys and ropes, to increase our mechanical advantage. The stone rested on top of the sled with skids on the bottom. The skids sat on top of rollers and the rollers sat on top of planks to keep from sinking into the soft ground. We attached the block and tackle to the sled and the other end to the tractor. We gained a three-to-one mechanical advantage and the sled moved! It traveled at a snail's pace, one quarter of the distance covered by the tractor to the end of the line. We reset the block and tackle each time, and slowly, slowly moved it up the hill with the mechanical advantage of the pulleys.

Winter came, and the sled slept barely more than halfway up the hill, covered in snow. When spring arrived, we worked on it again to complete its slow journey. We learned some important lessons about moving a four-ton stone. Finally the stone approached its permanent location.

To raise the South Stone, we hosted another workshop. Only about six or seven people paid to participate, which included lecture time and erecting the big stone. The group consisted of older, not very strong, white-haired women. Ivan looked at me and said, "How are we going to move this stone, we don't have enough people!"

I replied, "I don't know Ivan. I trust the process. Let's do the workshop and see what happens." I put the call out to the larger community to join the stone raising. Then we did the workshop and prepared the setup to place the stone.

Suddenly people started appearing out of nowhere. Some were just visiting Sirius who didn't even know about the Stone Circle, but, seeing our project, were excited to help. People from the neighborhood answered the call as well. By the time we were ready to move the big stone, 15 people had assembled.

We went ahead in absolute faith that we were going to move this stone and out came the people. It was similar to when we placed the North Stone; we called out and people showed up.

Once the people were assembled, we were reminded our stone was still just as enormous. We raised it up five feet above the ground, using fulcrums, levers, and a pivoting balance. We put two pieces of wood underneath the stone, near the center, to keep it from flopping over, and then as we raised one side of it, the weight of the other side helped lift it up. We rocked it back and forth and raised it up each time. And we got it five feet up off the ground, horizontally.

We positioned the stone and dug a hole, but I worried we might hit another big boulder as we did with the North Stone. Digging fourteen holes, it was likely we would hit some immovable ledge and not be able to continue. I was concerned that if we ran into more trouble, we could not move the coordinates a second time. But with patience and pry bars, we were able to clear the hole enough to continue.

We hovered the rock five feet over the hole. Ivan put a post under one end to maintain the balance. We pulled out one of the supports with one end on the ground and the other resting on one long single pole. We positioned it so that if you pulled the pole out, the rock would fall directly into the hole, all four tons of it.

The tension mounted as we placed this one pole and pulled out all the other supports except the two pivot points. We tied a rope to the pole and tried to pull the pole out so the stone would drop into the hole, but it wouldn't budge. We engaged in the most intense tug-of-war of our lives, pulling, yanking with every ounce of force in us. But the stone weighed so heavy on the pole that we couldn't pull it out.

Ivan declared, "We need to whack the pole with a sledgehammer and pull the pole out of the way as the rock falls. We looked at him in disbelief. But we accepted the task, and people gathered around again, picking up the rope. Everyone was chanting, Oming or meditating, sending energy for it all to go well as we prepared to give one more immense effort.

As I recall, I was elected to use the sledgehammer. I gripped the long handle and wound up as a dozen people pulled the rope taught with all their strength. Feeling the power of Spirit channeling through me, I swung the sledgehammer around and smacked the pole head-on, knocking it out of place. The rest of the crew flung the pole out of the hole with the ropes and the stone came thundering down into the hole, exactly where we wanted it.

But immediately it leaned over, and as it leaned, it twisted around.

We used the block and tackle and the tractor to raise the stone up to the vertical position, but it was facing the wrong direction. We wanted all the stones aligned with their faces toward the center of the circle, so we needed to rotate the four tons of weight, resting on its slightly rounded bottom. We lashed a huge 20-foot pole to the stone and with ten people twisting, exerting incredible effort, turned the stone so that it faced correctly into the circle.

We filled the hole with rocks, which hold the stone in place. Soil is too soft and unstable to secure such a massive, towering stone. Fist-size stones work best, which we used on the whole project. The filler rocks came from the land. We had amassed big piles all around our 90 acres from all our construction and digging and they revealed themselves to be an essential resource.

After many hours, we finally got the stone in its place. It was an adventure, but we felt the spiritual energy supporting us as a certain flow guided our work. Despite working incredibly hard and running into immense challenges, the energy flowed, and we never got completely stuck or discouraged. The process was divinely aligned and we were meant to succeed. I felt this during the entire process of building the Stone Circle. When I had doubts or concerns, new resources came and I felt playful as the flow of energy moved. It never felt insurmountably difficult or painful.

Building the entire Stone Circle would endure quite a long process of five years. We put some stones in place, and then we let it go because we were busy in the community. After we placed two stones, for over a year we did not work in it. Then the energy returned and we reminded ourselves, "What about the Stone Circle!" And we'd say, "Alright let's do another stone!"

East and West Stones: *Joy and Transformation*

We debated if east or west should come next. East represents the rising sun, the rotational movement of the earth, and how every day starts in the east and ends in the west. It stands for new beginnings, the awakening of the solar energy, while the west holds the qualities of sleep, quiet time and introspection. We listened and realized that ordering from east to west made the most sense spiritually. In reflection the choice was clear, we all felt the east was next.

So the east and west were the third and fourth stones placed in the circle, both erected in the same season. Once installed, much like the North and South Stone, an energetic link emerged between the two. When those four stones were in, magic blossomed in our circle. The conscious alignments created a new gateway for energy to flow in and out in the circle. Many people felt its significance.

Once the four directions were in, the whole dynamic of the circle changed. The four stones for each direction are associated with different elements. The Native Americans believe each direction embodies a type of energy and clearly define each direction to recognize the energy field present in each one. Worldwide, the four directions hold significance to traditional cultures. While my experience differs slightly, I feel an energetic field from each direction, which is hard to put into words. They each bring in powerful healing properties.

Some years we erected three or four stones. Some years we only put up one. The ease and interplay of energy was always present every time we returned to the project. When we were motivated for the next step, everyone wanted to do it and declared, "Oh, can I come help!" The excitement was contagious. Many women came and helped too. In the process of building itself, we embodied sacred ritual with inspiration and spiritual upliftment.

The enthusiasm amazed me because we faced such a daunting task. Overwhelming thoughts repeatedly flooded my brain, *Oh my god, we have to move all these stones! We have to search and search, just to roll them up the hill and raise them into the sky before digging for days and tediously dropping them down... It's such a monumental task to move these giant stones!*

Despite my fears, the project never burdened us. Overcome with excitement, we celebrated how much fun the whole experience was, which fired up our confidence. "We can do this! We can move these huge stones!" We didn't need a huge machine to dig the holes or lift the stones up. We achieved a beautiful rhythm and experience for all involved. We connected to an ancient ritualistic energy and we tapped into the energy of the past and the ancient stone circles of the world.

When I first heard Ivan speak about it, the idea to build one here came from a place of deep inspiration. I was not doing it just because I thought it was cool, I felt it on a spiritual, intuitional level, that I was receiving an impression from a higher level that this would be a good idea. This proved to be true every step of the way.

At the start, doubts and concerns trickled into my mind, but my guidance told me, "Do this, it will bring new energy to the community that will uplift and inspire people." The inspiration and guidance shone through and we persisted.

We created rituals and ceremonies on the site and my guidance proved to be true. People sit in the Stone Circle and meditate all the time. Other groups ask to use the circle for their ceremonies. A beautiful energy emerged during the process of building it that came to full fruition once it was complete.

The construction of the Stone Circle would be interrupted by the most physically devastating accident of my life. Faced with the choice between living through the pain or letting it all go, I felt the intense need to complete two projects before I went: finishing the Stone Circle and composing a book to share the lessons we learned in creating community here. I will explain what happened after telling of the Stone Circle.

Sirius Stone: *Perseverance*

We wanted to align one of the stones to the star Sirius in honor of our name and what the star represents. Sirius is actually a binary star system composed of two stars.

The Dogon tribe in Africa based their religion on the star Sirius. Digitaria, the orbiting white dwarf star, holds the spiritual power. It represents the feminine energy of creation. When Digitaria reaches the closest point of its 75-year elliptical orbit to the main star of Sirius, they glow more brightly and intensify their light emanations. Every 75 years, during this time of intensification in the stars' relationship, the tribe in Africa holds a three-day ritual and celebration. The last time it occurred was around the year 2000.

Many different spiritual teachings about Sirius and what it represents exist in the world. Other spiritual groups of the world, including the ancient Egyptians, recognize Sirius's significance. They believe the star Sirius holds an important spiritual presence.

If you view the star Sirius in a telescope, you see a blue-white light emanating from it, compared to other stars, which contain yellowish light. When I looked at it in a powerful telescope, I noticed this phenomenon.

The Star of Sirius rises in the same location every day. The time Sirius rises changes significantly, but it emerges every day at the same point on the horizon. I contacted a famous British astronomer and astrologer because I wanted to understand this concept. From a rational perspective, Sirius should shift because the earth shifts. They told us that it does stay at the same point each day because of its proximity to earth. It's the closest star to the earth, besides the sun.

She said, "August 4th is the day that Sirius rises with the sun. That's important for you to know; it holds great significance."

When we were ready to put in the stone that aligns to the rising point of Sirius, we dug two feet and hit solid massive rock. My fears about running into an impassable obstacle resurfaced. We dug to the left and right, but impenetrable rock ledges deflected our tools on all sides. In order to secure the stones in place, we must dig down at least three feet, or we risk the danger of a stone falling over and crushing somebody.

"*How interesting!*" we mused.

In order to fix the problem, we built up around the base of the stone. We placed it in the hole and added another two feet of soil. The Sirius Stone stood a couple feet higher than most of the stones in the circle, becoming one of the tallest stones, which felt appropriate.

Community Stone: *Unity, Aligned to New York City*

We heard about a contractor in Shelburne falls who recently dug up huge stones to build his house. We contacted him and he invited us over to see one stone in particular. The first time I saw the rock, I thought, *Eh, it's dirty and boring.* Yet my intuition persisted, telling me, *Yes this is the right stone*, so we hauled it away. At the community we washed it off, which revealed enchanting rings of quartz crystals! I knew we made the right choice.

It's the most unusual stone, dark in color, soft and crumbly and impregnated with veins of quartz. Moss grows all over it as its porous surface holds moisture. If you rub it, some flakes come off.

We call it the Unity Stone, and we purposely chose to align it to New York City to create a certain energetic field. The earth has specific chakras just like people, and New York City is considered the throat chakra of the earth. Just like in a human being, the earth's throat chakra holds the energy of creativity and communication. New York City contains incredibly immense energy and power as a mecca of creativity, expression, trade and business. In aligning this stone to New York, we tap into all of this energy and help create it here.

Mt. Monadnock Stone: *Love*

A granite stone aligns to Mt. Monadnock, the second-most climbed mountain on the planet after Mt. Fuji, held sacred in native traditions. We aligned to that sacred place full of people attracted to ascend the mountain to see beauty in nature.

Our unusual stone maintains and holds the sacred energy of the mountain. The solid granite emanates a striking beauty, energetically standing out from the other stones.

Our Monadnock Stone lay horizontally at the bottom of the hill for three years before we hauled it to the site. I walked by and found people meditating on the stone, with its magnetic energy attracting people to it. People would sit, sleep, and hang out on this huge stone.

Once we placed the Monadnock Stone, Ivan presented a particular challenge for our next placement. The Monadnock Stone would draw people in, but we needed some kind of energetic gate for people to pass through when they enter the sacred energy field of the circle. Ivan wanted two matching stones for the entrance, which seemed easy enough at first but eventually proved quite difficult.

Entrance Stones: *Clarity and Transformation*

The next two stones we placed have a similar size and color. They are sisters, both very reddish and narrow, perfect for the entrance.

We had bought a stone from the quarry during our original visit and found a similar stone to match as well, but the matching stone was way too big. It was so long it would have towered over the other, so we rejected it. We searched fruitlessly for a similar stone. Across the entire quarry we pored, with no other match in sight. Eventually we gave up and went home.

Eighteen months passed before we finally returned to find the rejected stone still lying where we left it. We examined it again, merely to be reminded of its excessive 15 feet in length. But I was amazed it still remained after a year and a half! They were selling stones all the time, constantly turning over their supply.

How auspicious, I thought!

But we knew we would not be able to bury such a tall stone deep enough in the hard ground at Sirius. We meditated on it and talked to Ivan. He said, "Yes, get that stone. We have to get that stone!" So we went back and loaded it up. The stone was so long, it filled up the entire trailer. It required extra effort to cart it up the hill, the awkward length providing all kinds of challenges. Finally ready to drop into place, we could see it would protrude way into the air above the other Entrance Stone.

Our only option seemed to be to cut the stone. I felt tremendous reluctance to cutting any of the stones for fear of violating them in some way as I so strongly wanted to honor them in their entirety. We meditated and talked to the stone and, tuning in, we received the message that it was okay. So we brought out the diamond cutting wheel, cut off the end and up it went! We used the piece we cut off as a flat altar on the edge of the circle.

Creation Stone: *Creativity and Manifestation, Aligned to the Amazon River*

Our neighbor Dagen experienced a vision of offering a stone to the circle. He described some kind of yellow quality to this stone. He came with us to the quarry, where we came upon a rare stone with a unique copper-yellow tinge. He knew it was the right one and we wanted a stone connected to South America, specifically the headwaters of the Amazon, one of the biggest, most sacred waterways on the planet.

A great deal of indigenous teachings abound about the bald eagle and the condor of North and South America. They say that when the eagle and the condor fly again together, it will be the great healing of the planet. When I traveled to South America, I visited the headwaters of the Amazon and also the pristine wilderness called Condor Park. I sensed the need for a healing that would bridge North and South America again.

Many of the people in South America embrace the spiritual awakening taking place. The United States' dominance over many of the economies and governments of South American countries has significantly hurt the wellbeing of the people and the environment. One of the first steps to establish a revitalizing collaborative effort between the North and the South is for the South to find their own power and independence.

In the last decade, many countries have torn themselves loose to find more self-actualization. Bolivia elected an indigenous president in South America for the first time ever. He refused to move into the presidential palace, instead living in a very simple abode, and he commits to protecting the environment.

We placed the Amazon Stone to establish a line of connection to

South America. So whenever people meditate or perform rituals in the circle, the circle acts as an energetic generator, sending rays of healing energy streaming out through each stone. In my sense, the stone enhances the positive spiritual connection between the two continents.

The reunification and upliftment of the Americas is part of the energetic shift that needs to take place for the healing of the planet. Now protected by the people, the condor and the bald eagle are both returning in strength. With a stone dedicated to the indigenous lands and people of the South, the next stone the circle called forth points to lands of an indigenous tribe in the North, the Hopi.

Indigenous Peoples Stone: *Honoring All Indigenous Peoples, Aligned to Hopi Land*

We call the stone pointing to the Hopi Lands the Indigenous Stone. The rock forms the distinct shape of an arrowhead, with its tip buried in the earth.

We believe Sirius was sacred to the native people, because of the ceremonial stone structures they left behind and from some mystical experiences we've had over our forty years here. We wanted to honor both the history here and the indigenous people of the planet.

We chose the Hopi because of their peaceful nature and their prophecies about the future and healing on the planet, and we resonated with their message.

To align with the Hopi Reservation, we honor the highest and best of the native traditions and embrace the ideals of peace and healing. For centuries, indigenous groups of the world were abused and mistreated and this stone helps to counteract all the abuse and disrespect. As this abuse becomes recognized, slowly more people respect indigenous practices and ancient wisdom. They recognize the horrendous abuse and genocide. This stone offers recognition and healing of those tragedies.

Amazon, Hiroshima, Hopis, I don't think at the time we realized that this was about planetary healing. A strong energy radiates out from our Stone Circle and creates healing energy on the planet. Next came the stone that reaches across the ocean to some of the community's deepest roots.

Stonehenge Stone: *Abundance and Expansion*

We first wanted to align to Findhorn as our roots and inspiration started there, but in meditation the guidance took us to Stonehenge. The people at Findhorn know of the ley lines connecting them to Stonehenge, and the lines connect all the way across the Atlantic.

When I visited Stonehenge, I had low expectations of the big tourist stop. Upon arrival however, the planetary cosmic energy completely blew me away. In placing the stone, I enjoyed making the energetic connection to such a strong earth power. It's the most famous stone circle on the planet, and after I felt powerful energy there, I knew why.

After placing the Stonehenge Stone, we nearly completed the circle, leaving only one space remaining in the northwest. And we had yet to address one of the most impactful traumas that ever struck the earth.

Healing Stone: *Healing for Earth and All Beings, Aligned to Hiroshima*

We stared at the empty space left by the lone gap in the circle with no clear alignments in that direction coming to mind. We explored maps and meditated, but no leads surfaced. Suddenly Ivan came to us with an idea. He plugged formulas into the computer and said "If you place the stone here and create an arc over the world, it aligns with Hiroshima. I think this stone should be dedicated to healing of the misuse of the nuclear energy of the planet."

The stone we chose also came from the ancient seabed. It blasted out of the earth in an especially unique shape.

We appreciated the opportunity to devote a stone to heal nuclear energy destruction in the world and we went back the site, placed the stone, and dedicated it to that process. After we placed it, the people expressed their gratitude for such an important cause; the misuse of the nuclear energy needs a lot of healing.

Everybody felt the energy up there growing, every time we put in a stone. The outer circle now complete, one final stone remained, and the most auspicious day was fast approaching.

Once we had the outer circle built, one more stone remained, which was the Center Stone. I called Ivan and told him with excitement, "We're ready to place the Center Stone!"

Center Stone: *Centering in Oneness*

The star Sirius, providing our community's name, is a significant channel to planet earth. While the sun and the stars rise from different locations on the horizon every day, one star, Sirius, always rises at the same place on the horizon. On one day of the year, August 4th, the sun and Sirius rise at the same moment. In the ancient teachings and wisdom, whenever a celestial body rises at the same time as the sun is considered auspicious. This concept is called the heliacal rising of a celestial body. The energy of love and wisdom from Sirius moves through the sun to the earth.

We decided we would place the stone on August 4th, because we tapped into this ancient wisdom. We planned a sunrise ceremony before we placed the stone, early in the morning at 5:30, so we advertised the ceremony on the list serve in our local community.

On the early summer morning, I walked through the forest to the gathering point beneath the black night sky barely turning twilight blue. Expecting about a dozen people to rise early enough for the ceremony, I sat waiting. A symphony of chirping birds serenaded the land as people began to arrive. To my delight, more and more people trickled in. By the time 5:30 rolled around, an astounding 75 people showed up!

We led a silent procession up the hill in the fading darkness. All the people filled the entire circle inside the stones, and Ivan led us in a series of chants. We meditated together and he led us in a dragon dance. All of us breathed in the cool morning mist and flapped our arms, twirled in circles and drew up the energy from the earth. The sun rose and the mist lifted. It was incredible.

After the ceremony, we placed the Center Stone. It's a smaller stone, about half the size of the others, but still weighed a ton and took some real work. Adorned in mica crystals, it sparkles with magic in the moonlight. We rolled it in place and raised it to its final position.

As the Center Stone rose into place, everybody felt the energy of the circle shift! We looked around at each other in wonder, exclaiming, "Whoa, what happened!"

The energy grew in magnitude with the final stone in place. During the rest of the day, people stayed to celebrate, cleaning up all the blocks, poles and wood, talking, laughing and sharing stories inside the circle in great camaraderie. The celebration proceeded with a pizza party and campfire, a day to affirm all our hard work and vision over the last five years.

After that day, people started going to the circle to write, meditate and hang out. The magnetic energy drew people in even more strongly than before. Now, each time I walk through the entranceway, I clearly feel energetically uplifted. A beautiful healing presence resides within those stones, which connects us to the earth and to the larger wisdom descending from the heavens. That cosmic energy runs deep into the core of our being.

Sacred Water Bowl and Meditation Hut

We still want to add one more addition to the circle. Many sacred temples in Japan and other parts of the world provide a bowl of water at their entryway. Worshipers wash their hands and splash water on their faces before entering the sacred space. We will place at the entrance to the Stone Circle a bowl for people to dip their hands with intention before they enter.

In the quarry I found a round stone, which is an anomaly for this type of granite to symmetrically form by itself. I carved out part of the bowl, but left it by the Longhouse, about a quarter of the way finished.

I cut it with it with a diamond wheel and then began to chisel out the bowl. Several people expressed interest in finishing it, but I have to teach them the method. I have a special pneumatic chisel that works on the stone. I hook it up to a compressor and touch the stone and it goes "chuk-chuk-chuk-chuk" as it chisels away the rock.

In the future we hope to build a small structure near the Stone Circle dedicated exclusively to meditation. It will be a sacred sanctuary where you can go any time, day or night, to meditate in quiet warmth. Such a space is dear to my heart. Findhorn and most spiritual centers provide places for this purpose, and it would be a great enhancement to the community.

Spiritual Center

We built this circle piece by piece, not aware of the greater ramifications of our work at the time. We followed our intuition and guidance, and the pieces connected. When we first began, I didn't think about the bigger ripples; I listened to what felt right. I didn't know anything at all about building stone circles, but we opened ourselves, felt that inner guidance and acted, as others caught the inspiration and joined us.

Later the patterns emerged. All the stones—particularly to the Amazon, Hiroshima, and the Hopi—created unity and healing. Upon reflection I realize our aim points toward planetary healing as well as connecting to sacred places. The Stone Circle through its energy vortex, radiates healing energy out into the planet. Finally we could step back in amazement at what we accomplished and say to ourselves, "Look how far we came, and how it changed us!"

Many times at Sirius, we received guidance for a task, but not until later did we realize the meaning and significance of it. I simply trust the inner process of these meditative decisions.

The Stone Circle offers a spiritual center in the community. It creates a magnetic energy field, where people feel spiritually uplifted when they arrive. The stones in their alignment were placed for that purpose. We created an etheric, energetic pathway that channels healing energy.

We all noticed the circle's completion create a shift within the community and how this shift helps with our spiritual process. Our ability to connect spiritually to each other, to this land and to the planet increased. Nearly halfway through the Stone Circle project, however, a fateful day would completely alter my life's trajectory.

The Fall

A LIFE-CHANGING ACCIDENT

16

For years I ran a successful business cutting trees outside the community. I employed people from Sirius, often seven at a time to work on a job. When I got a large contract, I paid $15 per hour, which created economic opportunities for people to have some part-time work. Because the dangerous work requires the proper skills and equipment, people pay top dollar. The contracts provided an easy way to make money, especially when we did the whole job from start to finish. I had done this work for years and years, and our work provided most of the wood for the Community Center.

In the early years we cut people's trees for free because we valued the wood we received. I took my apprentices and my building crew out, teaching them how to climb trees with spikes and ropes. It was a little risky, but I had been doing it for almost 30 years on and off long before I started my official business and was very conscious of the safety issues involved.

The business had been going for seven years and we received increased requests for our work. As our construction projects slowed, our need for lumber decreased, and we changed our model to start charging for our services. Our customers agreed, still asking us to do the tree work, so I invested in some serious equipment, buying a wood chipper and a bigger truck. We charged less than other companies, yet still made good money and brought home all the wood. It was a win-win for us and our customers.

I found my niche, enjoying the work while running a successful business. Nothing compares to the excitement of climbing trees in New England's enchanting forests. In our work we honored the trees with deep gratitude; we meditated with them, appreciating the mutual support we shared. At 62 years old I still climbed up trees with spikes, swinging from ropes and hauling chainsaws and branches up and down. I probably should have quit because I recognized my agility and awareness declining, essential qualities to performing this dangerous work.

Insurance companies don't like to cover tree work. They know a lot of people get hurt when people navigate rolling logs and massive chippers, not to mention dancing in treetops wielding buzzing chainsaws. Every year people die from this work; I knew two people in the local area who got killed and a few others who were seriously injured from it.

I sensed I should let go of it and do something different, but I couldn't resist the adventurous fun. The business helped support a lot of people I cared about, and I just didn't have it in me to stop.

One day I went out to Leverett with two crew members. We unloaded our gear in the shade next to a small stream. As usual we started our workday holding hands in a circle around one of the trees we would cut. We attuned and asked for the support of the trees and to work in harmony with the energy of the machines and the nature spirits. We gave a blessing for the products we would receive from the wood.

I fastened my spurs, slung on my harness and grabbed my chainsaw. I saw the largest pine was leaning too close to the house and needed its top cut off. Like I did many times before, I climbed as far as I could up a 40-foot ladder before jamming my spikes into the side of the tree to ascend higher.

When you climb a tree you smash off little branches with a baseball bat as you go so you can climb higher. If the limbs are too big to break, you cut them with a small chainsaw. You have two safety belts, and one is always hooked up while you unhook the other to fasten it to the branch above. As you ascend, you stay attached to the tree at all times.

Forty-five feet up in the air, I reached around a branch. I hooked one climbing line over the branch and unhooked the other, trusting all my weight with the top carabiner. As I leaned back into the belt, I watched the rope slide out of its carabiner in dismay. Somehow it didn't latch and I began to fall backward out of the tree. Suddenly I sank into complete freefall, whooshing through the air.

The only thought passing through my mind was, *Oh shit! This is not going to be good.* The forest blurred past me as I careened out of the sky and slammed into the earth, my back crashing forcefully into the ground like breaking glass.

Excruciating pain shot through my system as I lay on the ground screaming. "AAAAGGGHHHH!!" I couldn't breathe, couldn't move, couldn't think. My lung had collapsed, the bones in my foot were crushed and my back broke in three places, but still I remained conscious. I wanted the unbearable pain to end as I screamed and screamed. Desperately trying to escape the suffering, I clenched a stick in my mouth and bit into it as hard as I could.

My workers ran over to me in a panic, wondering what to do, and the owner of the house came running outside, waving her hands, exclaiming, "Oh God, oh my God!" Freaked out but keeping it together, she had called 911 before rushing out to ask me, *"How are you doing?"*

Barely able to speak, I gasped, *"I can't bear the pain! My back is broken..."* Pain pierced my lungs like a thousand daggers, my throat shredded in rawness. I heaved and squeezed, squirming like a decapitated worm.

"Maybe it's a good day to die," I uttered, as an existential feeling came over me.

With an earnest severity, the woman kneeled over me, looked me right in the eye and declared, "Today is *not* your day to go!" just like that, clearly with no hesitation.

I looked at her in surrender and responded, *"Okay!"*

It was a crazy moment.

Is this really happening?

Finally the ambulance arrived and the EMTs jumped out. I cried, *"Please help me! Take away the pain."* They injected me with morphine and loaded me in the ambulance. The drugs kicked in and the pain lessened, yet I still felt each bump in the road ripping through my broken body. They hauled me to the school field and tossed me into a helicopter to fly me off to the hospital!

I landed in the intensive care unit in critical condition, with a brace on my neck. They refused to operate on me immediately because my condition was unstable, but they filled me with more pain killers. My mind lost its focus and time went fuzzy as the ceiling turned pink.

At some point my wife and older daughter were at my bedside bending over me. Nurses came and went. I lay in the hospital bed, hurt and broken, swimming, lost in the depths of confusion. Disoriented, I asked, *"Whoa, what's going on!"* I was so looped out I would pick up something only to have it disappear in my hand. I saw flashing lights everywhere. While I could taste the euphoria, I couldn't stand the experience. It messed up my consciousness as my spiritual nourishment washed away. The drugs blurred my perceptual alignment process.

Teetering between life and death, a vivid vision appeared. Held in a sphere of unconditional love, in a beautiful place filled with light, I was shown I had a choice. I could either stay in my body or I could leave. My choices were free of judgment and I would be supported in absolute love no matter what I decided. I was shown that if I went back, if I decided to stay in my body, my experience would be difficult and painful, yet it would also advance my spiritual growth and evolution. But I could also let it all go.

As I lay there hovering between life and death, considering whether to live or let go, I saw my unfinished work, and an image of the unfinished Stone Circle popped into my mind. As the designer and planner, I initiated and held the vision for the sacred site. I knew if I didn't finish the project it would remain half-built. The soul impetus to finish it crept over me as I thought, *You've got to finish the Stone Circle before you leave! You're not outta here yet.* I knew I wouldn't do the heavy lifting anymore, but I could guide the whole process. This motivated me to heal, because of the project's significance.

Another strong desire called me to document my community life experiences of the last 40 years. I wanted to record the experiences, lessons and challenges we learned in building Sirius. Linda and I are the only two people who witnessed the whole history of the community and our lessons felt too important to let dissolve into the ethers.

I made a conscious choice: *No, I'm not finished yet; I need to go back and embrace what is in store for me.*

My condition stabilized enough that they began to operate on me, wiring me back together with metal rods, screws and bolts. I remained in critical condition with damaged lungs. With each breath, they pumped my lungs full of air, and gradually I started to stabilize.

For a few days after the surgery I was on morphine and opiates. Over the last 40 years, I allowed no artificial chemical into my body, not even an aspirin. Nothing. Occasionally, I used white willow bark for pain.

I told the staff, "You have to stop giving me the pain medication, it's completely whacking me out. I know people who went completely crazy from taking that stuff, and I'm losing my mind!"

The nurse replied, "You're in severe pain; you need this medication for your healing process," before admitting, "You have the right to refuse medication if you want."

I asserted, "I'm going to exercise my right. I don't want you to give me any more pain medication of any kind."

So they stopped the pain medication, but every half hour they would return to ask again if I wanted more pain medication. Every time I refused, though the pain level intensified, I used my inner process to cope. Through meditation I actually felt better than on narcotics. For 48 hours they kept asking me, but I continued to refuse until finally they stopped asking.

I thought, *Yes I'm in pain, but I have my ability to align my consciousness to a different state.* During the rest of my hospital stay I didn't take any more pain medication.

In the last year, as I have been sick with this kidney bladder condition, I've taken pain medication because the pain was so harsh for such an extended time. But now I stopped all that as well. I even tried a marijuana tincture, which disrupted my consciousness much less than morphine, but even that blurred my ability to make a clear conscious connection to Spirit.

Hospital Admission Miracle

As I healed, my care needs changed. The intensive care unit doctors wanted to move me to a rehabilitation hospital. But they divulged, "Rehab rejected you; they won't take you unless you have insurance. We don't know what to do with you!" My condition was still fragile. I was unable to walk or stand; I couldn't even feed myself. Going home was not an option. My care needs were greater than my family could provide, but the doctors wanted to remove me from the facility.

Outraged, I uttered, *"I can't even walk, and you're going to throw me on the street?"*

I knew I needed a miracle. I asked for the highest good in this situation and reached out to the Conclave, my network of meditators. Founded by my brother and his wife, people from all over the world link up regularly to meditate together. We gather once a year and share ideas and projects focused on improving humanity. I contacted Gordon and asked the group to meditate on my behalf. He said, "Alright, let me see who I can call." We asked the meditators to hold the situation in the light and pray for the best outcome, asking for the highest good. That night the network activated and everyone sat and meditated, sending energy toward me lying in the hospital.

The next morning, the same woman who told me rehab had rejected me walked in from the administrative office, holding discharge papers. Incredulous, she said, "I don't believe this...this never, ever happens. They agreed to take you into rehab hospital even though you don't have insurance! *They never do that!* I don't understand this!" I laughed, secretly appreciating the power of prayer to shift an outcome. Without focusing on a particular outcome, the Conclave surrounded the situation with light and love, and the circumstance dramatically shifted.

Power of Meditation in Healing

In recovering from my accident, I witnessed the influence of deep healing meditation. A group meditating collectively works to change situations and help people heal. Our thoughts and projections from our innermost self hold a powerful effect.

These ideas have been tested with patients in scientifically controlled experiments. People gravely sick in hospital received healing energy

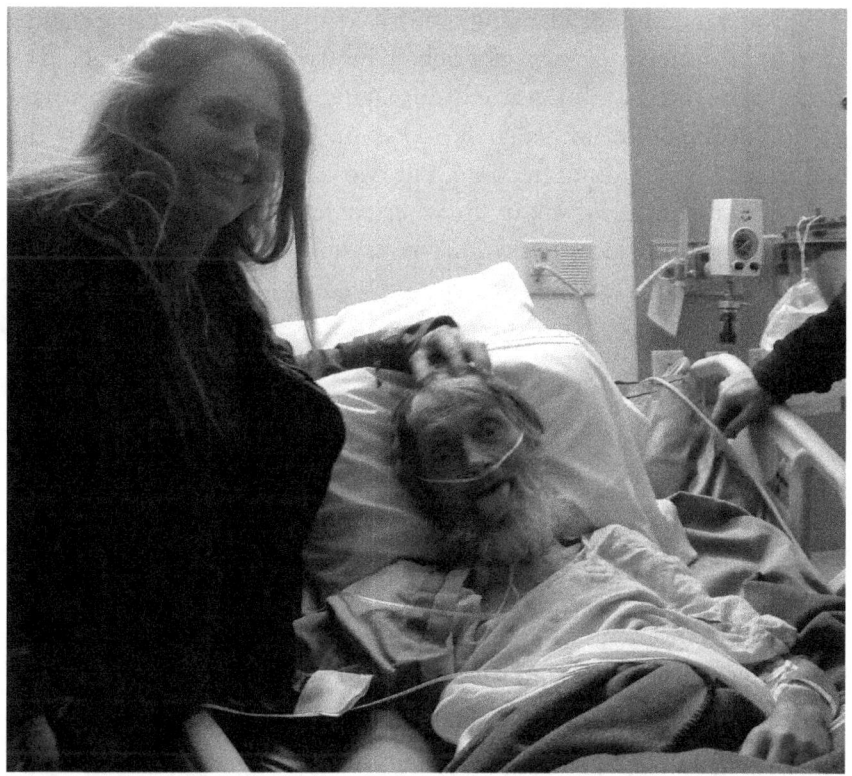

and love from other groups of people. The study compared them with others in similar conditions who didn't receive the healing energy. Those who received healing energy improved much faster.

This underlying spiritual principle shapes our lives. Who we are and what we project out from our being has power. We must project the highest good and the highest possible outcome and let go of our own agenda or idea of what the highest good looks like. If we attach ego and expectation to it, we diminish it. If we take the wonderful, infinite energy of possibility and stuff it into a narrow field, it just doesn't work.

Trust the process. If we limit the results based on our own desires and outcomes, we stop the energetic flow. We think we know exactly what needs to happen. When we let that go, something even better than what we imagined often occurs.

I've seen this pattern many times, with different groups in various situations. While living at Findhorn I experienced a humbling lesson in this regard.

I was a member of a healing group that attained remarkable results. One man came to us in a wheelchair he used the last 14 years. The group performed an intense session, laying our hands on him to aid in his healing. He immediately stood up and walked! Jubilant, he celebrated his newfound freedom, but two days later he lost strength in his legs again and fell back in the wheelchair.

During the process we didn't consider, "What's for the highest good?" Instead we intensely focused on healing his ailments to get him to walk. To release that expectation of our desired outcome proved difficult.

When he ended up back in the chair, the group completely flipped out and asked what went wrong. We meditated and received guidance that the highest good was for that man to stay in the wheelchair. For some reason, his ability to walk would not serve him, and even though we didn't understand, we had to accept it.

We realized we only focused on how to heal his deformity, which worked for a moment. But the condition returned quickly because there was a higher reason for him to experience his life the way it unfolded.

The event had a huge effect on the man in the chair when he saw that his condition showed up to catch his attention. He gazed inward and changed his perspective. This experience changed the focus of the healing group for the better, and we focused on the highest good rather than our own desires from then on. Sometimes when you let go, the message transmits more cleanly and clearly.

Pain: Lessons for a Lifetime

My experience in the hospital was a major life trauma. When I came home after six weeks in rehab, my whole life changed. I realized the extent of my physical limitations and challenges. I went from an incredibly active man, swinging from the tops of trees, to losing my basic ability to walk. Throughout my life I never became sick, and I could do anything for anybody. I could chainsaw, build houses, chop wood, and anything else that was needed. Now I couldn't even go to the bathroom without help.

When I first came home, my frustration soared. With time everyday challenges grew easier as I relaxed into my limitations. I understood what I could not do and learned to ask for help. It required mental awareness to embrace and accept the new me. Now I am less upset and more willing to accept what is.

This decline happens to all of us in old age, and for me it happened in one moment. I'm prepared for old age from this experience. When you can't perform simple tasks anymore, you feel your limitations front and center. You can choose to lament about your woes or you can relax into who you are. You can let go and be grateful for what you learn. Though the circumstance took away my physical abilities, it introduced an incomparable level of understanding to my consciousness.

My sense of compassion and understanding deepened for people I had judged as weak or disabled. Humbled, I learned spiritual lessons and maintained a level of peace and equanimity in the face of my injury. My 40-year meditation practice helped me be in the present instead of traumatized or depressed from my physical limitations.

I understand why people feel like victims and grow angry. When you are in pain and have extremely traumatic emotional or physical experiences, it feels like the universe is plotting against you. At times, I got a little bit depressed, but the dips in my mood were minimal compared to the overall experience. I learned it's possible to hold a high level of consciousness even in the face of extreme physical trauma. Because of the severity of the injury, my consciousness changed dramatically. It pushed me into areas of growth I would have completely avoided otherwise.

In rehab they didn't know if I'd walk again. I lay there in the hospital and thought, *Well my consciousness hasn't deteriorated; I still have my ability to connect with the Divine. I only lost aspects of my physical ability. Nothing else has declined at all!*

Perhaps breaking my back and being disabled even brought me into deeper connection to the Divine. I developed a deep level of compassion and connectedness to the moment. When you touch death, it changes your consciousness and each moment reveals a new presence and power.

In our speed track lives we lose sense of the present moment. Previously I had a meditation practice and I could enter a space of *being*, but most of my reality embodied *doing*. This experience changed that relationship dramatically.

Being present in the moment brings more love, light and joy into our souls. Right now is all we have, because we don't know what's in the future. Even if the moment is painful, we must work with it and bring goodness into it. Sometimes I lose track of the present as my ability to pay attention drifts, but I feel the sacred opportunity. The moment is truly beautiful and powerful.

Eckhart Tolle writes about how injury can bring us into the presence of Now as long as we don't identify ourselves with suffering. I didn't fully understand his ideas before this experience, but a new grasp of the Now has filled my understanding.

We might be caught up thinking, *What should I do next? Where am I going? What am I doing with my life?* A million thoughts run through our minds and we constantly flirt with who we want to be as we worry about what others think. Instead we could occupy this present moment right now, right here, to fill with joy, love and compassion. The focus of my life on doing has resolved to simply being.

My soul invoked this experience for me in order to alter my perception of the world. My calling in this life has been to grow spiritually and to understand deeper levels of consciousness. A dear friend of mine practices esoteric astrology, and when he looked at my chart he said, "If your fall hadn't happened, some other event would have occurred at this time to drastically alter your consciousness." For almost 40 years, the invocation to grow spiritually was my mantra. On the deepest level, I wanted to understand what life was all about. I wanted to plumb the depths of conscious and understand myself and the universe around me, and I gained a great opportunity to do so.

With this accident, so much changed and shifted for me. I had plenty of interesting life experiences, some of them very traumatic, yet this experience brought me useful lessons like never before. When boulders block our pathway, we can see them as opportunities and use them to grow.

Without painful or strong experiences of life we don't shift our soul rapidly. When we have to overcome traumatic life experiences our growth intensifies. It stimulates and creates a shift in consciousness and difficult circumstances develop spiritual strength and stamina. If we could be happy, loving people and still experience this shift, we wouldn't need all this. But we don't move in the same way. Why that is, I don't quit quite understand. But it does seem to be the issue. Practice gratitude for everything, even the most painful and challenging life events.

Tigers: *Facing Death*

The retelling of this story is based on recollections of Bruce's campfire storytelling rather than the interviews he intended for this book. While it describes his encounters with tigers in Israel, it is unlikely that any tigers roamed wild in Israel at this time. However, leopards certainly could have been encountered in the wild. We are preserving the nature of his storytelling and invite you to imagine the story as you wish.

In my life I have had many brushes with death yet many times have been spared because I had more work to do. On my way to Vietnam my orders were changed in transit, directing my life path away from the carnage. When I broke my leg in the car accident, I also experienced a tremendous life shift, reevaluating what is important and emerging with wisdom, insight and more spiritual awareness. I narrowly missed dying many times, finding new opportunities to live, grow and learn.

I also experienced a very close brush with death during my years at Findhorn. I made a close friend at Findhorn, Ishayahoo Benharon from Israel, who invited me to come tour his home country and stay with his family. I had a great time meeting his many relatives. He decided we should spend time outside of the city and explore the natural countryside, so different from any other place I visited.

We gathered our backpacks for a day trip and headed out into the desert environment. During the day we wandered and explored many of the canyonlands from above, admiring the red rocks and the sandy dry desert.

As the day wore on, the blazing hot sun started to color the sand with hues of red, orange and yellow, and we decided we traveled too far to make it home before nightfall. Concluding camping out would be our best option, we walked down a narrow rocky trail and passed some park rangers coming the other way. My friend stopped and talked to them. The ranger spoke in Hebrew at length, emphatically gesturing and shaking his head. I listened, silently wondering what they were talking about. The ranger gave us one last severe look and continued on his way.

"What did he say? What did he say?" I asked.

"Oh, he asked us if we were planning to spend the night out here.

He told me there are tigers out here and sleeping out would be a bad idea. I told him we were not camping and we would be out before dark."

I stopped walking and stared at him. "Um, I thought we were planning to sleep out, because it's so late in the day."

My friend shrugged, turned and kept walking as he replied, "Oh come on. There is nothing to worry about. I have only ever heard them a few times and they were always really far away. It's going to be fine." I gave him a hard stare and slowly picked up my pack wondering if I was making the right choice to keep walking.

We found a flat spot on the top of the plateau with great views and cloudless blue sky stretching in all directions. As the light faded, we tried to make ourselves comfortable with the minimal items we had in our day packs.

Mesmerized by the beautiful rocks on the ground, I started collecting them, wondering how many I could fit in my pockets to take home, when I heard a disturbing sound. My ears perked up, my muscles tensed and I dropped a half a dozen sandy pebbles.

"What was that?" I asked my friend. Faintly, way off in the distance, the thready sound of roaring reached our ears.

"What sound?" he asked.

"Listen." We both stood still, and this time we both heard the distant roar, clear and unmistakable.

My friend lightly punched me in the arm. "Oh, don't worry about it. Yeah that might be a tiger but they are miles from here. Miles. Relax. There is nothing to worry about." He sounded less convinced as he averted his uncertain gaze.

I frowned at him. "I don't like this, we are open and exposed on all sides. I think we shouldn't stay here." I convinced him to move our camp down into the bottom of the canyon where we would at least be protected on three sides. We climbed down to the lower part of the canyon, scrambling up and down over boulders, looking at rocks and admiring the cliff faces to arrive just as the last light slowly faded into twilight, hot, dry and orange.

We rolled our sweaty shirts into pillows. Ishayahoo muttered reassurances to me, but I think he was trying to reassure himself, "There is nothing to worry about. Remember the steep trail we came down? I don't think they can really come down here. We are much safer now that we're not out in the open." It was a dark, moonless night and the high canyon walls towering above us deepened the darkness. I tossed in a fitful sleep before eventually dozing off.

The next thing I knew I bolted upright as the canyon came alive with a terrifying roar. A snarling growl opened up into a horrifying eruption, *RooooaaaAAAARRRR!*

"Oh my god," I whispered, our backs against the canyon walls, peering into the inky blackness. Another blast of a roar reverberated against the walls, inundating us with a cacophony of horror, so loud the beast must be right upon us. My head felt like it would explode in the echoing noise. My hands started shaking as I fumbled on the ground for a rock or a knife, anything to hold onto for defense. We were stuck inside a canyon with no way out, rock cliffs on three sides and an invisible wild beast roaring at us.

RoooaaaAARRR! The walls echoed, with roars on top of snarls.

How many are there? I began to suspect we were being stalked by more than one beast.

Our hands shook and our muscles strung tight. We could barely breathe, staring into the darkness, waiting each second, each breath for a ferocious mouthful of sharp teeth to come lashing out of nowhere and tear us to pieces. On and on the minutes stretched, suspending our fear. I clutched Ishayahoo's arm thinking, *Oh my god, oh my god. Is this real? Is this really happening?*

Another roar pounded off the canyon walls, saturating our brains. All we could think about was the next breath, the next moment, wondering if we would still be alive.

Ishayahoo started praying. "Please god, save us," he muttered over and over next to me, his voice and hands shaking.

Eventually the sound lessened and the animals moved further away. In the silence that remained, we still stared into the darkness, rocks in our hands, mouths hanging open. We had no flashlights and our breath came hard and shallow in the inky blackness.

We sat there wide awake, wondering what to do. Getting up and trying to leave without proper lighting while the creature lurked would be unthinkable. My friend tried to reassure me the threat had left and we would be okay. "Everything's going to be fine. It's all going to be okay. We are fine. Breathe, we're fine," he kept repeating. I wanted to believe him.

We lay down in uneasy silence, neither of us able to go back to sleep. The all-encompassing darkness bore down on us like the walls of a prison cell. Despite my terror, I drifted off again in exhaustion.

RooooaaaAAAARRRR! I startled awake again to a thundering cry even louder and closer.

Oh my god. Oh my god. They're back. Oh my god. Only 20 feet from us, I could decipher the great animals pacing up and down, snarling in deep utterances before blasting open again. Petrified, we stayed huddled together, clutching rocks in disbelief. It was not over.

My eyes stared into inky black midnight. "Please God. Save us. Please just let them go away. Please, *please* let it be morning, let the sun rise. Please let it be over. I don't want to die."

Once again they walked in front of the cavern, up and down, roaring. Eventually for a second time they went away. We did not go to sleep again but stayed poised, ready for attack, waiting to defend our lives, with the desperate hope that we would live to see daylight. We did not speak but stared silently into the darkness.

To my exhausted relief, the first pink streaks started to appear in the east, far above our heads at the top of the canyon. We waited wordlessly, willing daylight to come faster. I stood up on shaking unsteady legs, sore from sitting still, huddled over a handful of rocks, my only defense.

Slowly I made my way to the end of the canyon and wordlessly pointed. Laid out in even rows less than 20 feet from where we huddled, the dusty tracks were outlined in the sand. Two sets overlaid on top of each other, wearing a trail into the dusty ground. Back and forth they traversed.

I let out a long, shaky breath. How gentle, sweet and life affirming the sun felt on my shoulders. In the light of day, we felt our joy reemerging as we trekked back to safety.

Ishayahoo and I were both extremely sick for a week after our experience. The amount of adrenaline that pumped through us gave us fevers, shakes and chills. Long after the event, I experienced flashbacks and nightmares, often bolting awake at night, sweating and shaking.

Later Ishayahoo sent me an article dated less than a week before our encounter. It described the death of a shepherd out tending to the flock who was attacked and killed by a tiger.

Fortunately I managed to walk away with little more than a good story and some rocks in my pocket. I guess God had other plans for my life but the experience taught me to value each breath more.

Close to Death: *Overcoming Fear*

I have almost died several more times, dealing with my injuries from falling from a tree. These circumstances helped me overcome my fear of death. As I lose my fear of death, I gain freedom, for what else is there to fear besides dying? If you really want to be alive and free, then walk with death close by. You are spiritually free when you embrace your own mortality, as it no longer rules your life. In our society and culture, we to try to stave off death no matter what. Change your relationship and know death, embrace and accept it. As we change this relationship, we are no longer ruled by getting old.

When I started meditating and gaining spiritual insight, I experienced stepping out of my body. My physical body could be in one place while my soul goes to another place, connecting with the entire universe and the Divine. Despite this, I was not totally free because I still had fear. My greatest fear before the accident was to be physically incapacitated. I feared becoming crippled and bedridden. Then it happened, and I was brought face to face with my own shadow. I thought, *Wow! The opportunity has arrived to overcome this fear.*

I immersed myself in this new reality as I realized I could free my consciousness from this last lingering fear. Afterward, I gained an even greater level of freedom. I still have some lingering fears about small challenges and I still get worked up when the day isn't going right. But now these small challenges don't affect my consciousness in such a detrimental way.

Since my fall from the tree, I recovered well. Gradually I regained my ability to walk again with limited mobility in my legs. Granted, I used a cane but I was mobile which was incredible. For about three years I lived nearly pain free. I had a little numbness in my legs and my left food did not flex well, but I was up, moving around the community, albeit in a different capacity.

Eventually my kidneys, bladder and urinary system started to malfunction, however. The last six months have been challenging. The level of pain pushed me into another state again.

Sometimes the pain is so severe I have to scream. The pain grows so excruciating, it feels worse than when I broke my back. I tried pain medications like morphine but the hallucinations became too much. Instead of taking drugs once again, I feel better off not taking anything. The drugs cut me off from the fundamentally nurturing part of my being and it numbs out our ability to connect spiritually, so I embrace the pain and work with it more consciously.

I search for the lessons and try to see it as a gift. When I am right in the middle of an attack, it doesn't feel like a gift but it does push me to more fundamentally appreciate the moment. Recently I've been in so much pain that when it subsides I see that life is so beautiful. The essence of life overwhelms me. When the severity eases up, it offers a new lens to perceive reality.

I appreciate when the pain leaves because it gives me lucid moments of joy. I savor the moment in ecstasy. A couple days ago during a normal day in my house sitting in my chair, I distinctly felt the presence of Spirit. I sat here with no pain and felt the peaceful beauty. I grasped the moment in gratitude, *What a miracle, the pain is gone!* The pain created contrast, awakening me to beauty and harmony.

Of course I would like the pain to stop, as it wears me down, draining my energy and tiring me out. But in the relief after the pain, energy floods my being and I feel my connection to all life. My friends and family pray and send me positive energy, which I distinctly feel as well. From my suffering, a shift within my own consciousness has occurred. I connect with the Divine and understand the constant presence of Spirit. The immediacy of life appears in each breath I take and in each moment that I find myself free from pain.

At some moments, I lose sense of this presence. Sometimes I wonder in desperation, *Oh God, why are you doing this to me!* Even Jesus, nailed to the cross cried, "My God, why hast thou forsaken me?" We are human beings with human emotions and feelings. I have them too and sometimes my emotions take over. Still, my overall experience is positive. There are days when I sit in the bathroom and I think, *Will this suffering ever end?* I don't have a perfect grasp of the lessons, but my understanding deepens daily.

In my life journey, my soul chose many difficult life experiences. I've made such a strong commitment to deeper understanding in order to grow spiritually. So on some level I've chosen these experiences to help me grow. Now I want to learn the lessons and shift my experience so that the pain can pass. This interest feeds my current daily meditation practice.

Relationship Changes

Reintegrating: Asking for Help

After the initial fall, I integrated slowly back into the community. Before the accident I held a major active role with my drive and experience. I fixed people's broken pipes and carpentry challenges and came to their aid whenever help was needed. I offered prayers and spiritual support, doing whatever I could to help people both physically and emotionally. Upon my return, our roles reversed, and I needed help instead of offering it to others.

The reversal proved to be a drastic challenge for me because I abhorred asking for help. I couldn't stand to be a burden; I wanted to serve. People showed up anyway and gave me healing sessions, drove me to appointments and helped in my garden. The amount of support I received was significant and consistent. I resisted help at first, but with time, I realized my behavior blocked people's desire to express love toward me.

As I realized how I stood in the way of positive interactions and important opportunities, I decided, *Okay, I'm going to accept and be grateful for what I receive.* I would ask for help when I needed it. I would allow the expression of love to blossom. The soul is the vehicle to give love, and to allow people to be loving and giving toward me helped them connect with their soul. My needs provided an avenue of spiritual growth for people. When I learned my resistance to accepting help prevented opportunities for people's spiritual growth, I changed my behavior.

I let go of my resistance and received tremendous support. In a community like Sirius, where I had a history of giving, the abundant flow of energy came back to me and I was held with love in my time of need. Over time, I grew stronger and found opportunities to return the kindness. When I first came home from the rehabilitation center, I was stuck in a wheelchair, wearing a hard plastic removable cast around the middle of my body. I couldn't easily go outside because of all the stairs. I was homebound, yet despite my physical limitations and my small travelling radius, I gave back by counseling people. Visitors dropped in to chat and I shared stories and heard about their lives and events taking place in the community.

Over time, I went from a wheelchair to a walker, then a cane, and I slowly got better. The experience, though painstakingly difficult, was good for me, and I learned when you reach out to help other people, giving your love and support, the exchange opens up a soul channel, moving the divine energy through you. It strengthens your soul connection with yourself and others. When someone acts lovingly toward you, you give them a gift by accepting their love. They are allowed to offer their loving expression.

We hold a responsibility to accept the love of others. We are not often taught how to do this. People struggle and claim, "No, I don't really need your help." When I say, "No!" it blocks the flow of energy. Before the accident, I frequently rejected offers of assistance, stating, "No, I can do it myself." I realized the drawbacks to this strategy. Today if somebody offers assistance, even if I don't necessarily need or want it, I still accept it as a gesture of love and goodwill. I embrace it and offer my gratitude because the act allows more loving kindness in the universe.

As I healed I realized what a precious gift I received in being blessed with some more time on earth. My obligation to share the experiences of 40 years of building community grew. I wanted to document the lessons, mistakes and spiritual insights. I wanted to learn from the past and apply it to the present and to the next generation going forward. A divine presence has always been here in our work and it has penetrated and interwoven itself through the land and all of us. Remarkable undertakings and unbelievable coincidences happened here. There was divine support for all we accomplished. We tried to create a community in line with the Divine and the higher good of humanity and this mission informed our decisions and practices.

We always faced challenges and difficulties, and there were many over the years. We dealt with money shortages, arson, interpersonal conflict, divorces and lawsuits. Even in the midst of all this, we believed in divine intervention and support, which helped us to more easily push through. When we came up against potentially destructive challenges as a community, the divine energy was always present. And as long as we held our alignment and connection to the Divine, the solution appeared, sometimes in unexpected ways. From this trust, I understand the concept of the higher good.

You can have those experiences in your life even without living in community, yet when a community works with these alignments, it magnifies the intensity. The divine energy is blatantly visible. The committed strength of a group of people creates more powerful experiences. A quote from the bible states, "When two or three gathered in My name, there I am in the midst of you." With a group, the whole is greater than the sum of the parts. It magnifies spiritual understanding.

Partnership

After my accident, my relationship with Linda changed dramatically and sometimes painfully. Through our lives together our relationship has always evolved. As a container, the maturing community shaped our growth, yet the accident affected us deeply.

In looking at our relationship as a whole, I see how far we have come. When we first met, we were attracted to each other. At the time I mused, *Wow, this woman is incredibly hard working!*

Linda was convinced that she was headed toward a nun-like monastic existence. She believed she would never be in a relationship again, until she met me. During our first few interactions, she had hesitations based on her past relationship experience. She talked to me about it, expressed her feelings and gradually we worked through it, coming together with common goals.

The aspect of love showed up strongly when we first met and has continued since. We made a commitment at the beginning of the relationship that our union was about spiritual growth and positive work in the world. The endeavor of our relationship would support our connection with the Divine. We committed to create working partnership and build sustainable, spiritual life on the planet.

Early on in my spiritual journey, even before Findhorn, I received guidance that I would create spiritual community. As our relationship deepened I felt the spiritual intuition that this would happen with Linda, and I sensed Linda's commitment to a spiritual path.

Over the last 40 years creating community, we spent most of our time together. We worked the land, meditated, ate meals, dealt with community challenges, and spent time with our children together. We've spent more time together than most couples and have always had a strong connection. I spent more time with Linda than anyone else in my life, and the intimacy of shared living deepened our connection.

We both have strong, often intense personalities. I was more physically inclined, swinging a hammer or wielding a chainsaw. She had important insights and intuition that I lacked. While I held a greater leadership role in the founding of community, she patched up the holes and fixed conflicts and disagreements, which is still true. With my accident, I lost my ability to hold central leadership and she stepped up, stretching to take on more responsibility.

Our conflict is rooted in our differences in personality. She's not a huggy, lovingly expressive person. She is a private person with a public role and often comes across as prickly when you first meet her.

At times our relationship hasn't been smooth; we have faced many challenges. We argued and disagreed, sometimes brutally. Our relationship dynamic is one of harmony through conflict. It taps into one of the energy patterns that make up the universe. She is aloof, which caused issues in our intimate relationships, but she tells me I'm not demonstrative in my love either, which is true.

Some patterns come out in community as well. Our different styles created conflict since she could be more abrasive while I would try to be more embracive. I often ignore or overlook patterns within people and the community that need to be addressed while she points out the issue and suggests steps to change it. We disagree on handling conflictual circumstances both in the community and in our personal lives. We discussed the best way to solve and handle conflict and while my pattern is to embrace and accept others' harmful behavior and patterns, Linda notices uncomfortable or unacceptable behavior and calls it out. She points out what isn't working and makes suggestions for how people need to change.

When we first met, this issue did not exist, but as we each developed into our personalities, it was obvious that we had different approaches. We practiced finding balance between the two.

She brings up crucial and important conflicts that haven't even entered my awareness. I temper down her severity, and say, "Yes, and let's embrace these people lovingly." When I recognize the off behavior, I try to address it with love and acceptance.

Our conflict lies in this different way of approaching life. I can also be severe, critical and even negative at times, so I'm working on those patterns as well.

Despite the intense conflict in the relationship, we manage to return to harmony at the end of each drama. Sometimes the conflict extended for a long time, but we never gave up the idea that we were meant to be together. Our relationship was divinely guided, as many events aligned to bring us together.

When I first met Linda I wanted her to behave in a certain way. I projected my expectation on her of what relationship should look like. I realized how those projections created disharmony. I decided acceptance was a better strategy. With time and practice, I learned to stop my expectations and projections toward Linda and others as I saw I cannot dictate how others behave; I must honor the differences in each of us. To project onto someone how we think that person should be causes harm. We must accept that we're all very different and diversity creates beauty in any relationship or group. If your relationship has occurring patterns and problems, you have to address them and try and find compromises; you cannot remake a person's personality to suit your own needs and expectations.

With my new physical limitations and injuries we stretched ourselves further and harder than any previous conflict. I lost patience with the daily challenges of getting dressed, going to the bathroom and eating meals. Through my subsequent decline, I expressed my impatience and frustration at her. The situation took so much effort and we were overwhelmed by this new life we did not expect. I had to greatly depend on her, and the caregiver role was new for both of us.

When I completely lost my strength, I tried to work on gratitude and acceptance of my new dependent condition and her role in taking care of me. This limitation pushed me deeper into humility and gratitude. She stepped up and took good care of me constantly and relentlessly, often at her own expense. She showed up day after day. My care is a full time job on top of her other duties, and sometimes her patience waned. She got overwhelmed. We had to readjust to a constantly changing, unfamiliar dynamic. With time, she practiced patience and examined her spiritual lessons as she found a new kind of internal strength. She tried to be patient and forgiving with me. It has deepened our connection, though it was not easy.

She really supported me and came to my bedside at the hospital over and over through the years as my illness continued. She cooked for me, helped me get dressed, took care of managing my pills, drove me to doctor's visits and did the laundry. She also took on all the tasks in the house that I previously held. She would help make me breakfast, then run across the property to water the seedlings, then check in with her work crew, then run back to help me get dressed and clean the kitchen, then go work for an hour and rush back to cook lunch.

The emotional roller coaster was traumatic and challenging for her. The new normal was that I was sick, which sometimes descended into an immediate crisis. Countless times she rushed me to the hospital sometimes in the middle of the night, not sure if I would live, before the doctors saved my life and bought me more time.

It's harder for her and the rest of my family than for me at times. She has watched me waste away without improving. She never knew when she would lose me. When you watch your life partner slowly but actively dying before your eyes, one day at a time, the emotional turmoil takes a toll. Overall it has deepened our connection. We understand each other so much better.

Lessons of Intimacy

Intimate relationships provide a powerful tool for spiritual growth. Sitting in a cave and meditating to experience higher states of consciousness is easy. The presence of God, nirvana and ecstasy are right there with you. But to apply the lessons to the intimacy of life rubs against our growth edges, especially when people start pushing our buttons. To maintain ecstasy and nirvana out in the world takes strength, effort and spiritual stamina. While the days of sitting in the cave and meditating had their place, we are moving toward a new chapter, and the deepest spiritual awakening invites us to apply these lessons to our daily interactions, uncomfortable situations and relation to the ones we love.

In intimate relationships, someone is in your face all the time, pointing out your judgments and your faults. Intimate relationships are the cutting edge to higher consciousness, because you must face your own shadows all the time.

The effort to resolve your conflicts strengthens you and aligns you to your highest self. To create an intimate, harmonious relationship involves finding a new ability to be more unconditionally loving.

Saint Francis of Assisi

The story of Saint Francis of Assisi fully demonstrates this concept. Saint Francis asked all his monks and disciples, "What do you think will bring you closer to God?"

They answered, "Feed the poor! Meditate for hours at a time!"

He said, "No, no, those are good things, but there's something that's even stronger."

Baffled, they inquired, "What is it master?"

And he replied, "You knock on someone's door to ask for donations for the poor, and they get angry at you, pick you up and throw you into the street face down in the mud! If you can get covered in mud, humiliated, and you look up and still see the face of God in that person, that will bring you close to God."

In my life Saint Francis was an inspiration and a hero. The movie *Brother Sun, Sister Moon* depicts the profound story of his life, and even before I saw the movie, I always felt a connection to him.

I related to his imperfect nature and his journey from his youth to his important work in the world. When he was young, he chased women and drank. He was not saint-like at all. Later in life, he undertook a transformational process, which matched my own journey. When I was younger, I was not spiritually oriented; I was materialistic and chased my desires with women and drinking. I drove a jeep and hosted beach parties; I had no spiritual awareness.

Saint Francis came from an extremely wealthy merchant family. As he grew, he saw the important parts of life and he rejected all wealth and materialism. His father wanted him to take over the business, and he said, "I don't want it." His father became angry at his decisions, with no understanding for his rebellious son. In protest, Saint Francis took off all of his clothes from his father, stripping down naked in the public square, and declared, "I don't want any of your wealth. All I want is what the Divine has to offer me." And he walked away completely naked!

He was a real master and saint. His profound love of nature and the animal kingdom touched me deeply. When animals crossed the road, in danger to be stepped on, he stopped and moved them aside. The animals befriended him, coming to his side; birds sat on his shoulder and saw his sensitivity. He saw the Divine in all life and exemplified spiritual principles to reach a valuable level of consciousness.

For me he is a huge role model. Though I don't model myself completely after the celibate monk, he exemplified values and spiritual principles I find worth emulating. I read his books, studied his work, and visited the town of Assisi in Italy. When I walked down the street, I saw the original church and felt a past life connection. I meditated in the caves where he lived with all his disciples. The place seemed familiar, like I lived there before in some capacity. The power to be in Assisi in such close proximity to where he lived, worshipped and died stuck with me. I felt his energy, echoing through time, living in the very stones and foundation of the church.

When I used to travel with little money, I experienced people making fun of me, and just like Saint Francis, I worked on holding them in love and kindness. I resonated with his story about connecting with the Divine by seeing God in others, no matter their actions.

Practicing this kindness and love is easy with strangers, but when I engage with someone I love, such as my romantic partner, the experience proves much more challenging. When someone I care deeply about projects negativity toward me, I must work hard to stay in love and not react. My defenses are down, because I don't expect them to hurt me, because they love me and should know better. But such expressions happen, and we need to work through the challenges as they shine light on our shadows.

If you can find the inner strength and the power within yourself to forgive others, you touch God. In abusive and harmful relationships it takes a huge amount of energy to overcome hurt and see forgiveness. If you can forgive them anyway for what they're doing, you invoke the most powerful healing.

These lessons and teachings of Saint Francis influenced my values and perception of life. He inspires me as one of my great heroes along with Gandhi, Martin Luther King and other spiritual teachers.

I studied the teachings and messages they offered and I learned what constitutes spiritual life and spiritual principles. Gandhi, Martin Luther King and Saint Francis were deeply spiritual people yet they actively participated in the world. They didn't hide away in a cave to reach their own nirvana. They were activists who stood for justice and practiced great courage despite facing extreme danger and death threats. They were amazing spiritual teachers who embody deep spiritual connection.

Sometimes spiritual growth and awareness arrive as gifts in many different forms. I never expected a gift from Catholic nuns, who rescued us in the early days when we ran out of food and money to pay the mortgage. I held onto projections about the Catholic Church and the harm it has caused in the world. Many of the Church's actions were not aligned to spiritual principles. All over the world, people of the Church killed, raped and pillaged in the name of God. They have been sexist, homophobic and racist, attempting to make people feel horrible about themselves.

Then the nuns came, and it changed me as I let go of my stereotypes. They exemplified compassion and service more in line with the principles of Jesus Christ. Their willing nature taught me to watch my negative projections. Though I don't particularly embrace the Catholic Church, it has pockets of good and graciousness. The current pope is humble and works closely with poor people as he breaks down old powers structures of the world. We recognize that goodness comes from many places. I have been surprised by goodwill in the most unexpected places.

Saint Francis of the Catholic lineage offers a perfect example of how we can illuminate pockets of goodness without succumbing to the larger organization. At first his mission was rejected because he committed himself to a life of poverty, but eventually the pope recognized his saintly power and accepted him into the Catholic Church, so he created his monastic order.

The Healing Garden

Last year when I was sick, I wanted to create a peaceful place where healing and joyful energy could flourish, so I felt the impulse to start working on a healing garden behind my house. I cut more trees to bring in sun in order to grow flowers and nourishing edibles.

This garden connected me to the soil and helped with my healing. I kneeled on the earth with my fingers in the soil, working with nature, meditating in the garden. I tuned in and cocreated with nature. The nature beings worked with me the whole time. I meditated and asked each step of the way if the paths and the beds were in the right place. I asked where to put certain plants to create balance. The inner guidance arrived, and I would install and create based on what I received.

I built it for everyone to share and I wanted people to wander the paths to be in a space of reflection, nurtured and healing. I added benches next to berry bushes by paths meandering around mossy rocks and bursts of color. Some beds produce annual vegetables with places to nibble while others host medicinal plants or vibrant flowers. The garden is a space I was guided to give to the community. Many people sit or wander in the garden and say they feel connection as they receive energy from the plants, animals and spirit of the garden.

In hearing people's experience, I see my original intention manifested beautifully into an edible meditation garden. Many of the plants are still young and as they establish themselves, more fruit will be available and the vibrancy will grow. The ongoing project motivates me toward healing as I derive great nurturance from the earth when I work so intimately with nature.

I love my garden, and I feel deeply connected and nurtured by the whole environment and vibe I created. I wander from bench to flower to berry bush, touching the smooth leaves and admiring the bright colors. I poke my nose in large lilies and inundate myself with the aroma of life, before delighting myself to nibble on sweet berries.

Often I stop and stare at a plant for a long time as I notice its presence and nourishing energy feeding me through the energetic web of nature. Gazing into the spirit of every plant, I feel our divine connection.

I don't have a favorite spot; just wandering and receiving the garden's gems inspires me. I feel reciprocity and when I give love and nurturance to the plants, they give it right back. Our symbiosis not only benefits the human kingdom but it also benefits the plant kingdom as we nurture the deep ongoing relationship between us.

When people come to Sirius and walk the land, they tell me how our forest feels more friendly than anywhere else they have been. They feel the presence of connection with the land. They feel the love and the care that we have offered here. This energy exists because the trees and the animals are open to foster connection with the human kingdom. When you go in the forest you can feel the reciprocal energetic magic taking place.

Spiritually, that connection is so important for nature and humans, because it nurtures and creates harmony in the world. The radiant energy field illuminates with reciprocal love. When I return from travels and I walk into the garden or the woods, I feel a wonderful presence of love, light and energy emanating from all the gardens and trees on our land.

This strong energy field didn't always exist here. It grew and strengthened through our care for the land. We see them as sentient beings worthy of our consideration and communication. We approach the land and the trees with care.

We don't abruptly tear up the landscape. We spend time meditating with the nature energies. As we create cooperation rather than dominance, this attitude raises consciousness and offers people a new lens. People come into that field, see what we are doing and gain insight. They practice a peaceful loving relationship with nature, which deepens their spiritual connection as they see the sacred interconnection of all life. Other sacred spaces on the planet such as stone circles, old growth forests, ocean waves, a starry night and sitting in the shadow of mountains also achieve this connection. When you witness the special sacred energy you feel awed and uplifted. You feel your connection to the Divine.

Into the Future

CHANGING FACES IN CHANGING TIMES

17

Speeding Evolution

As the world shifts and more people become aware of our impact on the planet, we are seeing new kinds of people come into the community with fresh energy, skills and talent. Through the decades, Sirius always received new residents and members. Some stay for a season, others for a few years, and some for decades, and each individual comes here with something to learn and something to teach us.

Sirius is an evolving entity that must change and grow so our consciousness doesn't crystallize. New participants keep us from getting stuck in an old paradigm and help us stay open to new ideas. We realize when our outdated methods of the past no longer serve us. Just because we've always done something one way doesn't mean it's the only way. Even if our practice may still be the best way, reexamination allows us to assess our effectiveness. New people push against old agreements and boundaries, and healthy questioning emerges. We always need to take stock, reevaluate and assess our work in the world and who we are. We reexamine our past patterns, break out of habitual tradition and find constructive new ways to work together.

The new transient young people change our group dynamic, helping to develop new concepts and affect decisions. They create the friction and fire, which stimulates growth and prompts necessary change. They shake up our patterns and push into areas that need loosening and reconsideration. New perspectives offer real stimulus for change for the good of the community and humanity at large.

From the early years of the community, if a person wants to live here, we ask about one's spiritual practice and if one embraces an intention to evolve and grow. Everyone must make a commitment to engage in one's own inner work when challenges arise. We don't ask what specific path people take to find their answers, because we honor the highest and best in all religious and spiritual traditions.

Projects and Follow-Through

Though we developed plenty of wisdom through the years, to rattle our perspectives around helps us expand, teaches us lessons and pushes our growth edges. Sometimes the lessons happen quickly while other times they demand more time. Our goal, especially for young people, is primarily to offer a space to grow rather than long-term residency. We try to create a formula to hear them, while remaining realistic of our bigger goals and we ponder how to respond to their ideas without being jaded based on negative past experiences.

When a new wave of people comes in, we start to realize how we are recapitulating challenges we've been through before and we reluctantly commiserate, "Here we go again. Do we need to start all over? It took us *years* to learn those lessons!" But we are repeatedly surprised to witness new members working through the issues in record time. Rapidly everybody gains a deeper understanding as our concerns of redundancy are recognized by the newcomers. A long-term member mused, "Where did that issue go? It just disappeared! We worked on that for *years*!" We would discuss old issues with new people and say, "You understand that *already*?" A higher level of consciousness manifested, which humbled us!

Currently a large portion of the community consists of people who have not been here for long who could be gone tomorrow or next year. The current paradigm of the younger generation generally reflects transience and exploration. Short-term residents hold less of a long-term stake in the vision and mission of Sirius, and while the new energy is welcome and creates a new dynamic, some long-term members struggle and have concerns with the instability it creates.

When short-term participants change the culture here, they sustain our natural evolution. We try to support this by letting people choose their involvement with Sirius regardless of whether they want to form stability and long-term relationships or to merely pass through for a few months.

When people stay a short time, they might propose new ideas and projects that they will not be around to complete. They question how we run Sirius and bring new energy that may or may not last. Young people are in a different life stage, not usually thinking of settling down. They want to travel, experiment and learn, which is vital when we are young. The freedom to experience life in an unfettered way is necessary, and I wasn't ready for a long-term commitment at age 25 either.

We must understand and appreciate the need for younger people to feel unfettered by extended commitment. Freedom to choose your level of experience is necessary. Imposing our boundaries never lasts or achieves positive end results. With a decision made from free choice, you feel empowered. While certain rules or agreements are necessary, fundamental decisions about your life have to come from yourself.

In the regular society, we are not given this freedom. Family and social impositions determine where we go in life and how we spend our time. They even impose interests on us, pressuring us to dress a certain way, make money, blend in and choose a career. The external pressure stifles our truest nature and creativity and keeps us from deeply knowing ourselves. We live in fear without pursuing our highest calling because of societal and family judgments. We have to find our inner courage to decide for ourselves what we truly want in life. Past Sirius members came here and discovered more clearly their gifts and dreams and have done some amazing work in the world.

In our thinking, we may judge lack of commitment as irresponsible. Yet if we step into a higher level of consciousness and put aside our judgment, we hear and understand the wisdom of young transient individuals. Even if they are not committed here, their ideas hold value. While recognizing the wisdom that comes with age and life experience, we can make space for their ideas.

Though we have a different lens from our life wisdom and maturation, it's not always the best, and our ways are not set in stone. While the experience of life provides insights, other souls may incarnate and contain more wisdom than us, despite our older age. The fact that someone is younger does not mean they lack great wisdom.

If we put our ego aside to see this we ask, "Can I look at a young person with less life experience, and see what they can teach me? Maybe they have certain insights and skills l lack."

In a group, people want the power to fulfill their passion, but individuals may want to pursue actions on the land different from our vision. The community works with individual proposals and tries to empower people. Instead of forcing our own point of view, we work with this idea of meditative attunement and guidance.

Good communication with honesty and effective feedback makes the process work. We need the openness to discuss our vision freely and the courage to hear criticism without being intimidated. Sometimes the process reveals painful difficulties as we run into the personality wounds that we all carry around. We may have taken a lot of beatings as children or in our experience of society itself.

As part of the dance, we use it as a consciousness raising tool. If someone wants to take action contrary to what we've done in the past, we ask the essential questions, like what resources are required, what support is needed from the community in terms of time, energy, money, etc., and harder questions addressing liability.

If the vision is brought up in a conscious way, others must take it to a deep level and dance with it. In the process, occasionally the Core Group changes its decisions, but generally individual perspectives shift and the person grows, gains new insight and releases one's attachment. Other times people get angry and frustrated, perhaps even withdrawing from the process and leaving the community by their own choice.

Sometimes an idea doesn't fit with the whole vision of the community and we protect against this with clear expectations. With each new idea presented, we ask if the project is in the highest good and how it might benefit all involved. Rather than saying, "No, you can't fulfill this vision," we ask questions that provoke reflection to explore what a project requires to succeed and what its impacts will be.

When someone demonstrates how deeply they have reflected on their idea, we recognize, "Wow, this person really *did* take into consideration all those questions! Now it's time for *us* to reflect on it." We will honor the investment and change our perceptions if necessary. *Do we need to let go of a past experience that is holding us back?*

We need to try to see if we're not understanding an important concept or if we are holding onto an outdated thought form. We have released attachments that we once thought were important.

Some young people proposed new projects and the community invested in their ideas though some did not last. The person who had the ambition often leaves the community and the energy for their creation fades out. While some think energy is wasted, this change doesn't present a huge problem. People are curious and tend to ask what happened to a project they are no longer hearing about.

One example of this was our involvement with the Global Ecovillage Network. One individual spearheaded the project and generated interest and connected with people. The energy brought conferences and new faces to Sirius. The main focalizers left and no one had the same passion to continue the work. It faded away and went into dormancy, and people missed it but its absence didn't create a huge problem.

Some people don't like this pattern at Sirius because we already hold so many projects and each department has its own focuses and priorities. The challenge of who decides to give priority to which projects often leads to conflict. Some people might want new buildings to house equipment while others hope for a better website or kitchen management. Some might desire to increase food production and add chickens, but some may believe the space is better suited for the children to play.

New people come in and say, "The community needs to do *this* or *that*," as they present new ideas. They may receive community backing, but then find disappointment when residents don't volunteer to step up to do the necessary work because they already have their hands full. So we must agree on how best to use our community resources and time.

Often the imagineer doesn't realize that each project needs a champion, with unrealistic expectations about what one's project takes to implement. Disillusioned, they ask, "Why doesn't the community support my vision?"

Any project is only as good as the enthusiasm and time people have to offer. Unless someone is passionate enough to carry it forward, it won't last. We are already engaged in our work and if the envisioner leaves, we can't muster the same amount of passion for the idea. The community only has the means to support the project if the passion and individuals to work on it are present. But we cannot guarantee its success after they leave.

Champions of Change

When people come here to learn, the environment sparks fresh ideas and passion. People apply the knowledge they learn here and birth new projects. We plant the seeds and provide inspiration for similar work to be carried forward out into the world so others gain familiarity with the concepts.

One example of this expansion is the permaculture gardens installed at UMass. A young man named Ryan Harb came here and enrolled in our Permaculture Design Course. He got very excited about the concepts and ideas, and as a student at UMass he crafted his senior graduate project based on permaculture. He turned his lawn in Amherst into an edible forest garden. With his personality and social media talent, he rallied students and some faculty to get interested and involved. He popularized the concept of permaculture in the university culture. After he graduated, he lived at Sirius and maintained ties to UMass. With the experience of his first home-based project under his belt, he pitched a proposal for a permaculture garden next to the dining hall at UMass.

While somewhat supportive, the university remained reluctant, skeptical of the project's chances for success. But Ryan marched forward with the energy and motivation to succeed as he worked his connections with the students and showed the administration how many students supported the idea. Because of all the student enthusiasm, the university warmed up to the idea as it gained popularity and publicity. His proposal required sincere persistence, and other students supported him with long hours to fine tune the document. Eventually the university granted him permission to transform the lawn in front of the dining hall, saving it from becoming a parking lot.

The university recognized this project would attract new students who would find inspiration from such a sustainable innovation. They could promote their green image and everyone would win.

They formed a student committee and a design team and eventually they built the permaculture garden. Students participated and classes were set up to teach permaculture. Local elementary schools took field trips to the site to offer their kids the opportunity to shovel and plant edible delights. With its public location, students' interest grew, and each new installation piqued everyone's curiosity. The team publicized their work in the local newspaper and organized design meetings with permaculture educators in the area. After the initial installation, they worked with other sites on campus and added other gardens, often on damaged landscapes.

They became one of several projects nominated for President Obama's Champions of Change award for young people in educational situations doing good work in the world. The winner would be determined by an online vote with many contestants addressing issues on social justice from housing needs to climate change. Intent on winning the award for the school, the team poured endless hours into social media and maximizing their social capital. As the contest progressed, they saw they had a real shot at winning, and they mobilized the whole student body to jump online and vote. They made one huge surge at the very end and amazingly won the contest!

Ryan, along with other students on the committee, traveled to the White House to meet the president and receive the award. With all the publicity, their reach extended far beyond the campus as other universities learned of their success, hoping to replicate their design. The students started a yearly "Permaculture Your Campus" conference to share everything they learned and apply it to other schools. Ryan became a consultant and traveled to universities all over the country advising them on their projects.

A little seed was planted and grew with hugely successful results. The initial idea went further than anyone expected at the outset and now gardens are sprouting up in universities and schools all over the country.

The university uses vastly more food than what is grown in the garden but the contribution they make is important. The site acts as a demonstration to the student body as they watch food grown practicing sustainable permaculture techniques.

Permaculture gardening meets the mandate for organic and local production. It increases plant and animal diversity and to see the garden growing right outside the dining hall demonstrates a new model. The small scale food system effectively changes our future, and the current paradigm shift starts with awareness and education.

This project affirms values we believed in for years. We carry out our mission because we believe society needs to shift, and hearing the ideas embraced by the mainstream reaffirms our years of work. The motion toward embracing sustainability differs from the dominant mindset of the past. So many people are choosing to use sustainable gardening practices now. We no longer exist in an isolated, insular community; now our model demonstrates new methods for the future of humanity.

We want the mission and organization to continue beyond our individual lifetimes. We see positive change as the young generation takes responsibility for the future. The young people *are* the future. They will be here when our strength and capabilities decline, and they must step up and do the work. We will be the elders to give advice, but our roles will shift.

The roles of leadership that Linda and I held involved lots of responsibility in the community, more than necessary at times. When we were away travelling, I saw the community get stronger. That responsibility was not equally divided, so in our absence, people had to rise to the occasion and take some leadership, which strengthened our work. Since my illness in the recent years, I am not available in the same way and others taking the lead is a shift that will continue.

Over the years there were others who played key roles, but Linda and I held the center. And now that's changed in a positive way. My daughter Llani comes in and asks me carpentry questions all the time. She's now the one actually doing the work. As her skills developed, she asks fewer questions with more carpentry competence, and she knows the systems of Sirius. Right now we are transitioning out the leadership which we held for decades, which is a kind of leadership in itself. We want a group of responsible people stepping up and taking the vision forward. It will change and new leaders may not hold it in the same way we did, but I am inspired and see a positive future.

Changing Attitudes

Sirius experiences many iterations over the decades. Each generation and world event affects our work. In the early years, we existed as an isolated anomaly, protective of its insular nature to remain somewhat separate from mainstream society. At the time, in order to fulfill our vision outside of the societal paradigm, the isolation proved necessary. We lived too weird a life for society to support our ideas and visions. To create a new model with different goals and principles to survive, we had to create our own orb outside of the society.

As times change, the world awakens and a new paradigm emerges. We must redefine and change our role in the world as some of the boundaries and protective layers fall away and we open up to the penetration of society to share experiences relevant to the current times. We have developed and learned lessons useful to greater society. This change poses no danger to our survival because, established in our identity, we offer a great value to ourselves and the world in reaching out.

While my life experiences helped the expansion of consciousness progress, as new generations come in, they will continue to expand these ideas and experiences even greater. I hope the stories, the lessons, and the mistakes I share help push you and humanity forward in our evolutionary process. The lessons are already being learned faster and faster. Here in the community, I have witnessed how quickly people learn lessons that took me years to understand. In this short period of time, young people take the wisdom to another level, and I feel heartened and humbled by the change.

With a new generation, the evolutionary cycle is affirmed. We witness the acceleration of growth and our ability to change faster. We recognize we aren't here again going through "the same old thing," but instead the same lessons push us ahead further. Understanding and expansion of consciousness goes deeper than in previous generations and forms an outward spiral through which we evolve without stagnating. I always learn from the younger generations in the spiral of life. Interestingly, watching the growth of today's youth stimulates my own spiritual growth. Any feeling of separation between my identity and others breaks down. Different levels of spiritual development exist simultaneously. Not everyone moves on the same level, yet we move together as an evolving consciousness. Some of us have been around longer than others, with different life experiences and levels of consciousness.

Our lives merge and interconnect in a new way. As I grow I stimulate others' growth, and as others grow, they stimulate mine. My ego dissolves, and rather than seeing myself as a great wise individual deserving of reverence, I recognize I am simply part of an evolving consciousness. I have my individual soul consciousness, yet it isn't separate from the greater consciousness.

You and I dance in a mutual movement of expansion, both learning as our interconnected soul consciousnesses evolve and grow together. We embrace the interconnectedness of all life. Ego and individualized beingness start to dissolve without disappearing completely. The boundaries blur and we see our humanity in every individual.

Why Not Dance?

This new understanding speaks to simplicity. Ram Dass, a fascinating spiritual teacher, described how you might as well dance, because life is the only dance there is! Your life experience may go many ways, and you can fight against the evolution, or you can consciously move with it, because in reality, it is the only dance.

So why not? Why not dance with the universe, in a way that creates more joy, love, wholeness, and wellbeing? The opposite only creates friction, tension and disease. It makes no sense to do anything else. Human beings unnecessarily complicate their lives, but to move back into absolute simplicity and radical acceptance of what is moves us with the flow of the universe. We might write or meditate or choose to spend time alone in the woods. You can stop your combativeness against it and in each moment ask yourself, *How much love, generosity, goodwill and light am I generating in my being?*

In a moment-to-moment, day-to-day basis, make choices that stimulate this reality. In every moment, and every situation, we receive a choice in how we feel and respond. Deep within us we know how capable we are of making this choice. With a practice of more attentively listening deep within ourselves we hear the guidance and messages that allow us to dance in our life journey.

We must activate our ability to listen deeply and practice listening to our soul. I faced hard lessons in my life of not listening or learning. Even the hard lessons proved necessary. I suffered as life woke me up and brought me great difficulties. The challenges interrupted my direction and made me look deeply inside myself. Even though they were painfully difficult, I feel truly grateful for those experiences.

We can choose to listen and move with that dance or we can choose not to dance. We have the choice to sync with the process or we fall out of harmony with the flow. As human beings, we have freewill to move and the choice is ours alone. Despite our free choice, karmic energy eventually pushes us in the direction we need to go. So life is the dance, we can choose to dance, or even if we choose to step out of the dance for a while, we will be brought back into it. Whether we accept it or not, we are all evolving and growing into more spiritual awareness.

The Dalai Lama once said, "All people want the same thing, they want to be happy." The road to happiness helps others fulfill their own happiness. We recognize direct experience of spiritual awakening is the most important tool. Helping and supporting the growth of others and the wellbeing of the planet gives us joy and purpose. When we choose these positions of service, we feel a surge of energy beyond our normal feelings and experiences. Recognizing our wholeness is vital for us to feel loved, seen and connected. We are not imagining this change, but believe in the possibility that something new will happen.

Because of this book project, I reflected deeply on the profound questions of our time through my life experience. In that reflective process, I hope my insights help other people.

I am gaining new wisdom and understanding, which inform my own growth and evolution. In these chapters, we submerged into deep personal spaces, and the project gave me a voice to transmit my experience and express my profound pain and suffering both physically and emotionally in my life. In these words I can transmit the lessons forward, knowing their benefit to others.

Recounting all these memories of realization benefits my own understanding of myself and my life journey. During this project, ideas and lessons lingering on the peripheries of my consciousness came to me. While at first vague and undefined, naming and speaking about the concepts brought them into concretized reality. Some ideas we discuss here truly emerged through the reflection process, with more clarity than ever before. The evolving recording process surprises me as concepts and ideas come into my consciousness that I've never before spoken about. Suddenly the idea has come alive, so thank you for helping me learn. May you find value in my experience to apply in your own life.

Epilogue

BY LLANI DAVIDSON

The last time I saw my father alive, he was lying in a hospital bed, grey and emaciated from six months of not walking. I held his hand, staring at his swollen fingers. I stroked his arm and touched his hair as my throat tightened. So this is how it ends. Seven years passed since the tree accident, enduring multiple midnight trips to the hospital, jumping every time my parents' number popped up on my phone, and so many tears shed for the lost years we won't have together. Lucid, he smiled at me and said, "I hope you have a really great life." Then he shared a joke and stuck out his tongue.

Two months earlier, on one of his visits in and out of the hospital he told us, "Well I may be dying, but I don't want you to be sad. I want you to have fun; I don't want this experience to be heavy and miserable." I cried all the way home anyway, driving through the darkness with my husband beside me. I wept for all the grandchildren he would never meet. I cried for all his skills and knowledge that vanished with him. I cried for my mom, for my sister and for my uncle. I cried until I couldn't breathe. I got out of the car and my legs shook. "Honey, can you help me, I'm not sure I can walk."

Bruce died the next day. His suffering was finally over after a long and intense journey with pain. The days of oxygen machines, wheelchairs, dialysis, and bed pans were over. The chaos of tangled bed sheets and pill bottles strewn about lay forgotten in his room, his glasses perched upon the desk. And just like that, he was gone.

Over 200 people flooded into the Community Center to remember his gifts and 69 years of learning, growing and teaching. Pictures of Bruce as a young man in military uniform littered the table. His brother told stories of his years at Findhorn. Others praised his carpentry skills and expertise in building the Hartsbrook Waldorf School. We learned of his role as a leader, mentor and spiritual advisor.

The dining room was alive as everyone ate the famous meal he lovingly served to guests on Sundays for over 30 years. Silently everyone walked up the path in the dark with an unlit candle. Our faces in shadow, the light grew as each candle lit the next, slowly passing around the circle. Voices echoed out into the night, sending his soul on into the otherworld, honoring his life.

People who missed the service wrote to us from all over the world, sending their love, condolences and stories. They spoke about how his life had changed or impacted them. My email inbox overflowed from people I had never met. I sorted through it all in tears, seeing how much this one life mattered, seeing how much the power of my father's ideas and 40 years of shining light at Sirius offered to the world. He was remembered in the phone calls, emails, and condolences. He was remembered in the cement, wood and rebar, and the floorboards under our feet.

And now he is remembered in these words you read.

Eulogy

We didn't know it yet, but the day my father reached for a tree branch and came up short, grasping onto air in the stunned moments of wondering what happens next, was one that would change all of our lives. Would the next breath bring life or death? He fell hard, he fell shattered. He fell into surprise and pain. "Well I guess it's a good day to die," he said amidst screaming, chewing on a stick, crying and suffering.

Thanks Dad, for choosing not to die that day. Thanks for suffering through the pain for the next seven and a half years, because we weren't ready to let you go yet. In grief and gratitude, I feel the immensity of this loss that sits so heavy in all of us.

My father's life was one of daring. Daring to be different, daring to push edges and to dream into what seemed impossible, daring to reach beyond his home and roots and to live large. Daring to come back to this country after being gone four years, and along with his brother and sister-in-law, armed only with faith, tenacity and a dream, to try and start this community, with no address in the US, no money and a family to support. Thanks for dreaming, Dad. We are sitting here today because of you.

As a little girl he could hand me the world. He came home at the end of the day smelling like wood shavings, warm fleece and gasoline. He offered us goofiness, stories and play. Strong and powerful, he seemed to know how to do everything. He would take us on his lap and tell us stories about the magic lion, about the fantasy world of Nanini and Wapole and this land where everything imaginable was possible. I loved sitting on his lap as he swept me away to magical lands. I loved his joy of being alive. He would drive all the way down the hill to Whole Foods on a whim for an ice cream pop, just because they tasted good. We made candles together, mixing colors, smells and sizes, getting wax everywhere! We played silly games and tromped around on piggy back rides.

Sometimes his daring to be different left me confused as to how the rest of the world worked. I sweated through years of embarrassment with friends who came over and awkwardly stood over the composting toilet while I tried to explain how to use a common fixture that looked like no one else's. As I grew up I often felt like a foreigner in my own country and realized how many people thought my life was outrageously weird or fascinatingly unique.

I realized that many people were seeking what I had been handed, what I had been born into. My title as Bruce and Linda's daughter, which brought me status in certain circles, was either admired or completely misunderstood. In some contexts, it was just too weird for some mainstream suburban mom of my friends to wrap her head around. "Like, do they believe in electricity where you come from?" Other times people treated me like an exotic species in the zoo that everyone wanted to poke, admire and take pictures of.

"So what was it like to grow up in community?"

Really? Now? I haven't even have my breakfast yet. Do I have to explain it yet again?

But in the long run, I am grateful. Grateful that my father and my mother gave me a life that is so much more rich, deep and colorful than what I could find inside a box for the low price of $99.

My father gave me the gift of community. How many Sunday mornings we spent hanging out in the farmhouse with him in his frilly apron, pots steaming, while I attempted to make the cornbread, trying to keep most of it off of the floor. How many guests did he welcome with a good story and a kind word for all those years? He gave me huge bonfires behind the farmhouse with swirling sparks, watermelon rinds tossed at flying bats and running away, shrieking into the dark, while we danced to my aunt's scratchy record of Paul Simon's "Diamonds on the Soles of Her Shoes," munching down huge bowls of popcorn.

Community gave me 90 acres of adventure, a span of bumpy roads for bike riding and unending neighborhood houses with open doors to run in and out of. I had access to plenty of adults in the community who loved to hang out with kids. I met countless people who walked through these doors over the years, leaving an impression on my young mind. I saw their humor, kindness, weirdness and flaws. They left me behind, off to the next adventure which only added to the allurement of what was out in the big wide world out there. Thanks Dad for providing community in my life.

My father has a profound connection to nature which he has passed on to me. He loved being with the trees and in the water. He never found a swimming hole he didn't like, even if it was just a pipe coming out of the ground in the middle of a third world city. He took us on our first backpacking trip in the White Mountains when I was ten, which either fostered my love of nature, or scared me beyond belief. No trip would have been complete without leeches on my sister's foot, bushwhacking through the undergrowth with him thinking, *I know the shelter is around here somewhere,* while three little girls tripped over tree logs and stumbled as the darkness descended, freaking out and crying that we may never make it back home again. But somehow I walked away hungry for more. And I felt the profoundness and the wildness of the land. Thanks Dad for teaching me to connect and honor the wild and sacredness of this land and in all life.

My father gave me the gift of travel and adventure. His stories created the allurement of the "world out there" and all that we can be. I mean come on, who else's father dropped out of society to hitchhike around the country and become a bonafide hippie trying to find God? Who else's father almost got eaten by a tiger in a cave in Israel? I wanted to have stories like his…stories worth telling.

He gave me freedom to choose my own path, to drive off into the sunset looking for the allurement of adventure, to meet people gnarled with missing teeth, stooping in their small shacks on dusty roads… To watch the sunrise on cold windy mountaintops… To run after dirty smog-filled buses with all my possessions on my back, to bicycle 2,000 miles through deserts, swamps and cities… To camp in the dusty desert near howling coyotes and rattlesnakes… To see the stars upside down… To experience spring in September… To chase cows while dodging wet cow pies… To pick lettuce in the freezing cold sunrise. Like him I have stories worth telling.

My father fostered my love of tools, machines and carpentry, starting with my very own tool box with a real hammer, saw and tape measure when I turned 12. His skills shine in all of the walls around us. He literally built our house up from a patch of forest with not much more than tenacity, a few carpentry tools and a copy of *The Builder's Guide to Timber Framing*. He let me be a member of his crew when I was 14 and hang out on the Octagon rooftop putting down shingles. He taught me how to use my hands, to make piles of wood become walls, siding and cabinet doors. He showed me how to pound a bouncy nail, how to level a board, how to see with precision and to bring critical thinking to each step. Even when I impatiently wanted to do it my way, he showed me how to square the corners of a house, precise, plumb and accurate. He gave me the ability to see potential in every piece of wood. He gave me livelihood and skill and inspired me to bring my gifts into the world.

My father gave me the gift of spirituality. He taught us to meditate at a young age despite our giggles and squirminess and interest in beating the sacred drum rather than actually sitting still. He taught me to always seek and ask questions about my existence. When I called him on the phone after breaking my collar bone in a mountain bike wreck, he could only ask me what lesson or message the universe was trying to give me, a message that often I did not want to hear. Sometimes I wanted him to give me direction, tell me what to do, where to go, how to live, but in the end I suppose it was up to me.

He had the psychic ability to tune in when I was in trouble. He was expecting me the moment I called him from the side of the road by a lonely cornfield in Nebraska, right at dark with a broken down car. Another time, inside his head, he heard me on the opposite end of the property yell when I put my foot through the top of a wooden file cabinet. His ability to tune in always amazed me.

My father had a social, outgoing side, yet he was also a deeply private person who refrained from sharing much of his inner emotions. He did not often know how to talk with us about our feelings. It's been in the last few years of his illness that I have come to see him as more than my father, but a person with his own internal feelings, pain and conflict, a person robbed of his familiar identity. In the fall from the tree, he lost so much. The strong, capable, tree climbing, chainsaw-slinging carpenter had to let all that go and become someone else. And somehow he still was able to learn from it. He went back and thanked the tree later. But he did not want our pity. He tried his best not to complain. His ability to endure served him well.

As his daughter, it has been hard to watch him suffer so much. It lends itself to a certain helplessness. It's been hard to see his physical mobility taken away from him. Despite the challenges his life was still full of spirituality, community, nature, connection and inspiration to others.

We hoped for a long time that somehow he would beat the cancer, beat the odds, that he would still be here, that he would get more time, more healing, a second chance, and the ability to live a full life. But in the end, facing the challenges of decline proved to be the journey.

If these last seven and a half years have taught me anything, it's that you can never have the joys and ease of the past back again, that we must embrace our lives. Let his legacy teach you to love deeper, laugh louder, be more present, take risks and follow your heart. Speak truth, do your work and keep trying.

Thanks Dad for being my father even when you felt like you didn't know how. Thanks for playing hard and working harder. Thanks for living your life so large and dreaming ferociously... Thanks for mattering to all the people reading this message.

Go joyfully on. You are free and I love you.

LLANI DAVIDSON, DECEMBER 2017

www.ingramcontent.com/pod-product-compliance
Lightning Source LLC
Chambersburg PA
CBHW051938290426
44110CB00015B/2027